Colour and Contrast

Artwork of Jindrich Degen

Arranged by Eva and Alex Peck

Artwork: Jindrich Degen
Photography: Jindrich Degen, Alex Peck
Photo editing: Jindrich Degen, Eva Peck, Alex Peck
Text: Jindrich Degen, Eva Peck, Alex Peck
Design: Eva Peck, assisted by Alex Peck and Jindrich Degen
Front cover design: Jindrich Degen. Background image: "Flowerage" by J. Degen

National Library of Australia Cataloguing-in-Publication entry

Author: Degen, Jindrich (Henry), 1923- artist.
Title: Colour and contrast: artwork of Jindrich Degen /

artist Jindrich Degen;
editor, compiler, graphic artist Eva Peck;
editor and compiler Alex Peck.

ISBN: 9780987500366 (paperback)

Subjects: Degen, Jindrich.
Still-life painting.
Nature in art.
Portraits.
Spirituality in art.

Other Authors/Contributors:
Peck, Eva, editor, compiler.
Peck, Alex, editor, compiler, photographer.

Dewey Number: 759.994

This book can be purchased online through http://www.henrydegen.com or http://www.pathway-publishing.org . Available on Amazon and elsewhere.

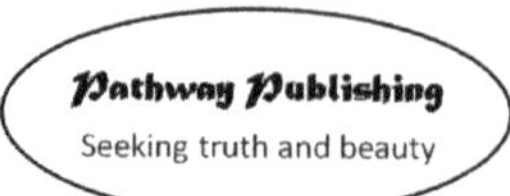

I dedicate this book to Eva and Alex
in appreciation for their work on it.

Other Books Featuring Jindrich Degen's Work

Artistic Inspirations - Paintings of Jindrich Degen arranged by Eva and Alexander Peck

Faces and Forms Across Time – Artwork of Jindrich Degen arranged by Eva and Alexander Peck

Floral and Nature Art – Photography of Jindrich Degen arranged by Eva and Alexander Peck

Volné verše, Jindrich Degen (poetry in Czech)

Verše pro dnešní dobu, Jindrich Degen (poetry in Czech)

The above books can be viewed and purchased online:
www.henrydegen.com
www.pathway-publishing.org

What Others Have Said About Jindrich's Art

Thank you for your paintings in which I see light and hope. I like the harmony of colours and shapes which give the impression of movement. Your artwork reflects optimism.
Ali D. (United Kingdom)

The colours in Jindrich's art are very positive, reflecting optimism, as well as purity and wholesomeness. His versatility is amazing – the way his artwork ranges from impressionism and abstract to portraits and still lifes.
Col B. (Australia)

I like colours, freedom, and the resulting joy. This is exactly what I feel when I look at Jindrich's pictures. I can imagine having some of them in my home.
Radka S. (Czech Republic)

I looked through Jindrich's artworks and found them fascinating. I especially like the painting "In the Forest". There I feel that I understand the forest – being able to perceive how it lives, grows, and receives nourishment from the roots.
Drahomira O. (Czech Republic)

Many thanks for the gifts that you have brought to us all through your long life of music and art. We are all the richer for your presence! I was interested to see so many mandala-like pieces – conveying a sense of completion - though I think my favourite work is "In the Forest". Once again, thanks for the inspiration!
Erica M. (Australia)

ACKNOWLEDGEMENT

I would like to thank my daughter, Eva, who with the help of her husband, Alex, was the leading spirit behind this book. She did a great job in creating the concept for the book, as well as preparing the pictures for print. Many thanks to Eva and Alex. Their work in publishing other aspects of my artistic work, as well as their own edifying publications, is also greatly appreciated.

CONTENTS AT A GLANCE

CONTENTS

What I dream of is an art of balance,
of purity and serenity,
devoid of
troubling or depressing subject matter.

Henri Matisse

INTRODUCTION

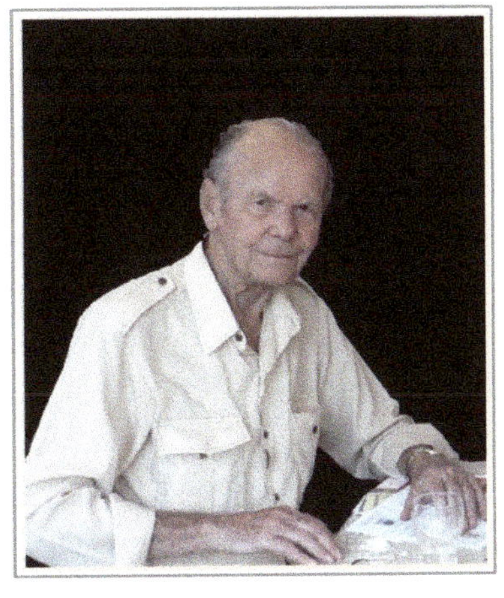

Born in 1923 in Prague, Czechoslovakia, Jindrich (Henry) Degen has enjoyed drawing since childhood. After completing secondary education, he chose to pursue his other great interest, music, following in the footsteps of his father. From 1943 until 1979 he performed as principal oboist in various symphony and opera orchestras in Prague (now Czech Republic), Gothenburg (Sweden), and Melbourne (Victoria, Australia). He also published educational music for oboe in Prague, England and Germany.

After his retirement in 1979, Jindrich moved from Victoria to Queensland where he began devoting himself to art. While living on the Sunshine Coast, he took a three-year art course at the TAFE (Technical And Further Education) institute in the area. Later in the Redlands, as a member of the Yurara Art Society, he attended workshops conducted by prominent artists, Irene Amos, Jan Jefferies, Jack Oudyn, and Michael John Taylor.

Jindrich's subject repertoire is diverse, directed by his personal mood or idea at the time. He enjoys painting realistic subjects, such as portraits, townscapes, still lifes, and nature themes. Through colourful semi-abstract or abstract art, he seeks to express his subconscious feelings in images using various media (such as oil, acrylic, pastel and watercolour). Many of these can be seen on his website www.henrydegen.com, as well as in an earlier publication entitled *Artistic Inspirations, Paintings by Jindrich Degen* (published in 2011).

A respected local artist, Jindrich continues to take part in various art activities and exhibitions, especially those of the Yurara Art Society. In addition, during March-April 2004, he had a solo exhibition in the Redland Art Gallery. In July-August 2010, he displayed a selection of his mandala paintings at the same gallery. Another exhibition is planned for 2014.

This new book of 184 pictures is a selection of Jindrich's paintings featuring both realistic and abstract art. Organized under twelve categories, it contains many of the art pieces found in a previous publication entitled *Artistic Inspirations* (2011). The paintings in this book, however, are each featured on a separate page. The collection contains still lifes, landscapes, city scenes, real-life portraits, as well as abstract images representing nature and spirituality themes.

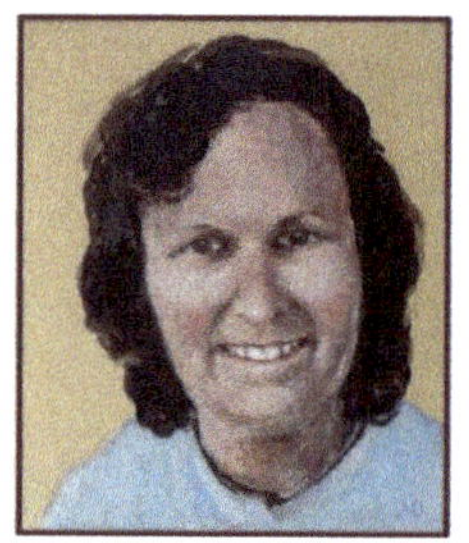

This collection of art works has been arranged by Jindrich's daughter, Eva, with assistance from her husband Alex. Jindrich actively participated in the various production steps including final selection of the works, photographing his art, guiding in the computer editing process, writing and editing text, choosing the quotes used on the divider pages, and advising on the final layout, including the cover design. He also painted the portraits of his daughter and son-in-law featured

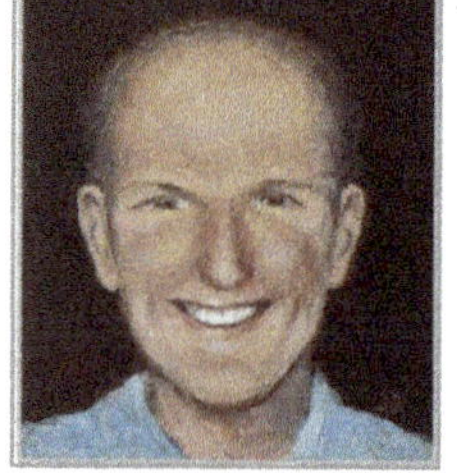

on the preceding page and designed the cover using his art piece “Flowerage”.

The artist hopes that this varied and colourful collection of paintings will leave visitors to this "gallery in print" uplifted and inspired.

If we could see the miracle of a single flower
clearly,
our whole life would change.
(The Buddha)

The subject itself is of no account;
what matters is the way it is presented.
(Raoul Dufy)

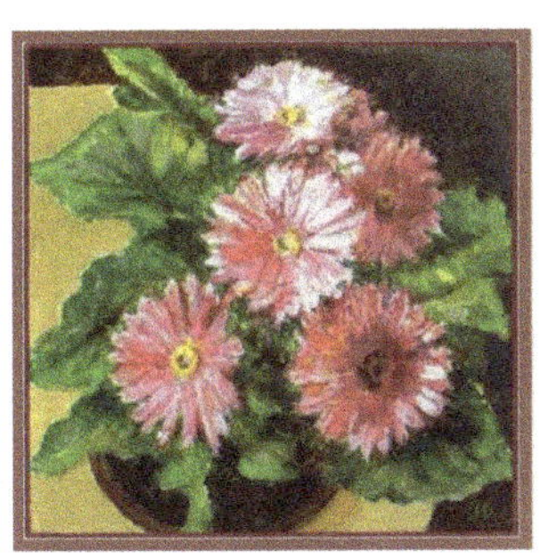

Still Lifes

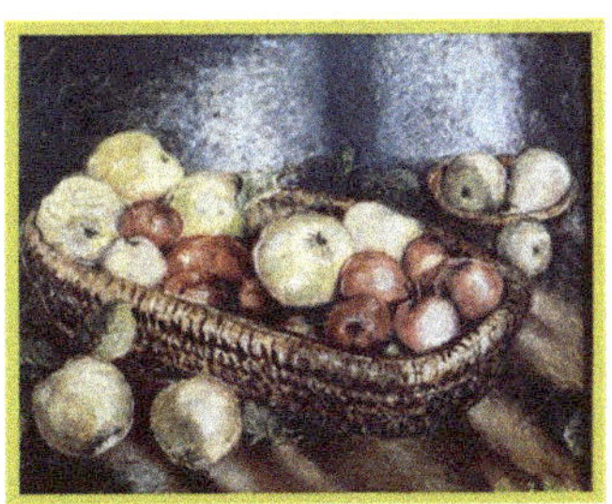

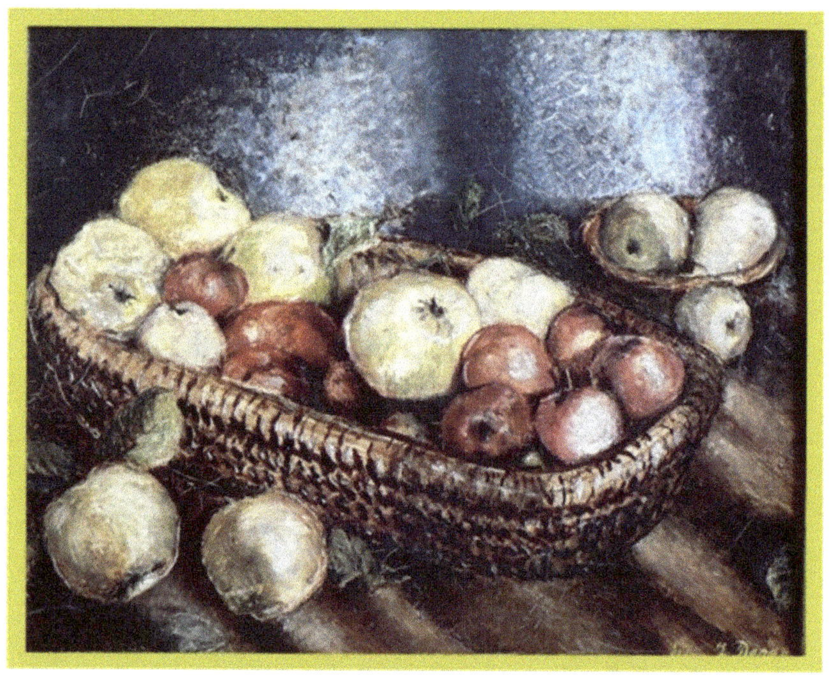

Apples in a Basket

Oil on canvas, 26 x 31 cm, 1941

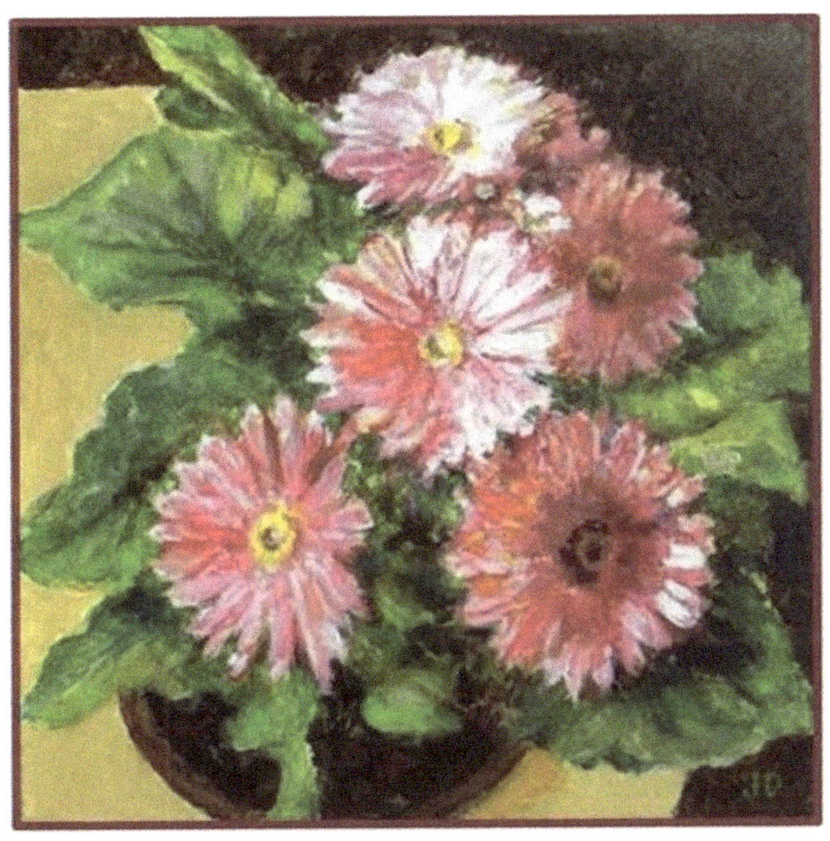

Gerbera

Acrylic on canvas, 31 x 31 cm, 2010

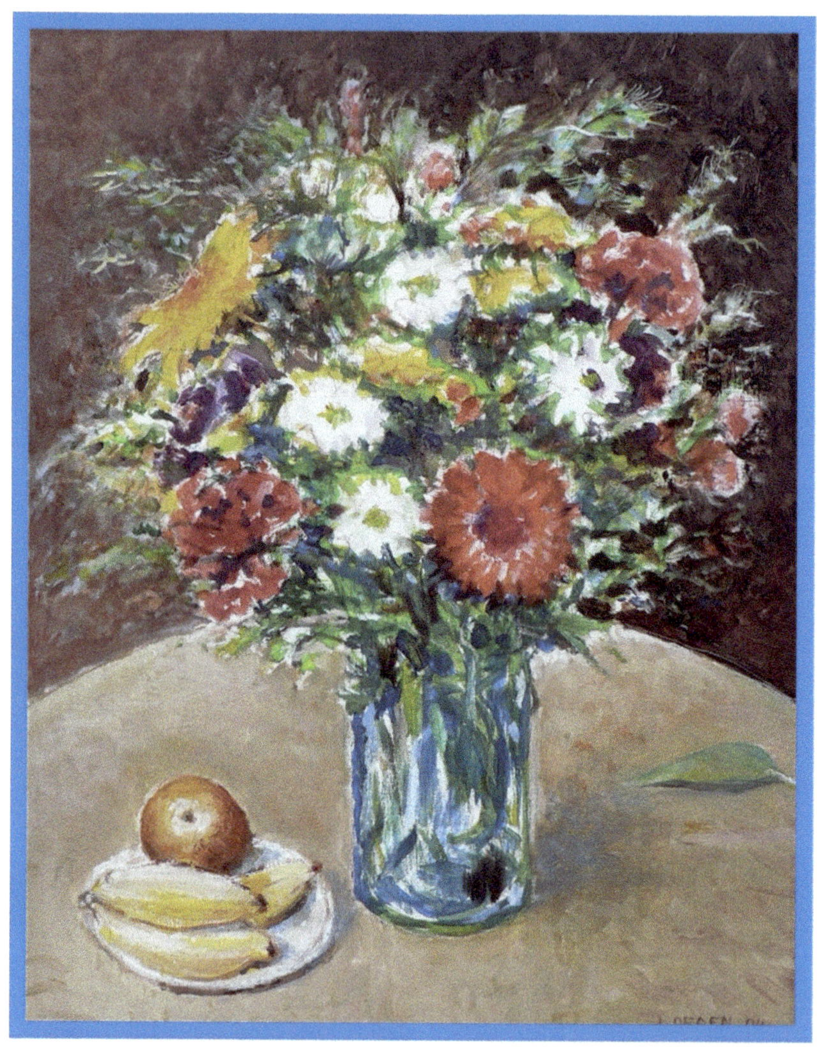

Blue Vase

Acrylic on board, 57 x 42 cm, 2005

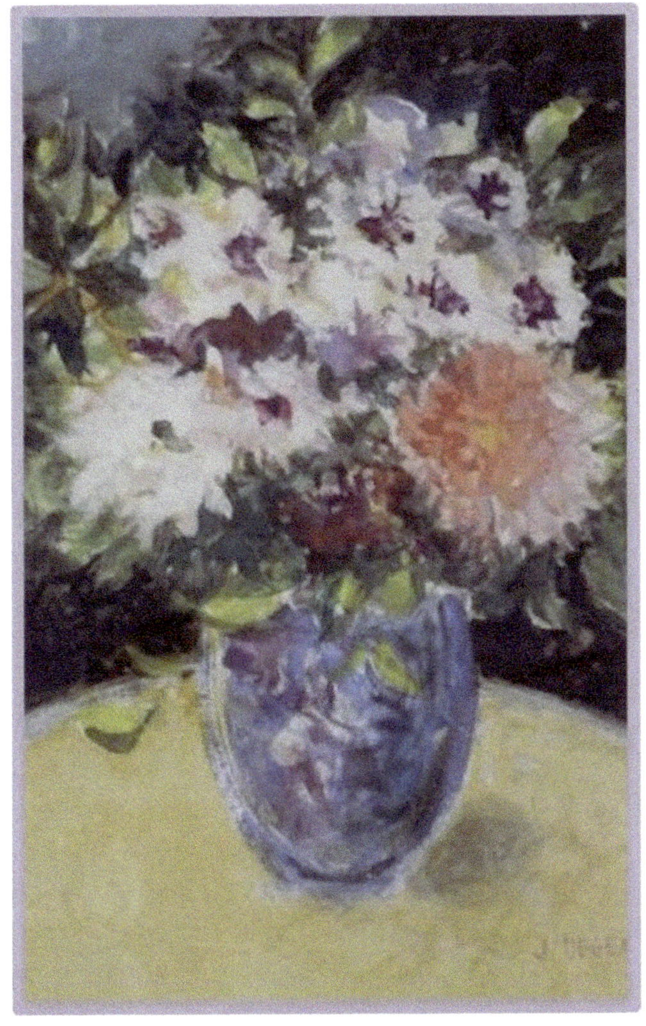

White Flowers in Violet Vase

Acrylic on paper, 32 x 27 cm, 2006

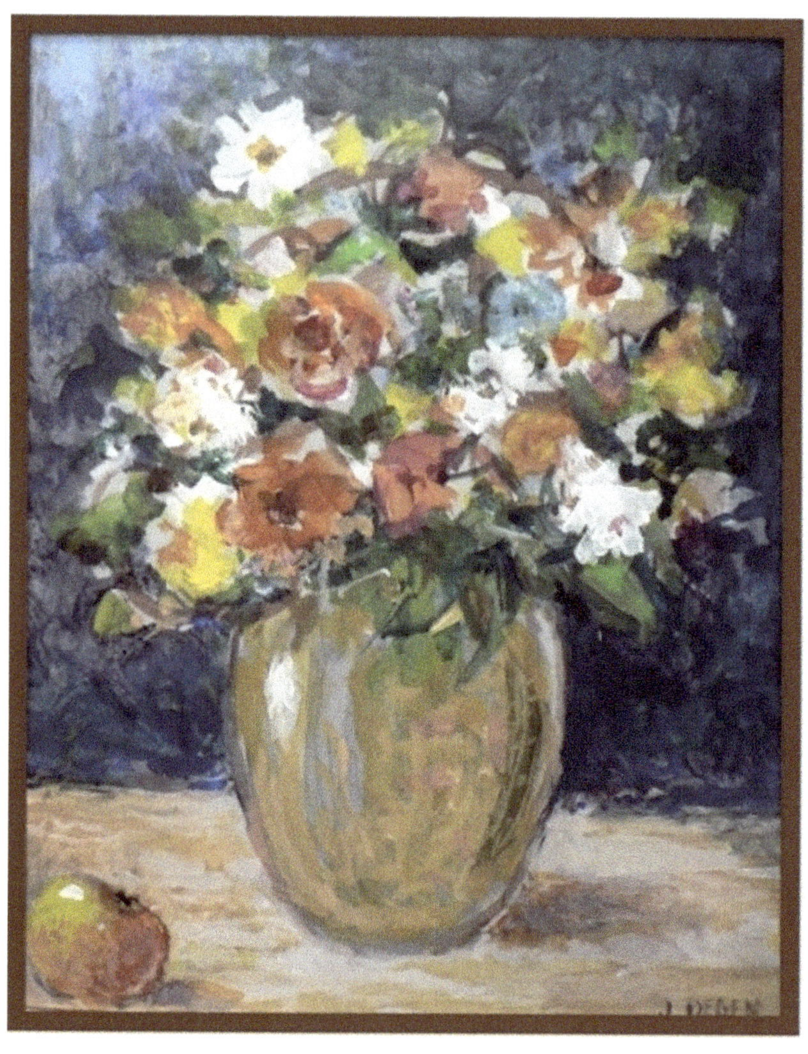

Brown Vase

Oil on board, 28 x 22 cm, 2009

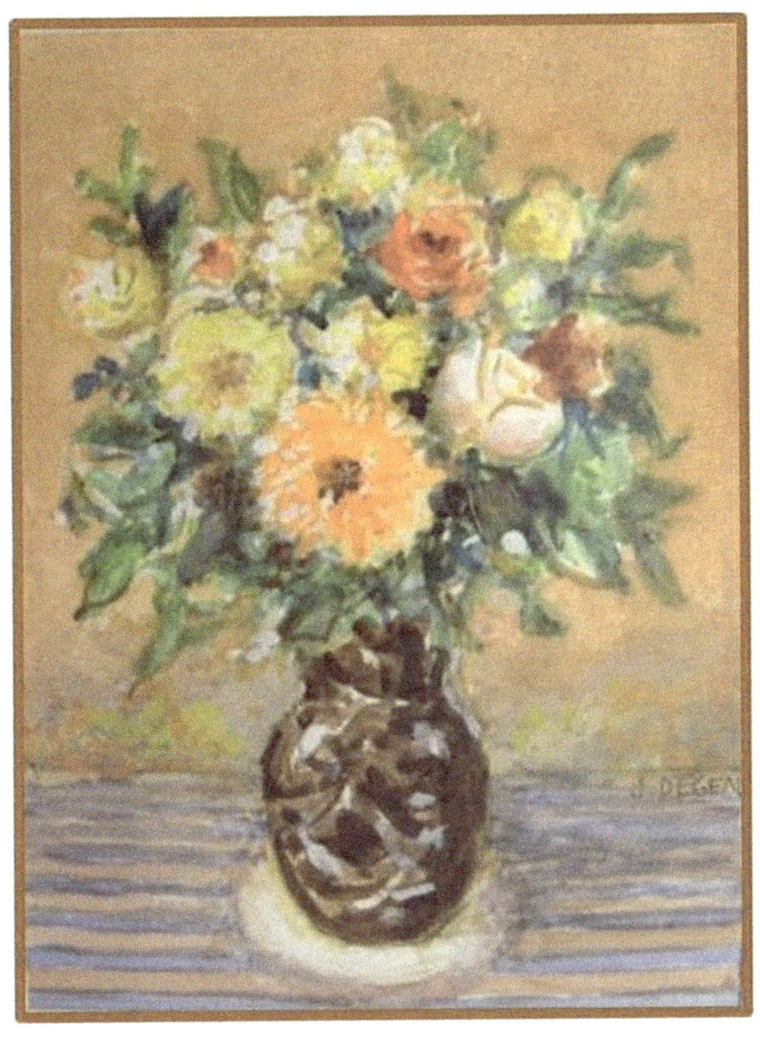

Bouquet

Watercolour on paper, 38 x 28 cm, 2011

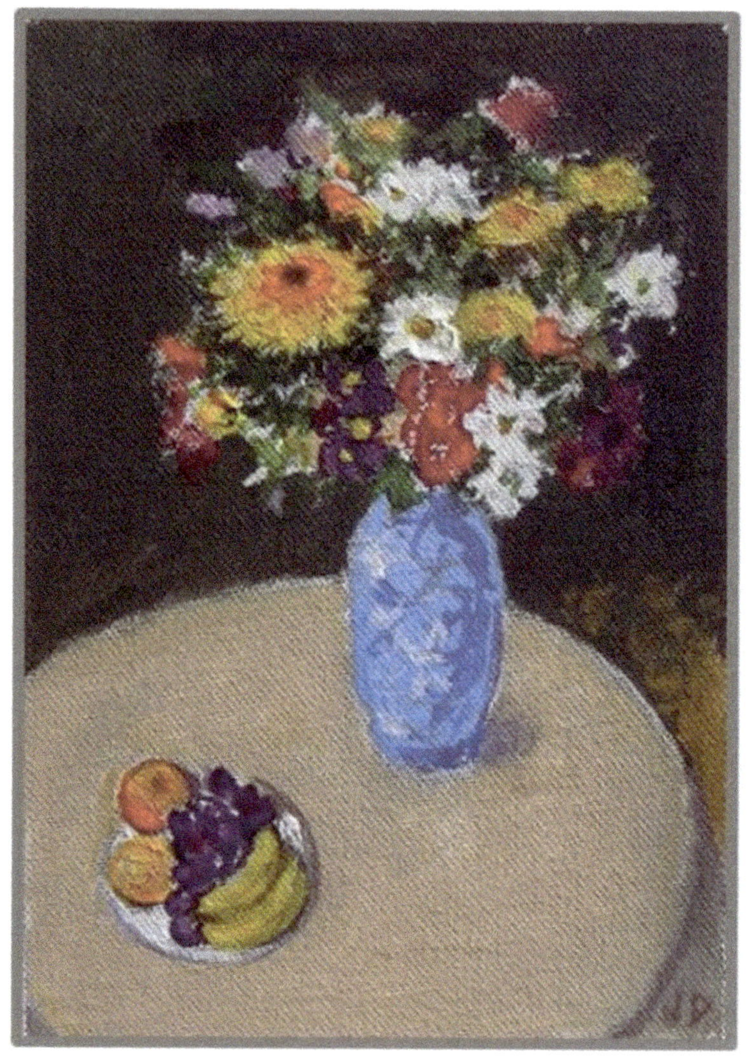

At Home

Acrylic on canvas, 20 x 14 cm, 2011

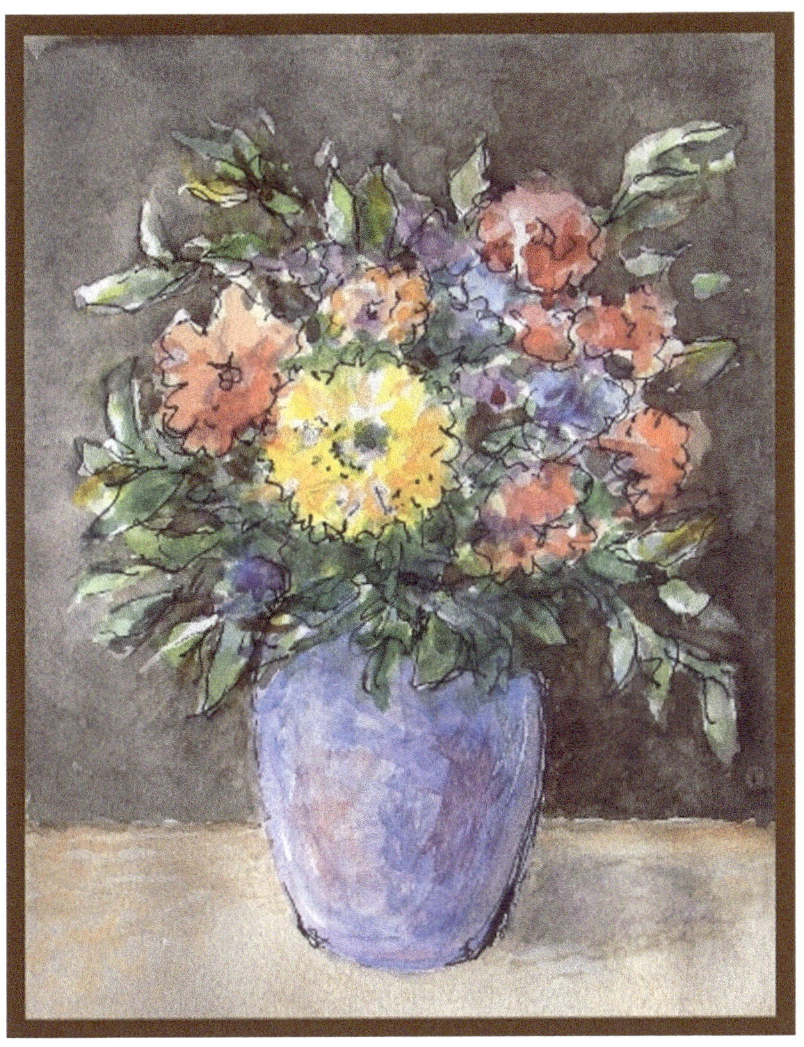

Violet Vase

Water colour on paper, 29 x 22 cm, 2009

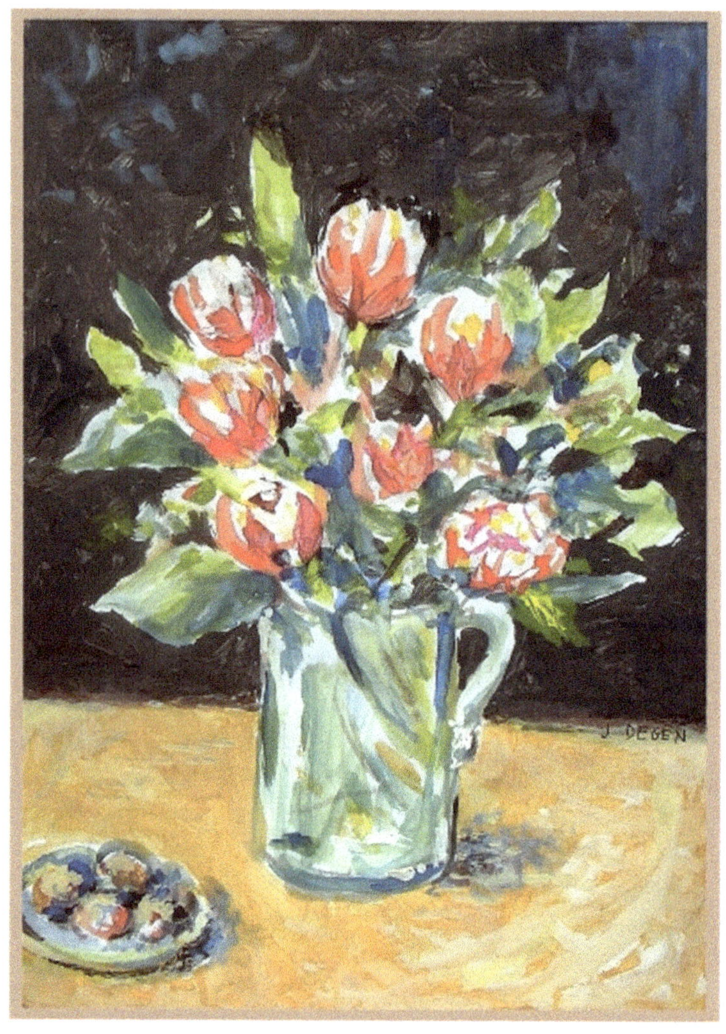

Tulips

Acrylic on paper, 37 x 25 cm, 2009

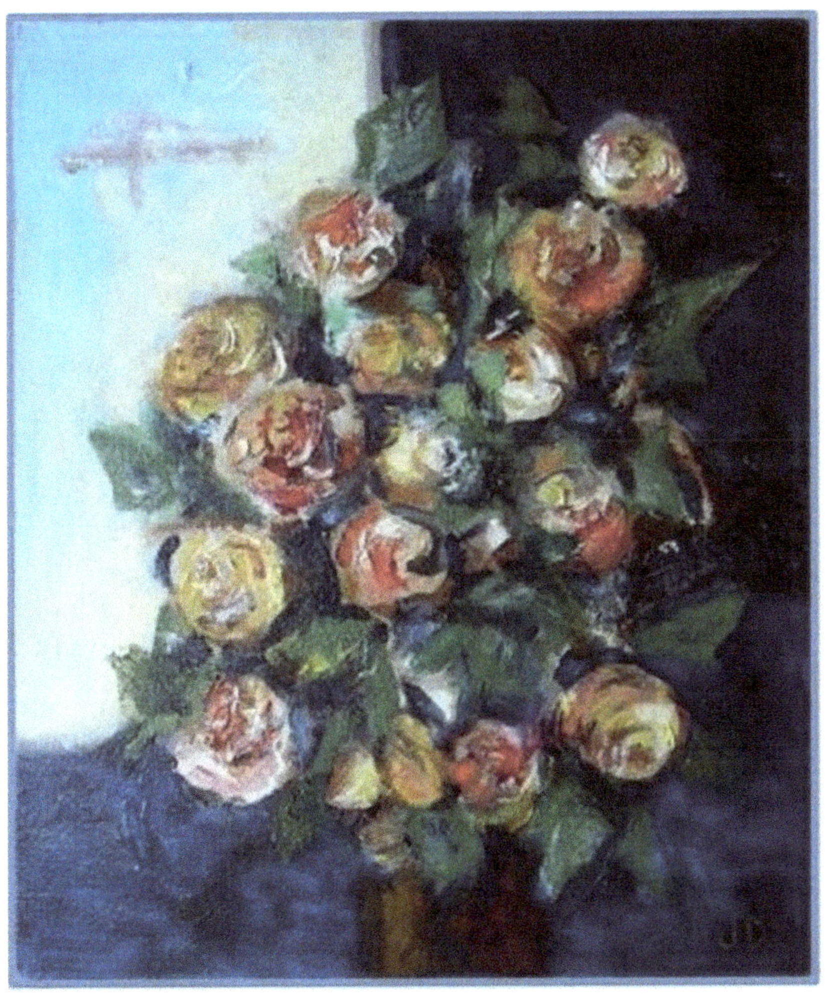

Flowers

Oil on canvas, 30 x 25 cm, 2010

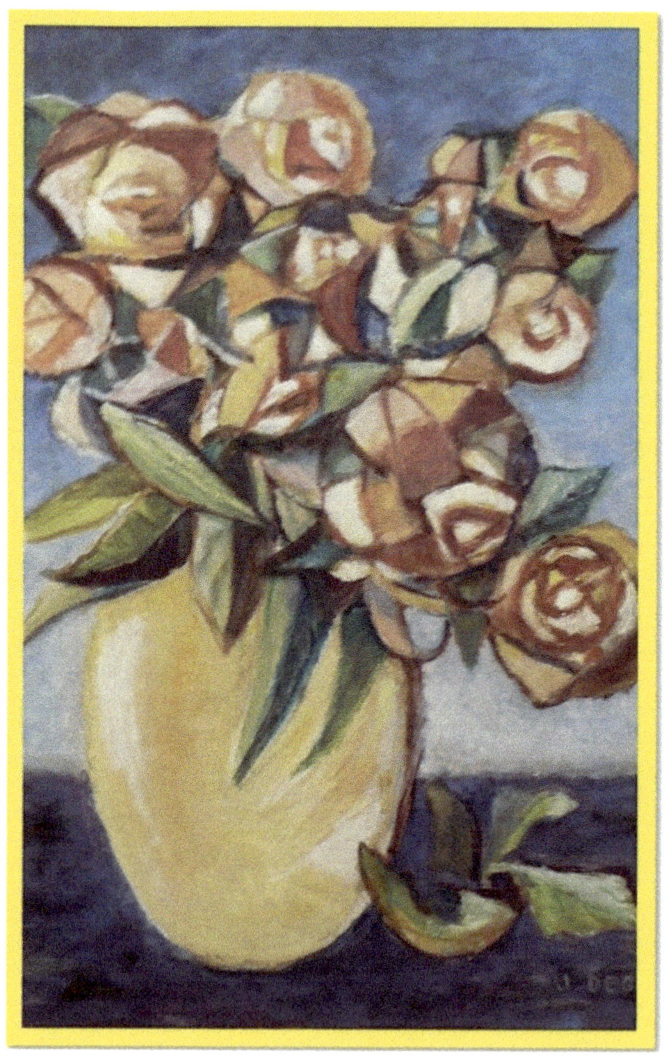

Yellow Vase

Oil on board, 40 x 32 cm, 2002

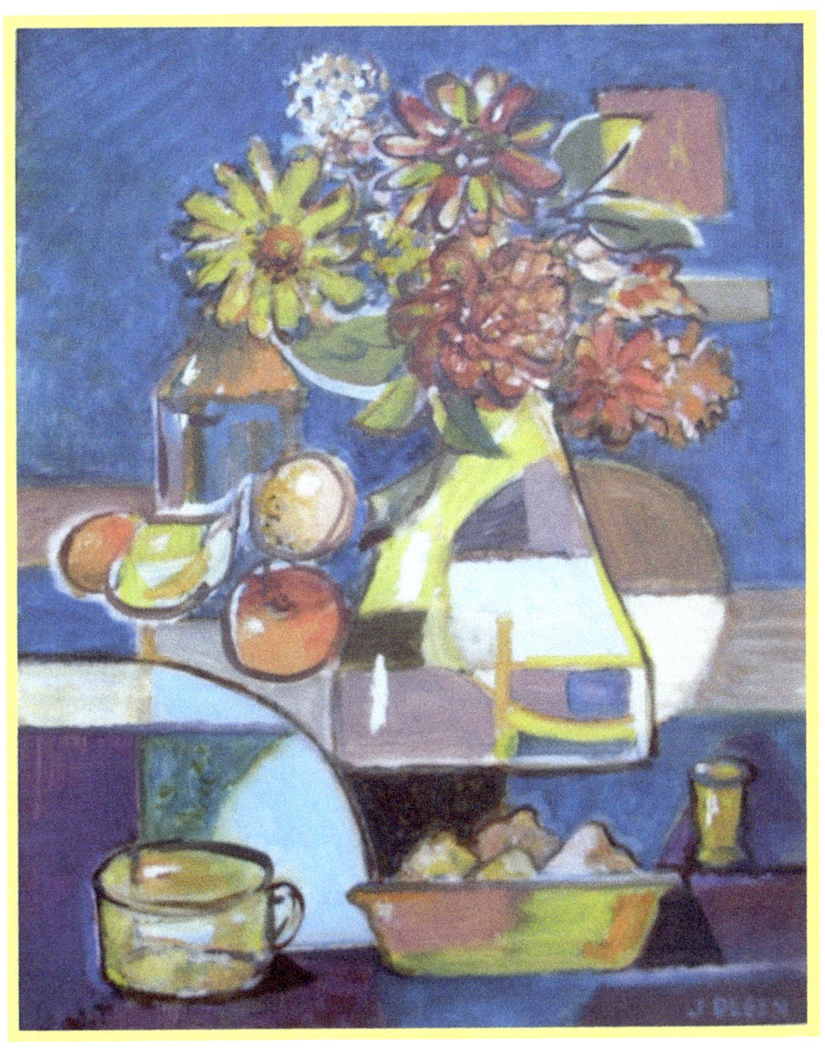

Still Life

Oil on board, 58 x 45 cm, 2002

God made the country,
and man made the town.
(William Cowper)

Though we travel the world over to find the
beautiful,
we must carry it with us,
or we find it not.
(Ralph Waldo Emerson)

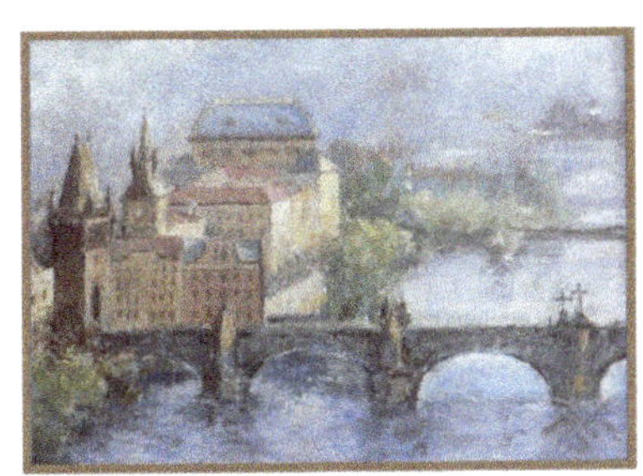

City & Country

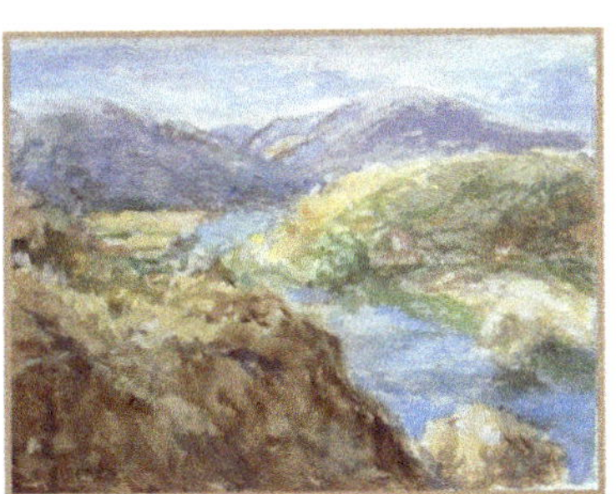

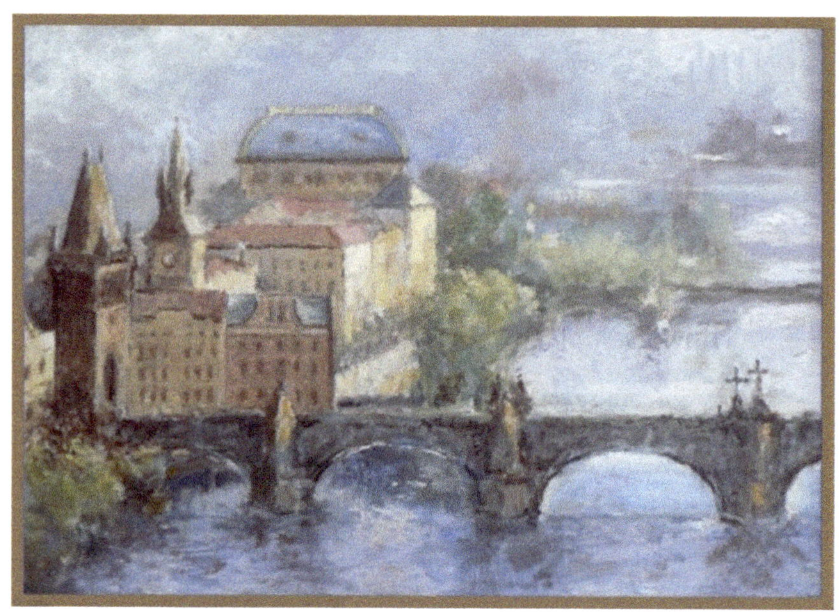

Prague

Oil on board, 28 x 39 cm, 2004

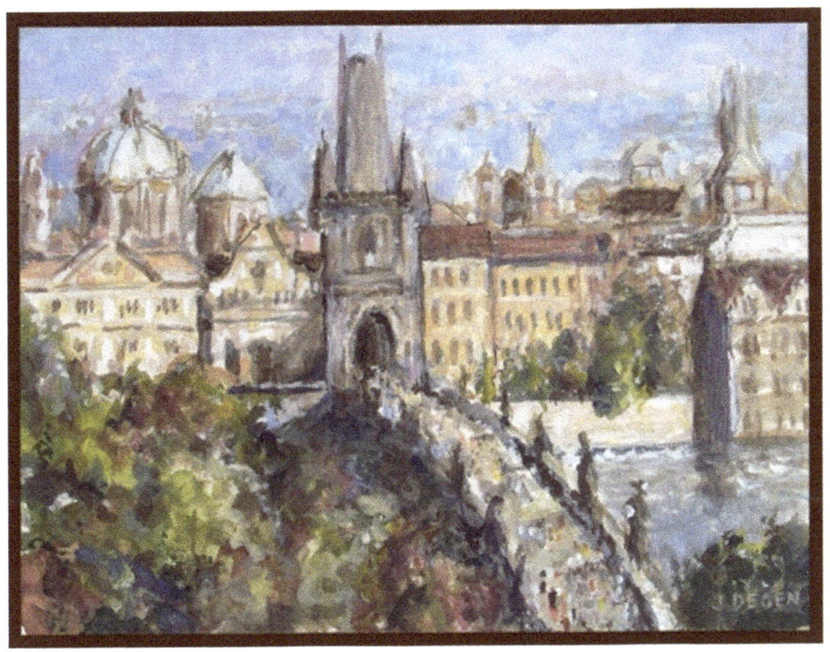

Charles Bridge in Prague

Acrylic on paper, 27 x 34 cm, 2009

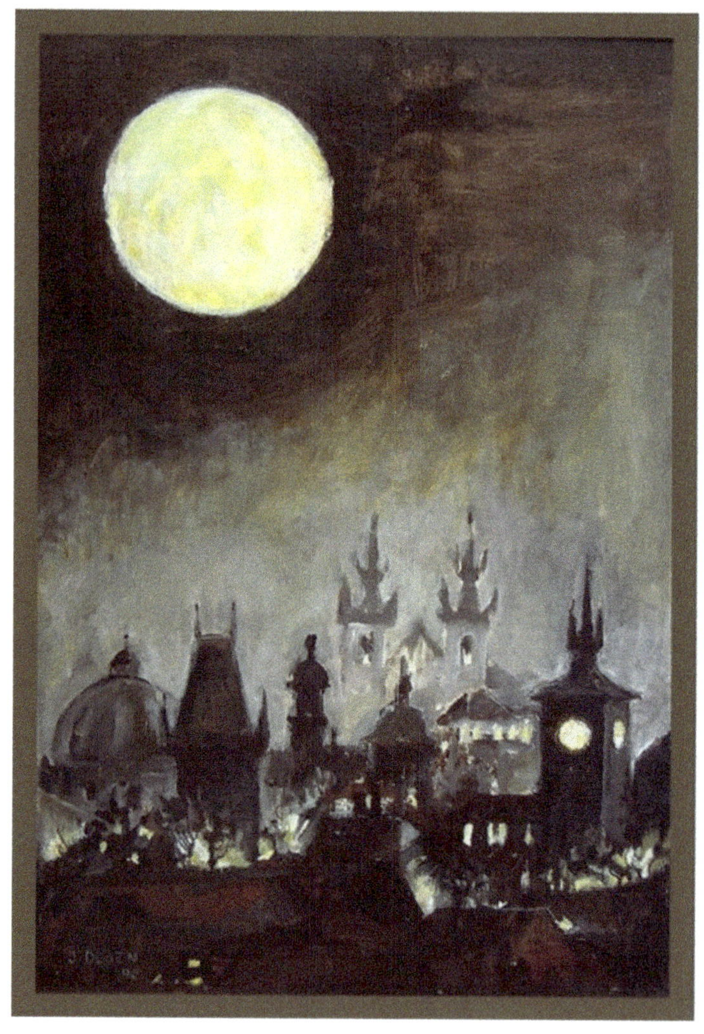

Prague Nocturnal

Acrylic on board, 72 x 49 cm, 1990

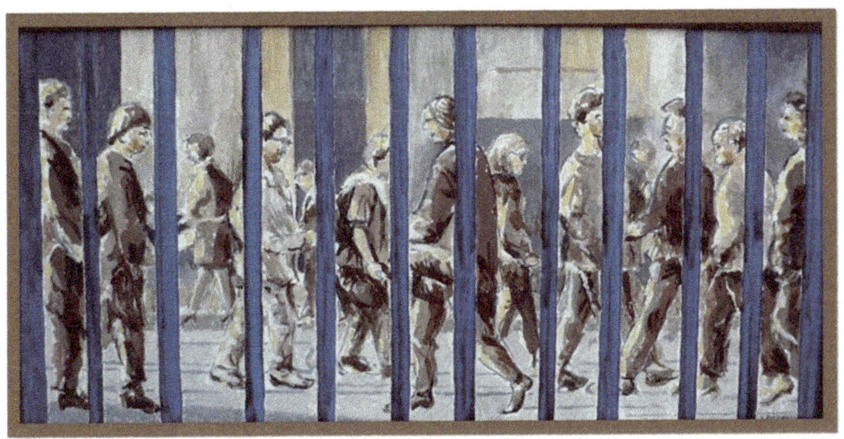

Faster and Faster - Speed is the Jailer

Acrylic on board, 29.5 x 60 cm, 2007

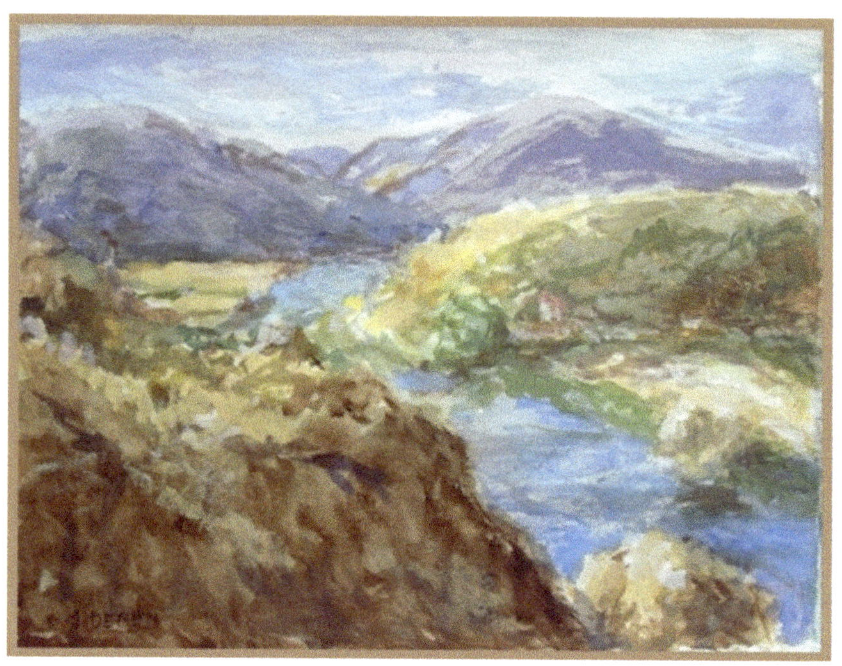

Berounka River

Mixed media on paper, 30 x 39 cm, 2009

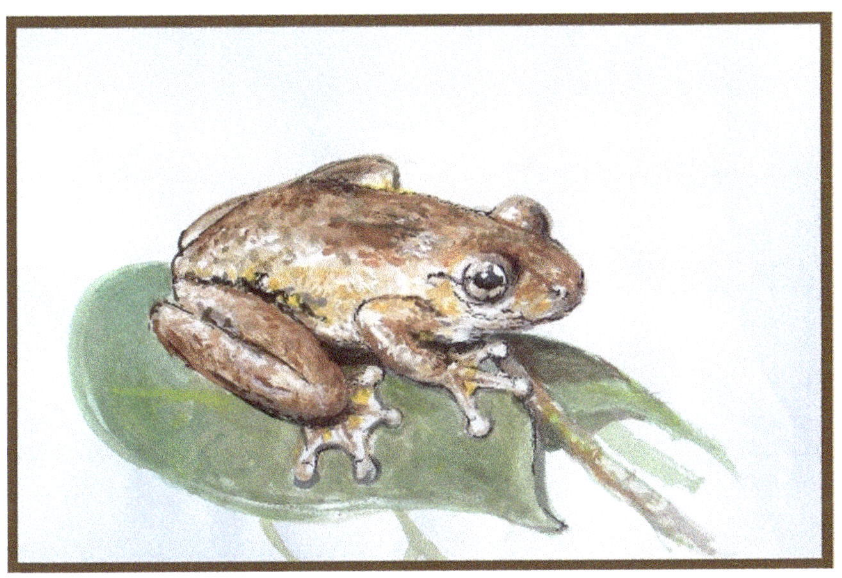

Friendly Frog

Acrylic on board, 26 x 38 cm, 2009

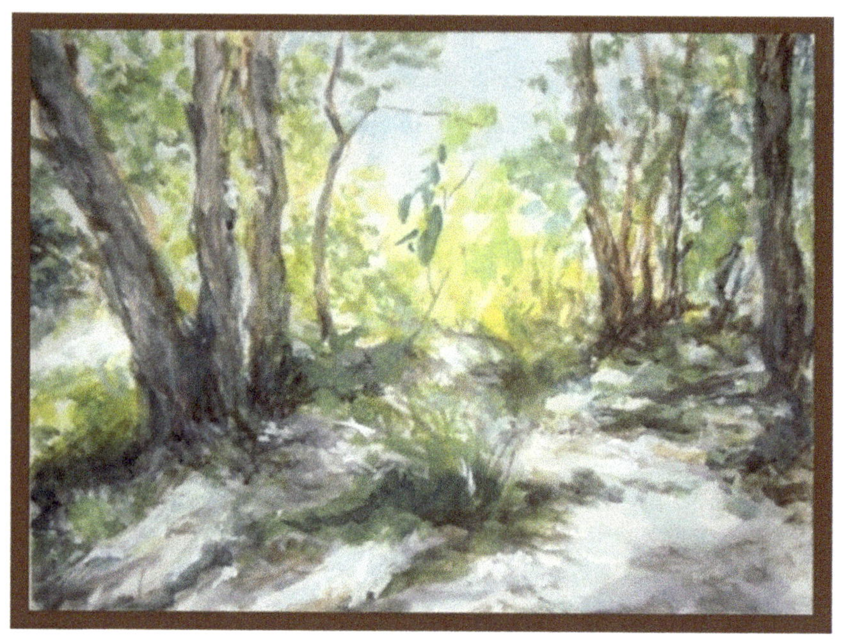

Black Swamp, Cleveland

Acrylic on paper, 29 x 39 cm, 2009

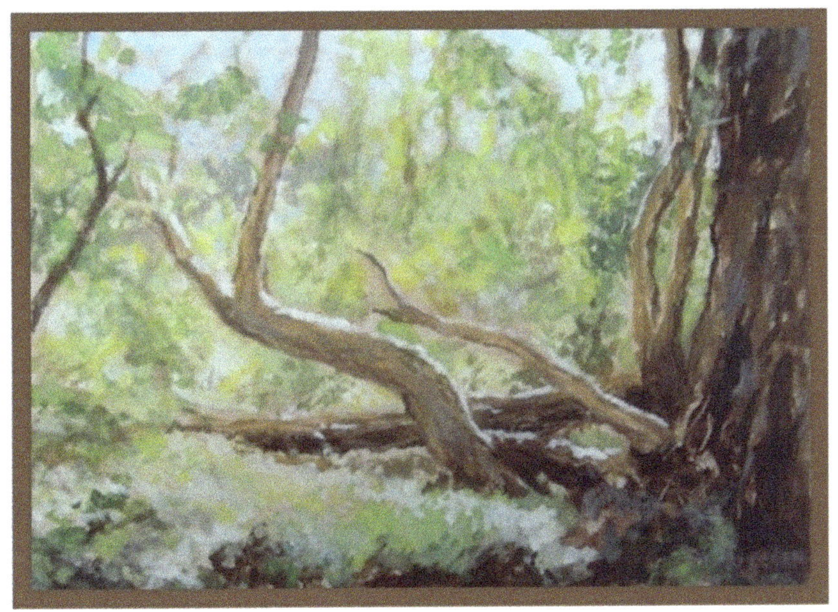

Sunny Morning

Acrylic on paper, 27 x 38 cm, 2009

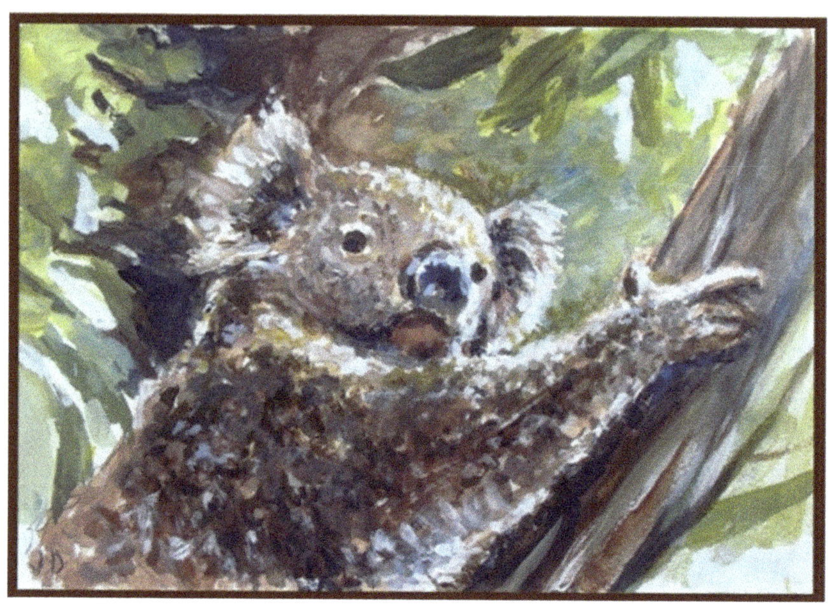

Koala

Acrylic on paper, 29 x 39 cm, 2009

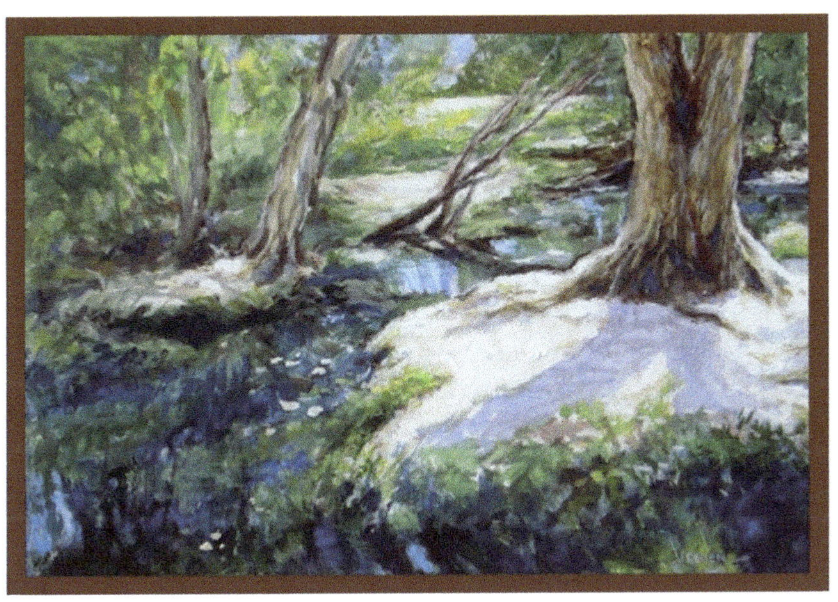

At Hilliards Creek

Acrylic on board, 59 x 84 cm, 2008

Are we to paint what's on the face,
what's inside the face,
or what's behind it?
(Pablo Picasso)

The body always expresses the spirit
whose envelope it is.
(Auguste Rodin)

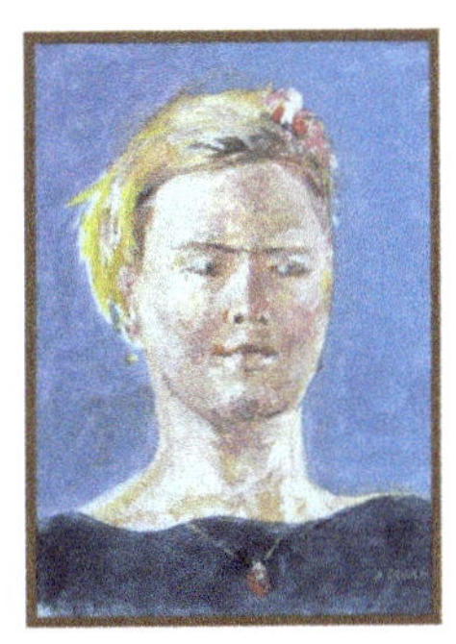

Portraits

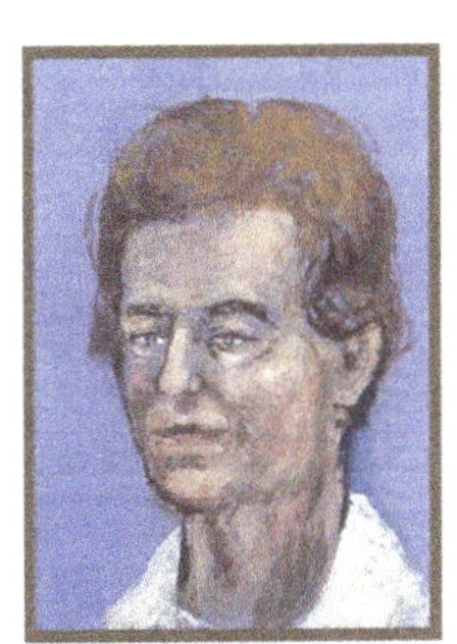

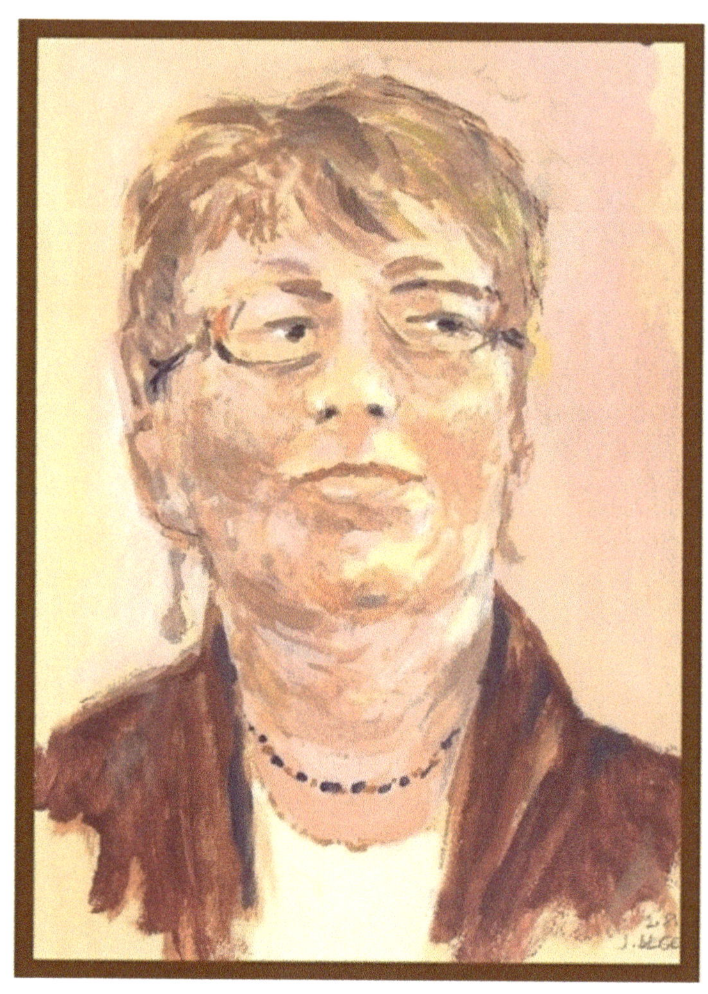

Auburn Hair

Acrylic on paper, 39 x 28 cm, 2009

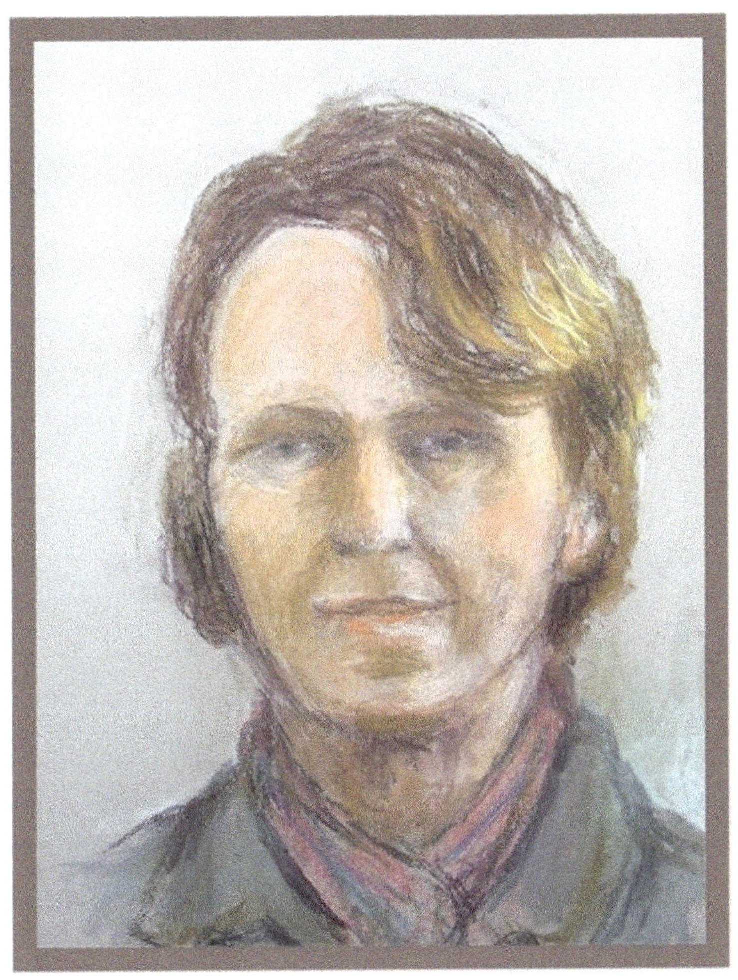

Sue

Pastel on paper, 38 x 28 cm, 2009

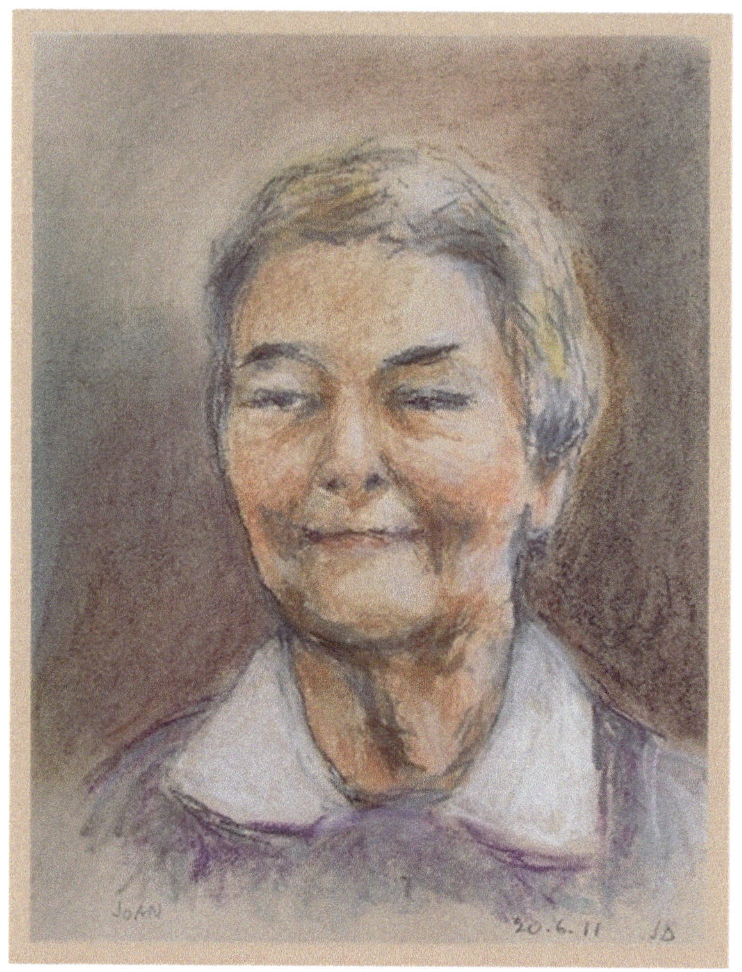

At Peace

Pastel on paper, 32 x 26 cm, 2011

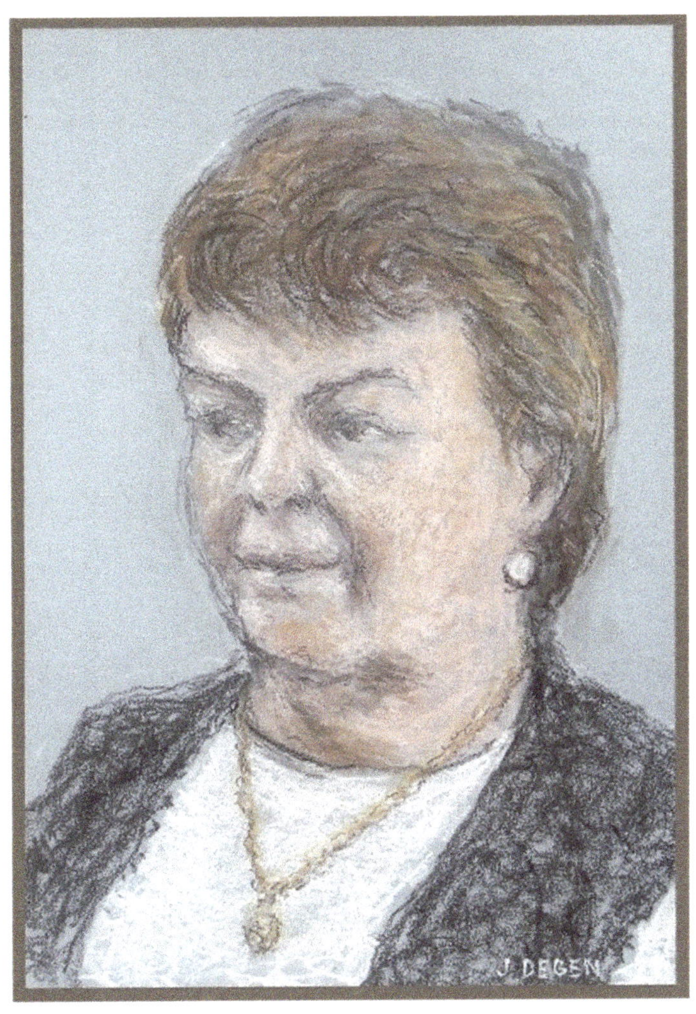

Lost in Thought

Pastel on paper, 35 x 23 cm, 2010

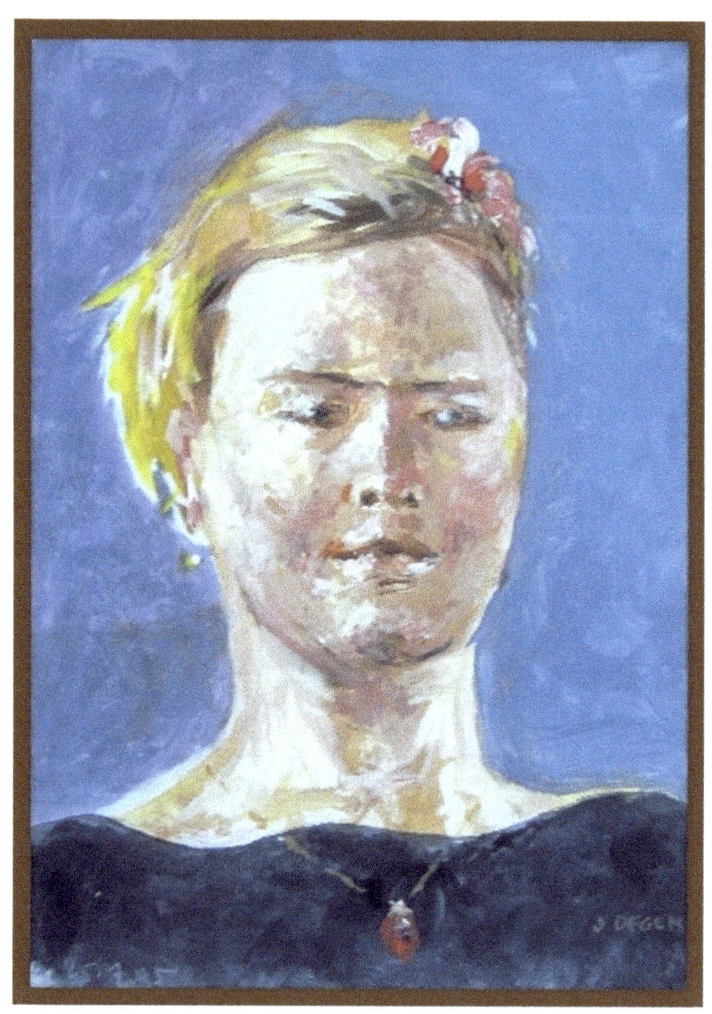

Young Blonde

Acrylic on paper, 40 x 30 cm, 2009

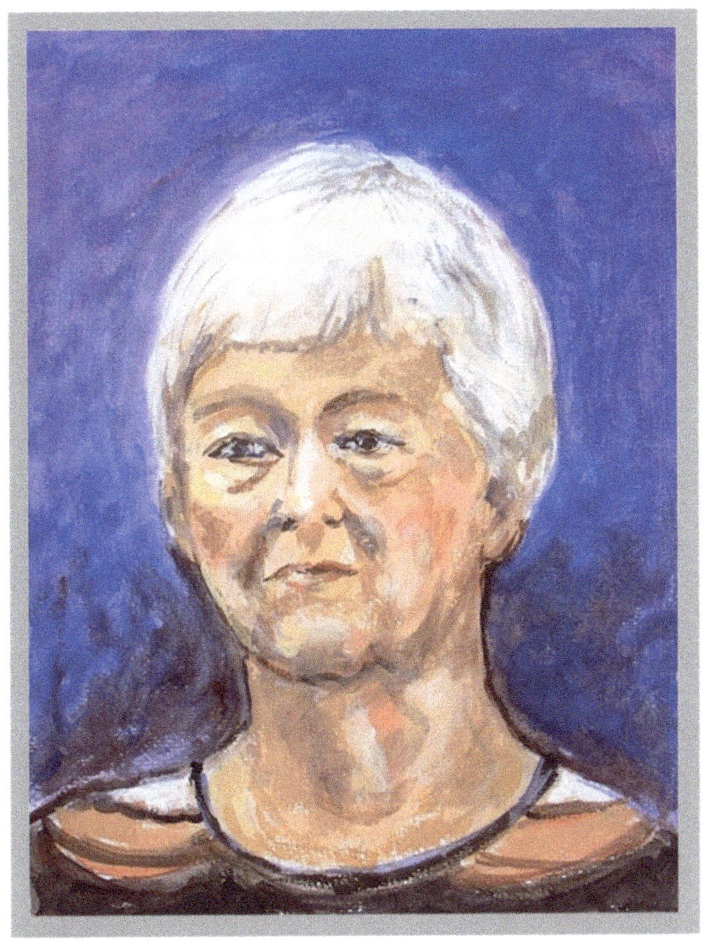

Subdued

Acrylic on paper, 32 x 26 cm, 2007

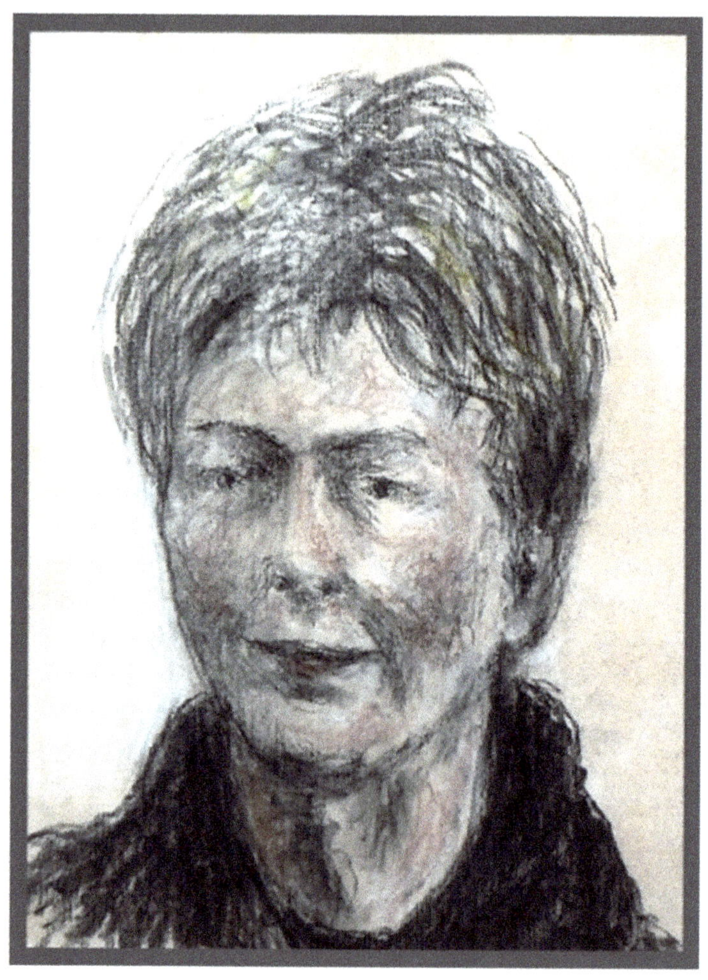

Portrait of a Lady

Pastel on paper, 38 x 28 cm, 2009

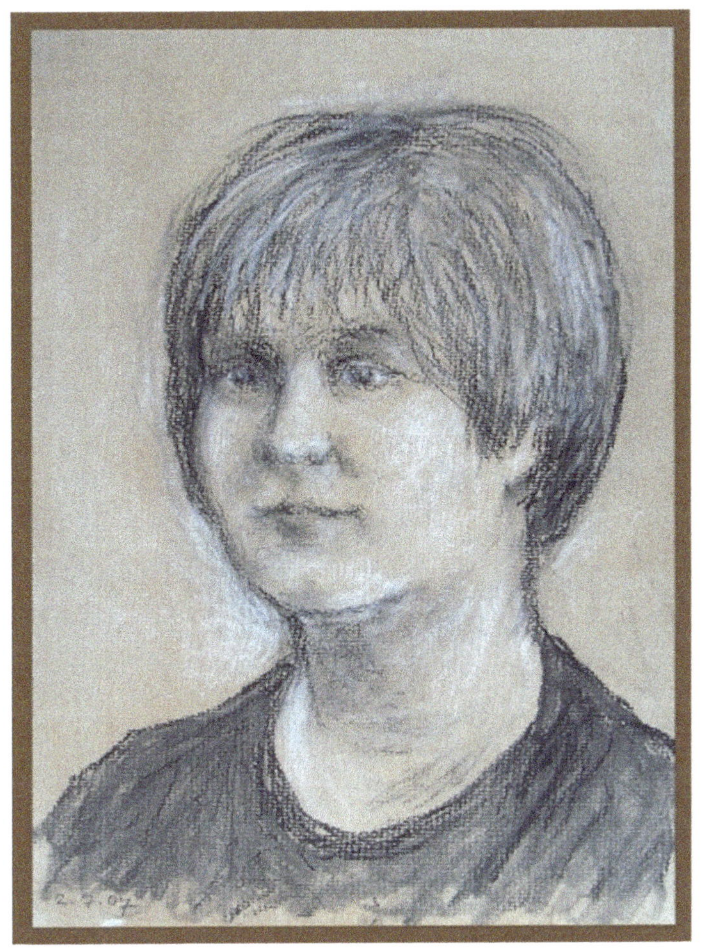

Youth

Mixed media on paper, 40 x 28 cm, 2009

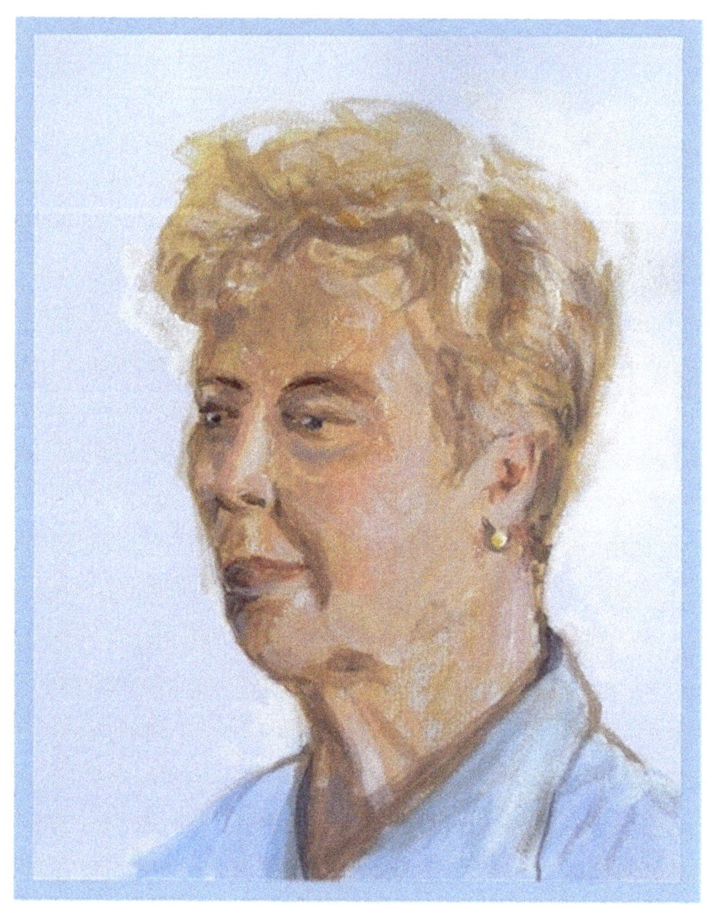

Portrait Sitter

Acrylic on paper, 30 x 25 cm, 2008

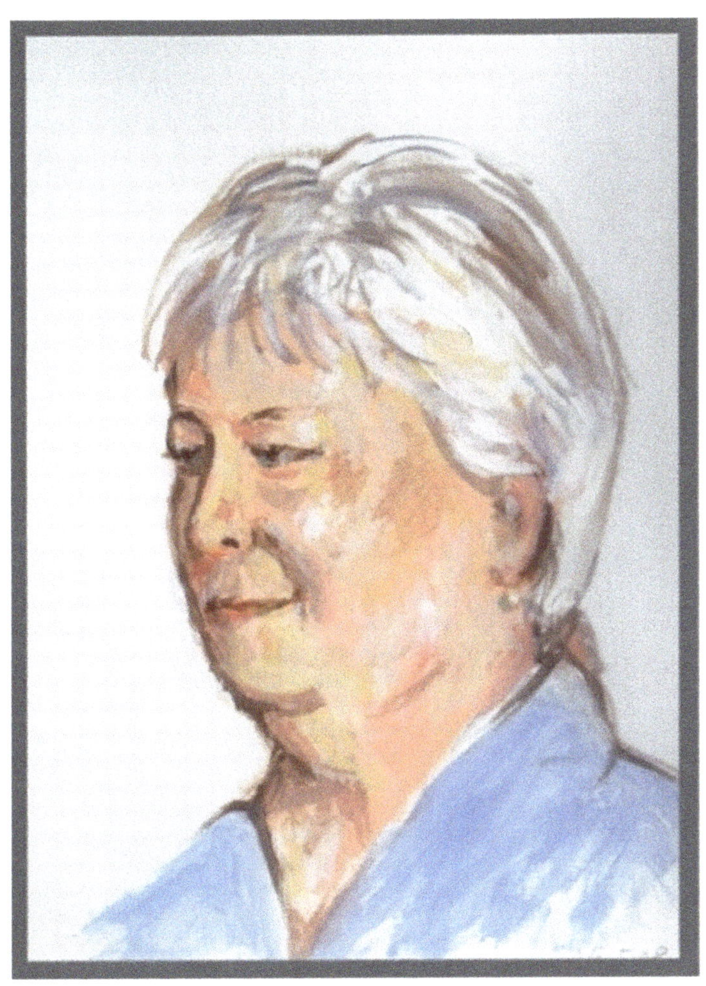

Contentment

Acrylic on paper, 37 x 28 cm, 2008

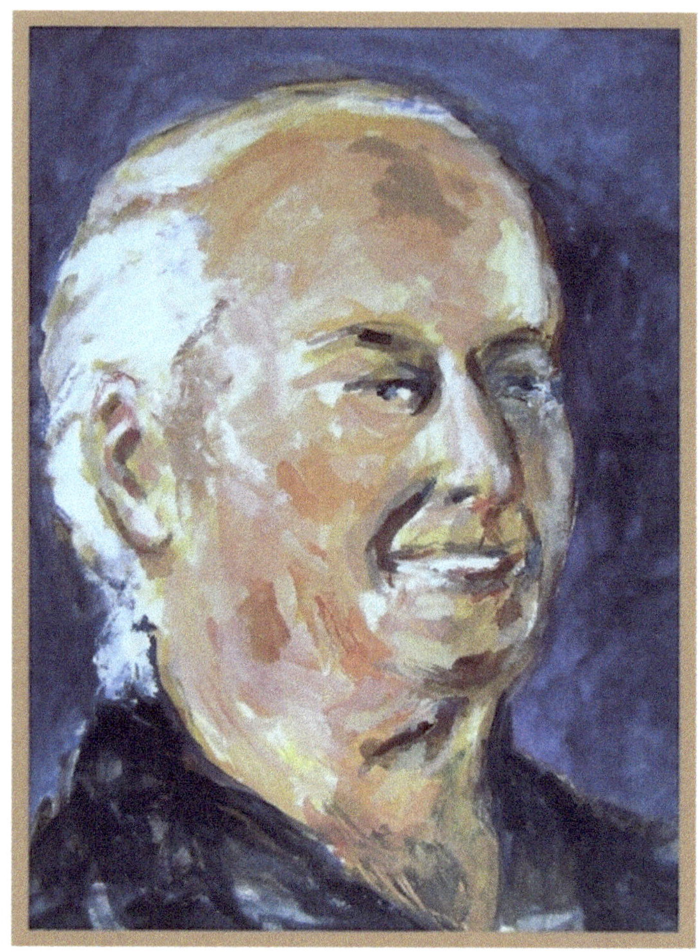

Eric

Acrylic on paper, 40 x 30 cm, 2009

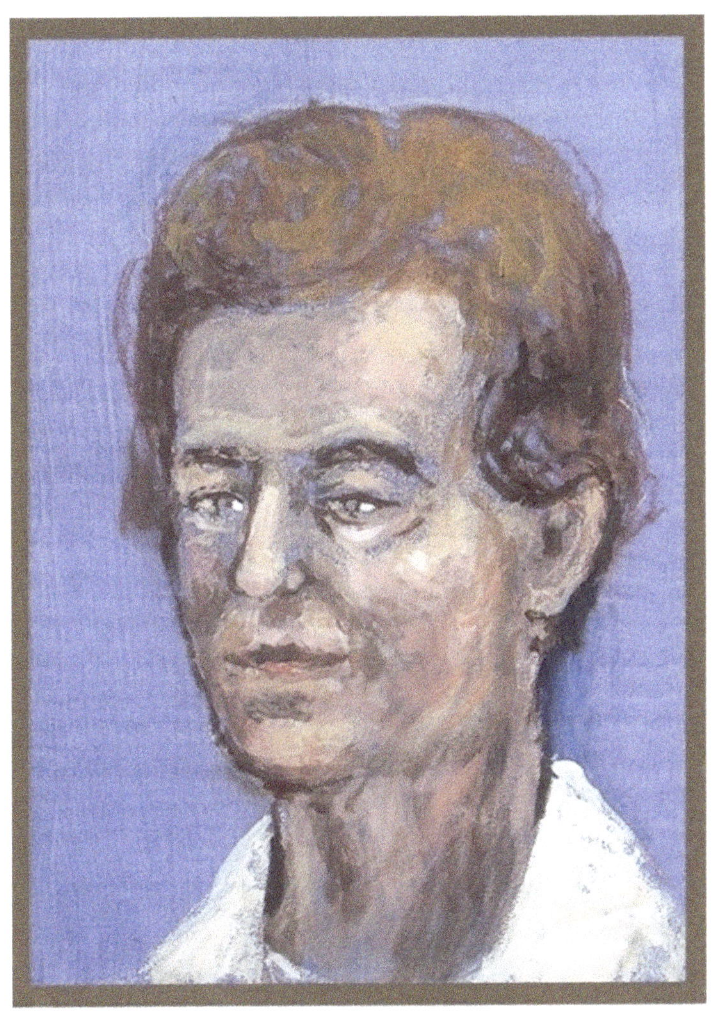

Pensive

Pastel on paper, 30 x 22 cm, 2008

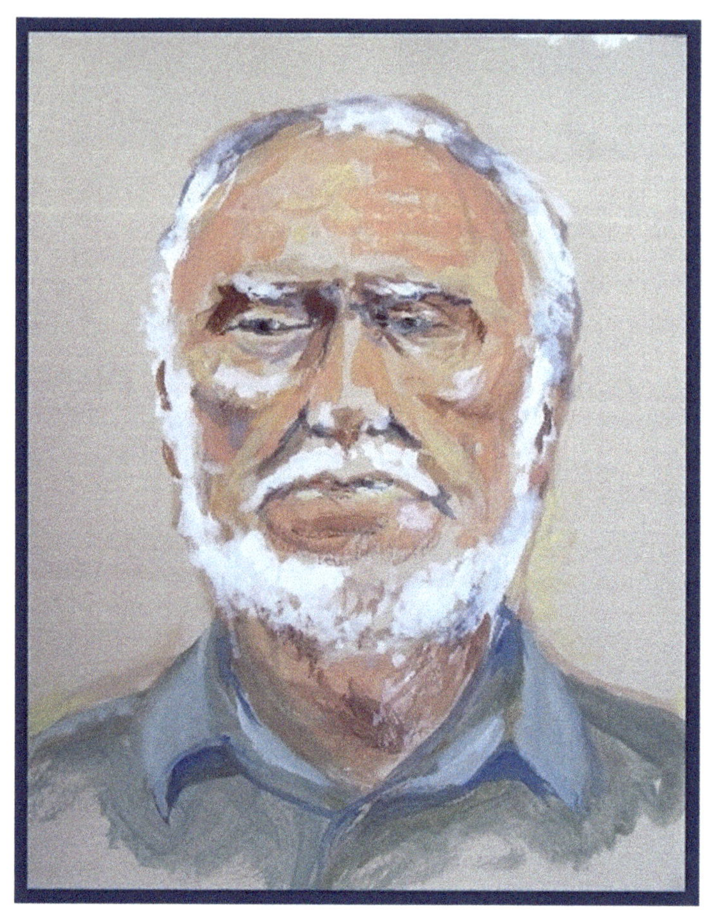

Robert

Acrylic on paper, 40 x 30 cm, 2009

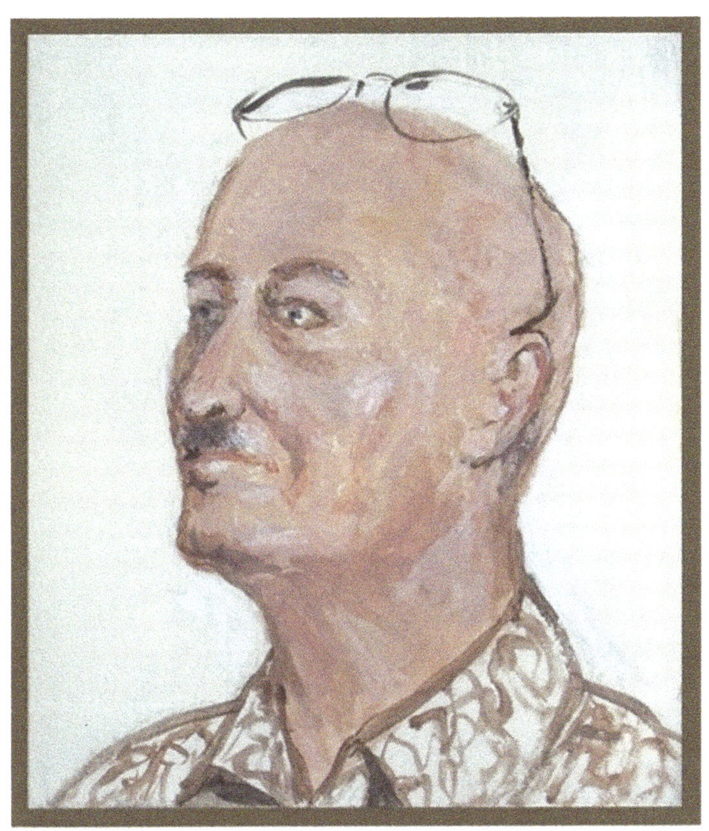

Dave

Acrylic on paper, 26 x 22 cm, 2008

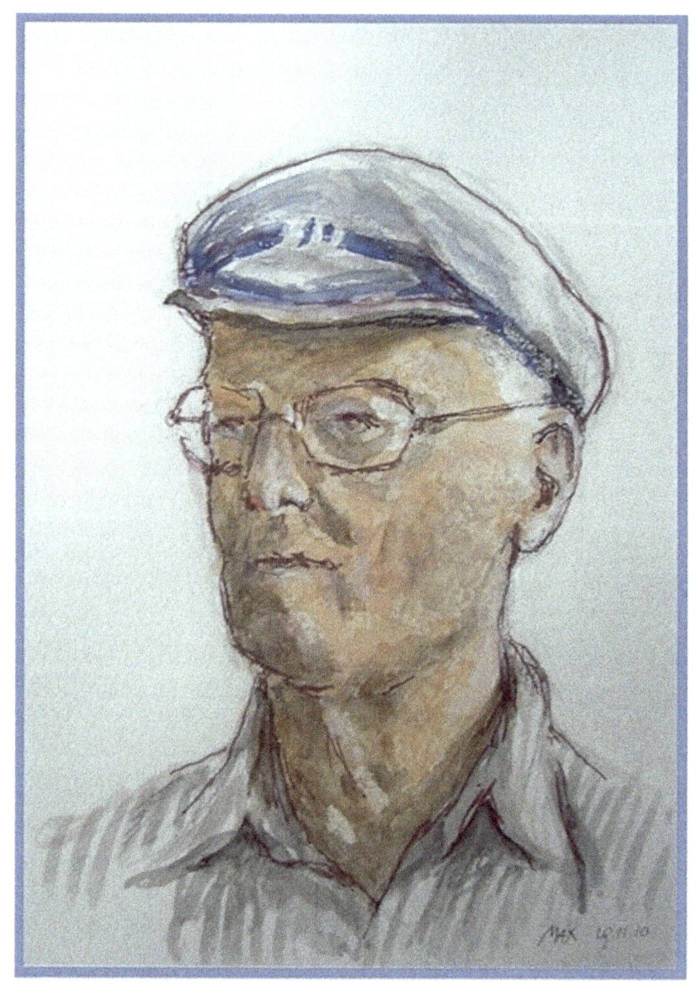

Max

Acrylic on paper, 38 x 28 cm, 2008

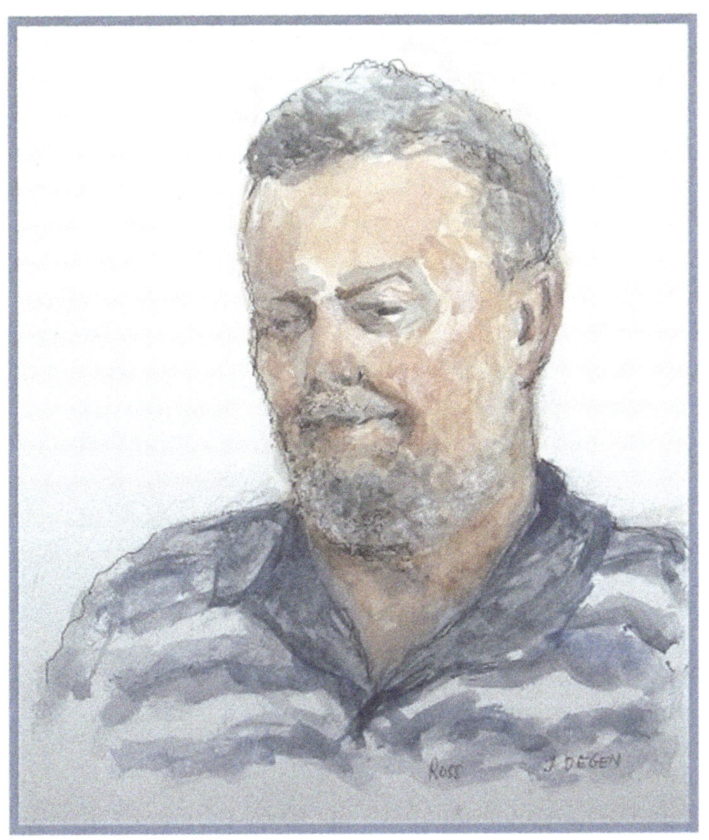

Ross

Acrylic on paper, 38 x 28 cm, 2010

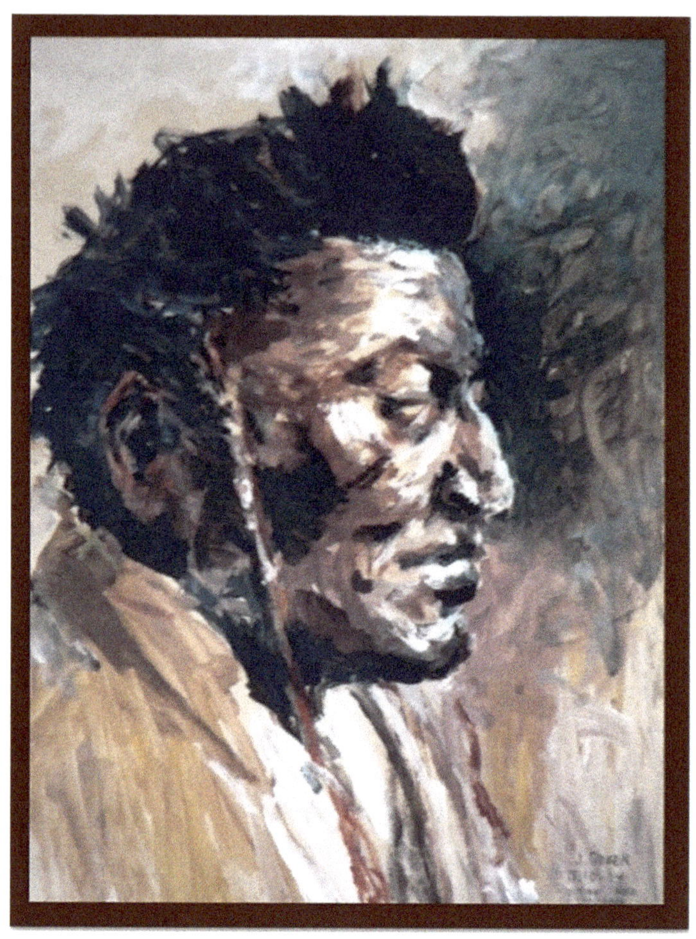

The Red Man

Acrylic on paper, 39 x 29 cm, 2005

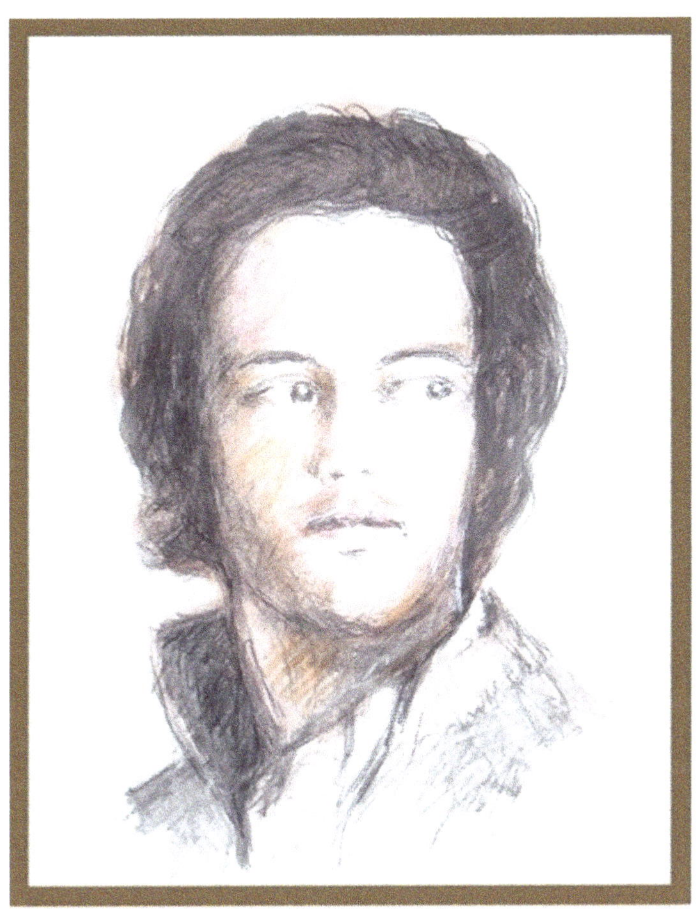

Young Man

Pastel on paper, 30 x 25 cm, 2010

Art will never be able to exist
without nature.
(Pierre Bonnard)

Art does not reproduce the visible;
rather, it makes visible.
(Paul Klee)

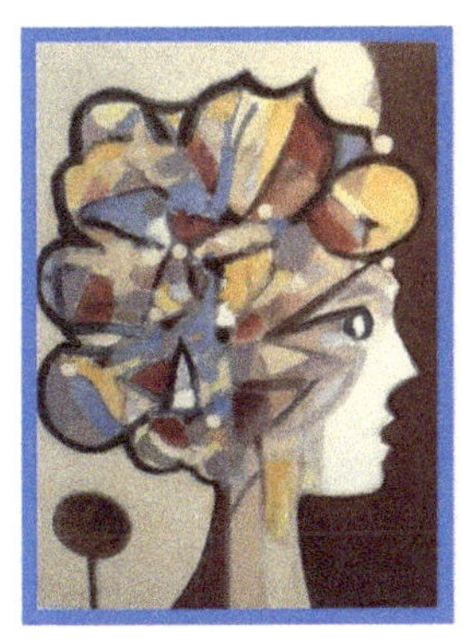

Inspired by Nature

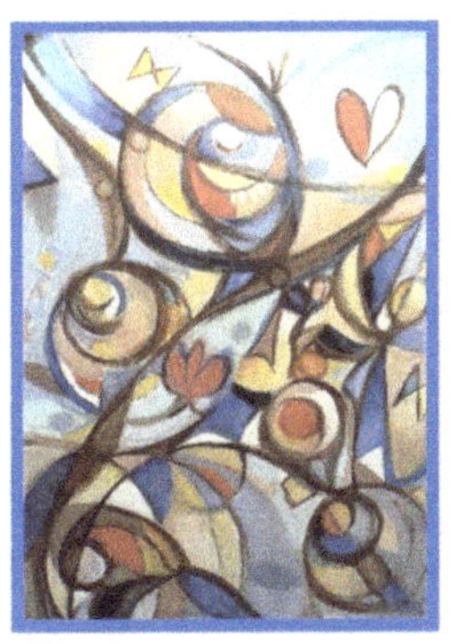

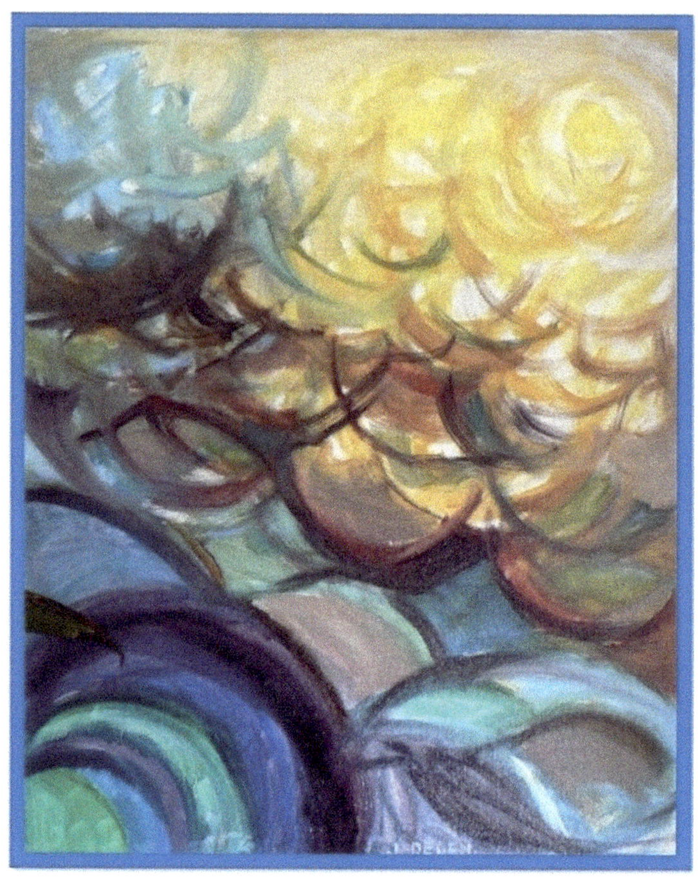

From the Abyss to the Sun

Oil on canvas, 50 x 40 cm, 2005

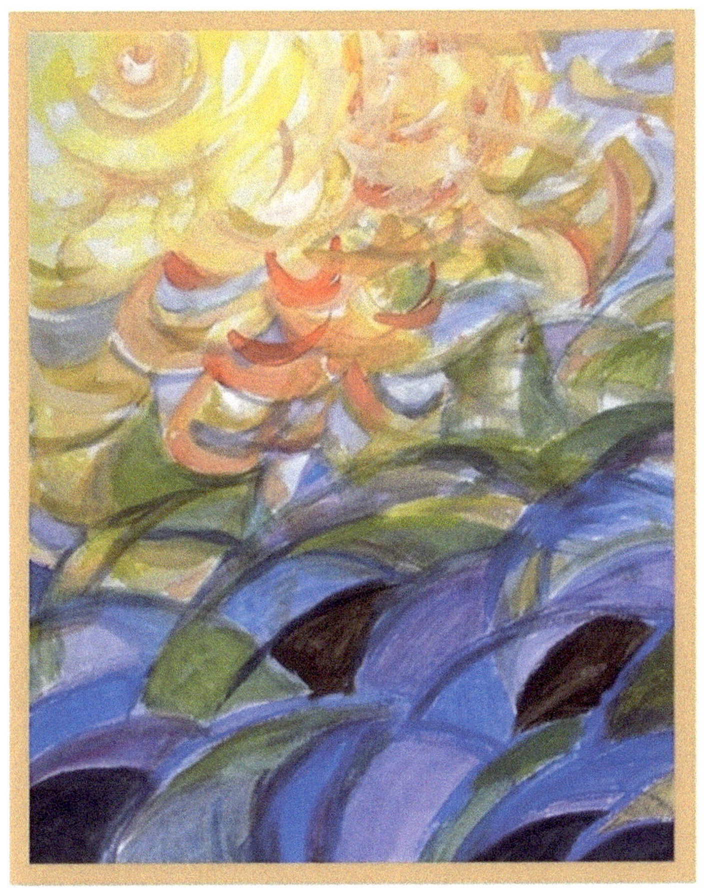

Flow in the Sun

Acrylic on paper, 28 x 22 cm, 2009

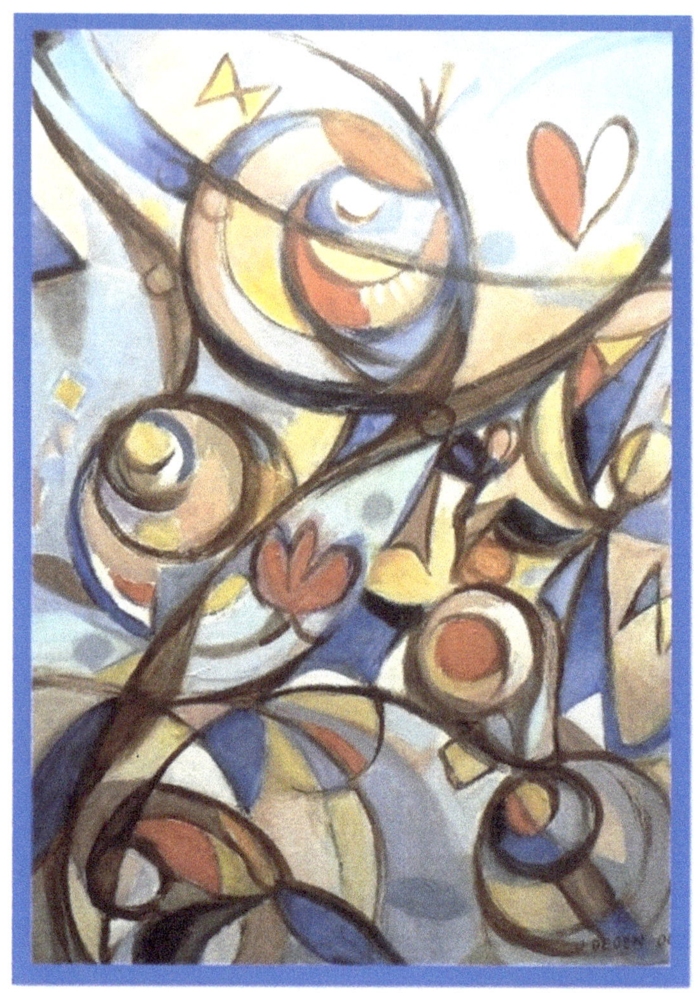

Something in the Air

Oil on canvas, 60 x 45 cm, 2005

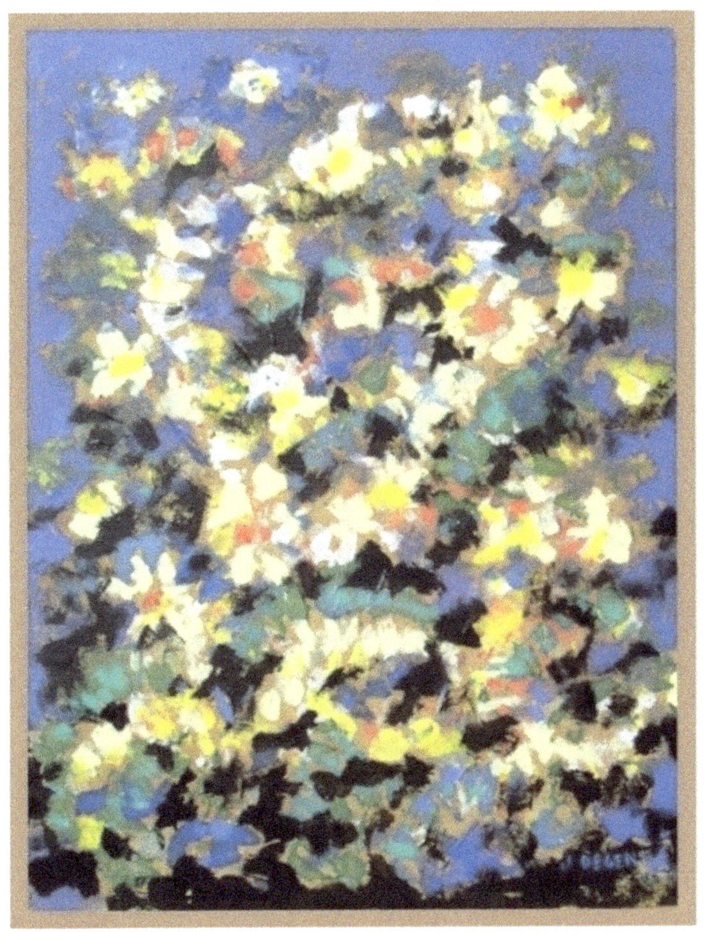

Summer Feeling

Acrylic on board, 40 x 29 cm, 2009

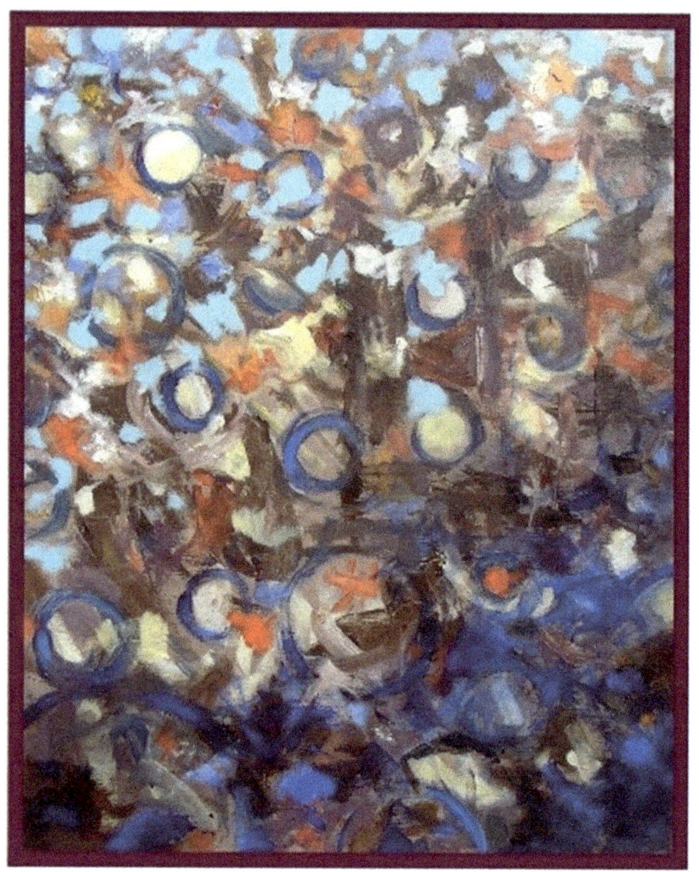

Meadow

Oil on canvas, 51 x 41.5 cm, 2009

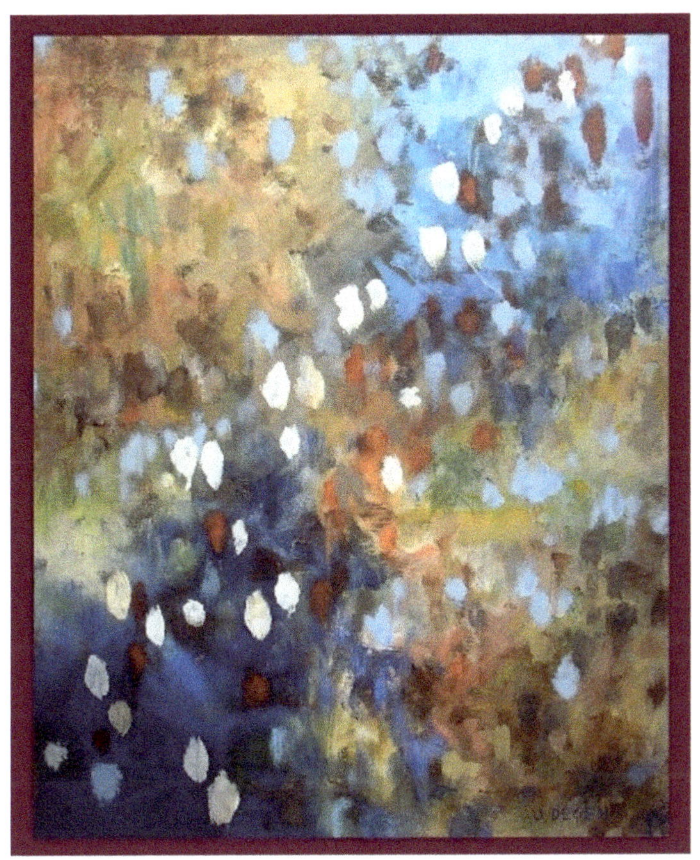

Flowering Meadow

Oil on canvas, 51 x 41.5 cm, 2009

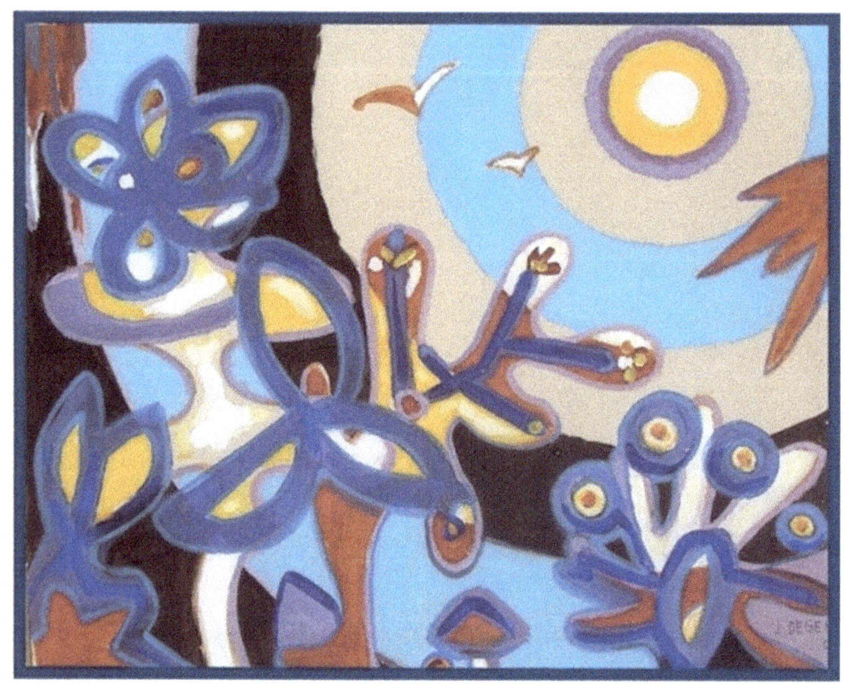

Place in the Sun

Acrylic on board, 37 x 45 cm, 2003

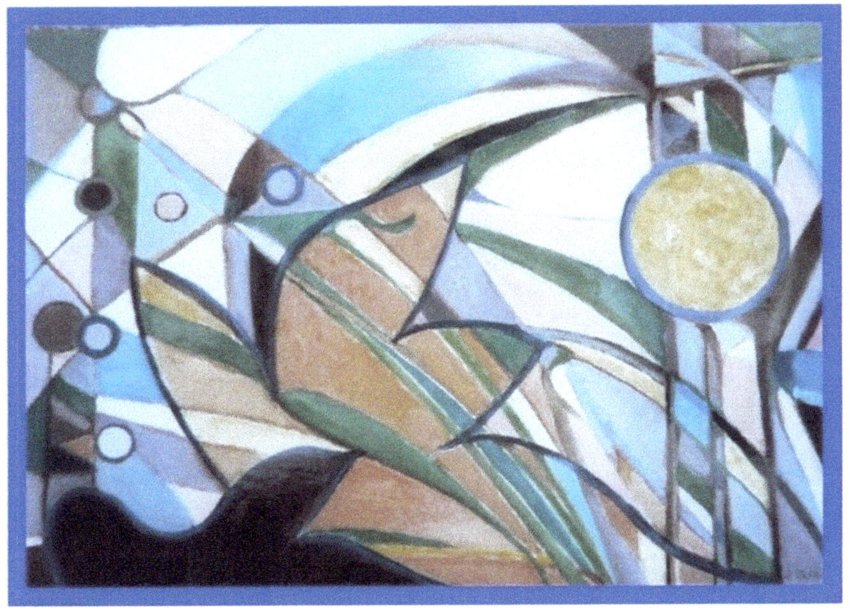

Tropical

Oil on canvas, 51 x 76 cm, 2005

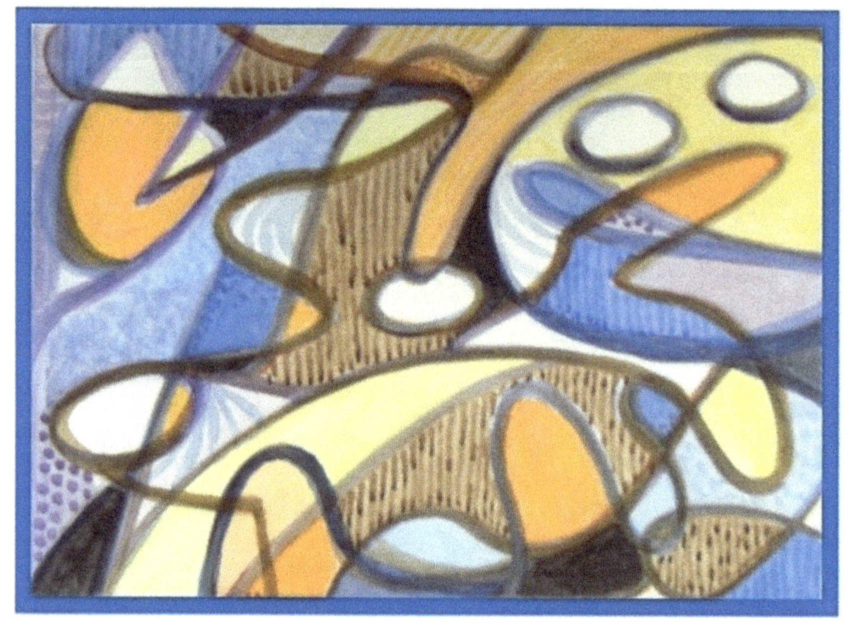

Waves

Watercolour on paper, 28 x 37 cm, 2009

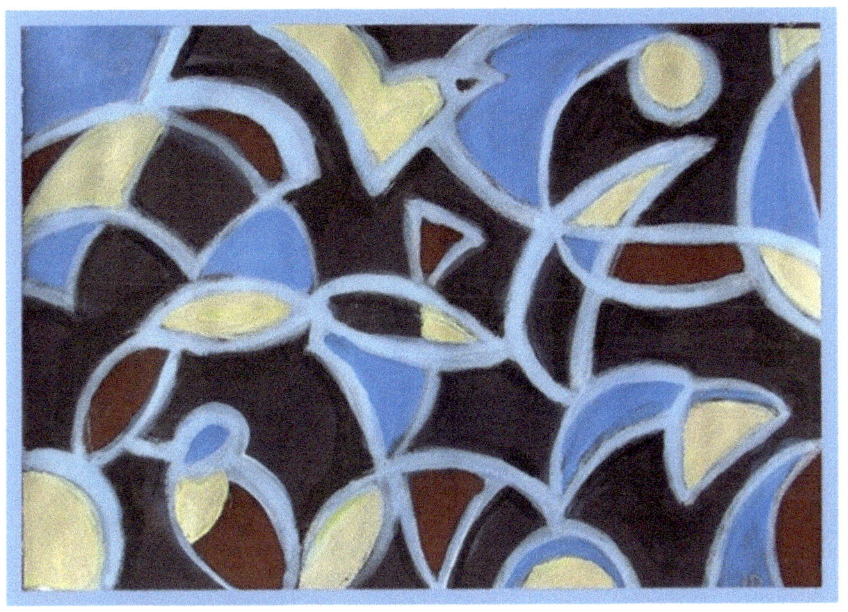

Friends in Nature

Acrylic on board, 47 x 60 cm, 2010

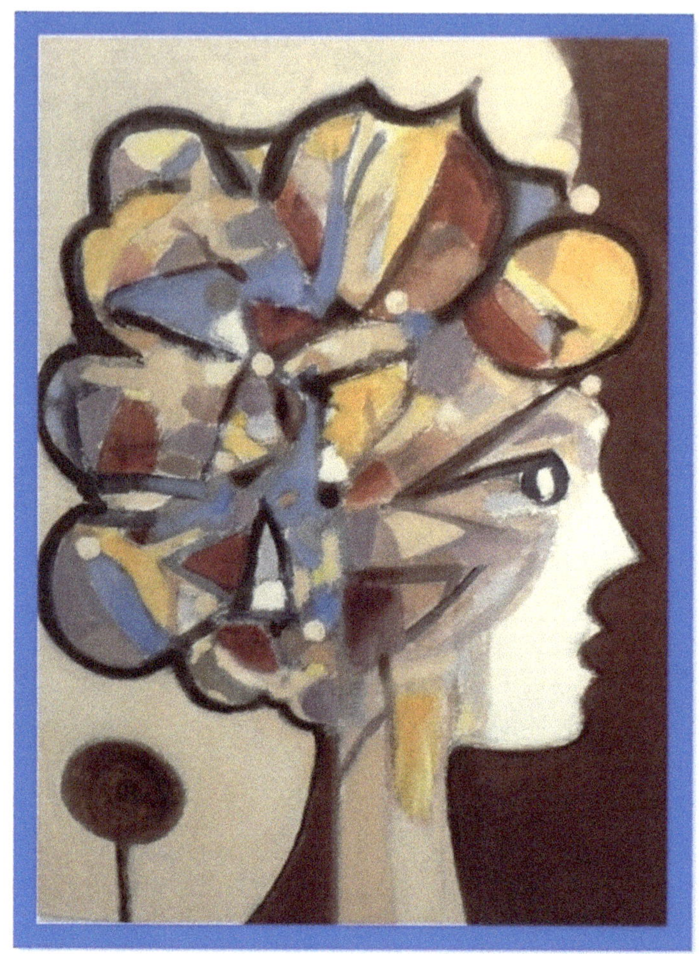

Lady of the Trees

Oil on canvas, 51 x 41 cm, 2005

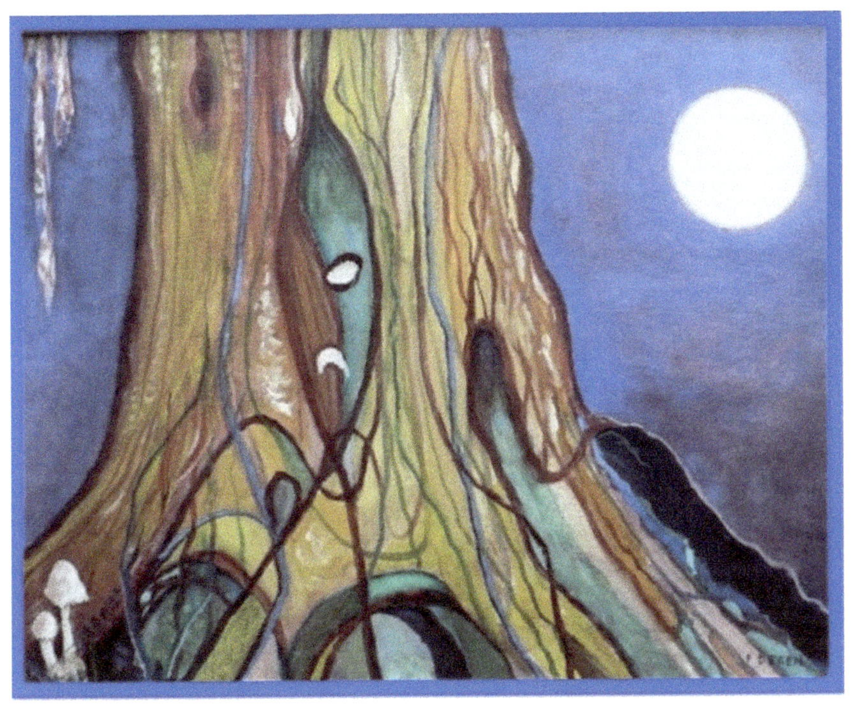

In the Forest

Oil on board, 43 x 58.5 cm, 2002

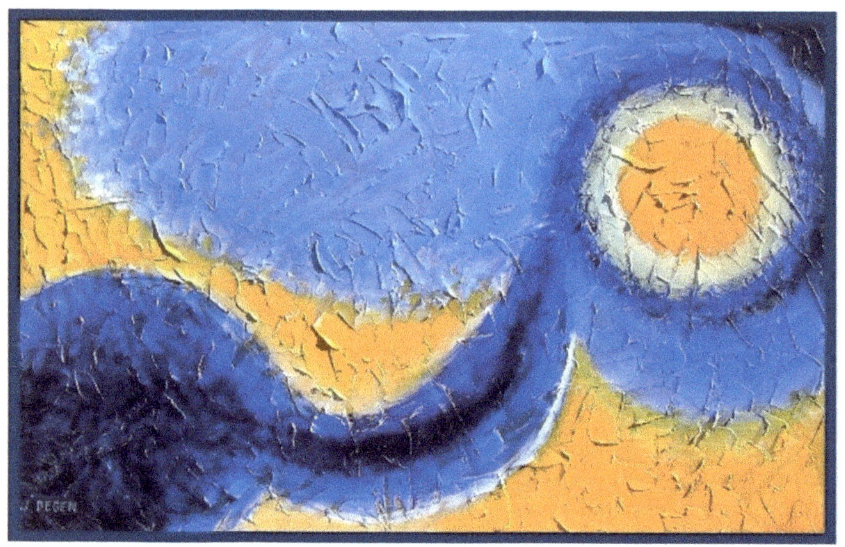

The Sun Under Attack

Acrylic on board, 60 x 90 cm, 2009

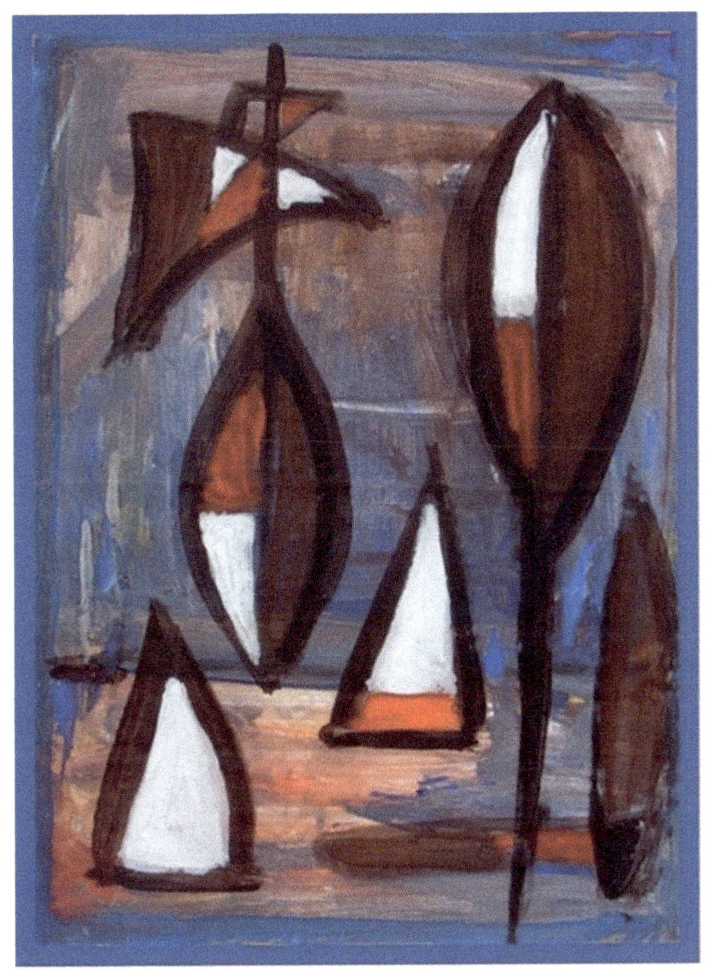

Red Tide

Acrylic on paper, 30 x 22 cm, 2011

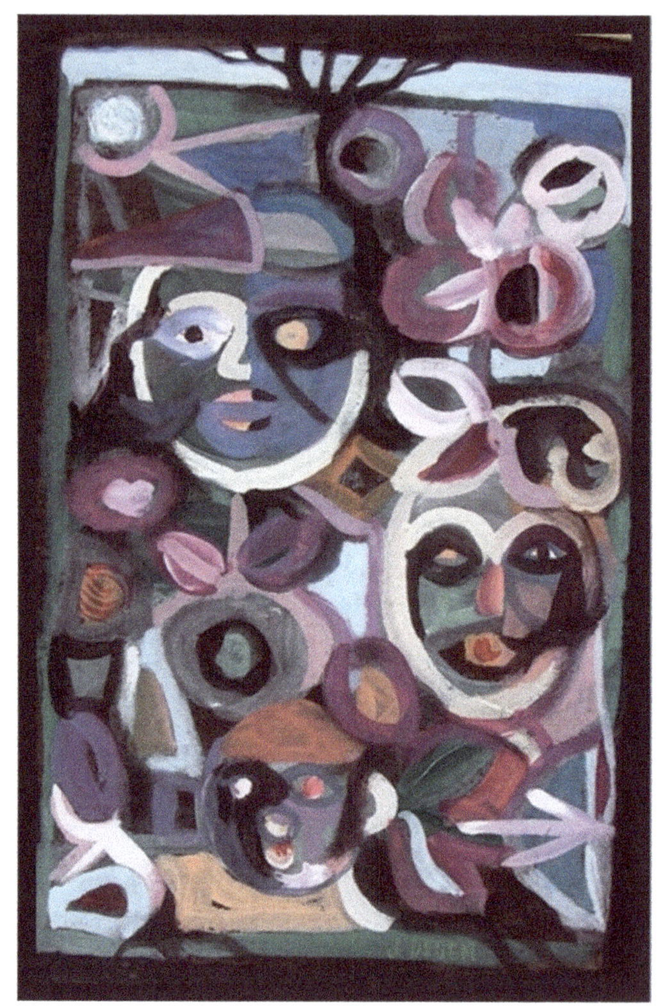

Nightfall at Camp

Acrylic on paper, 31 x 23 cm, 2005

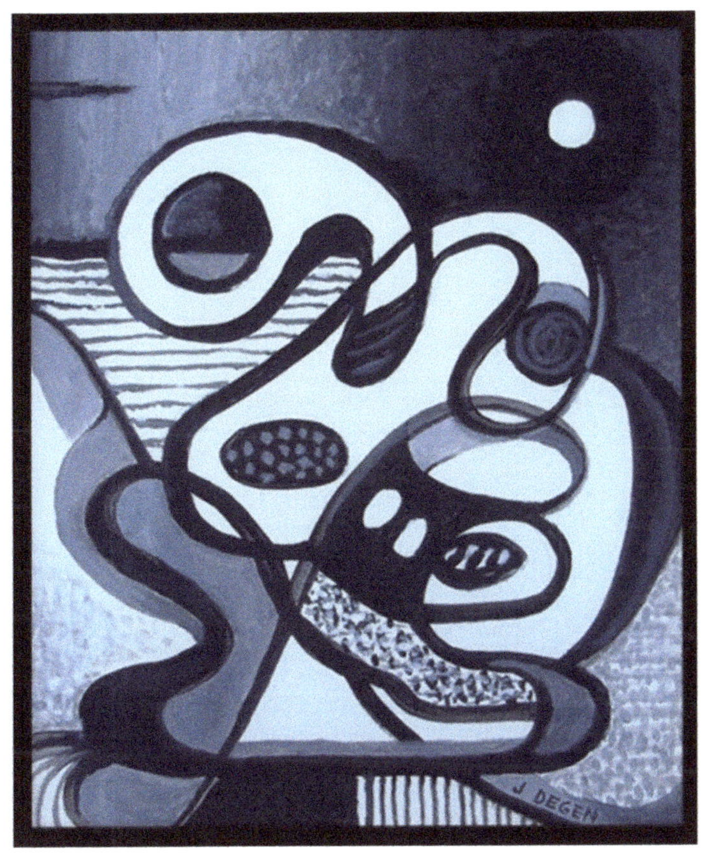

Living Night

Acrylic on board, 30 x 25 cm, 2009

Art is the unceasing effort
to compete with the beauty of flowers
and never succeeding.
(Marc Chagall)

Though short-lived - a symbol of our
impermanence -
flowers remind us of the inner beauty that will
flourish
if we conduct ourselves well in thought and deed.
(Lisa Tenzin-Dolma)

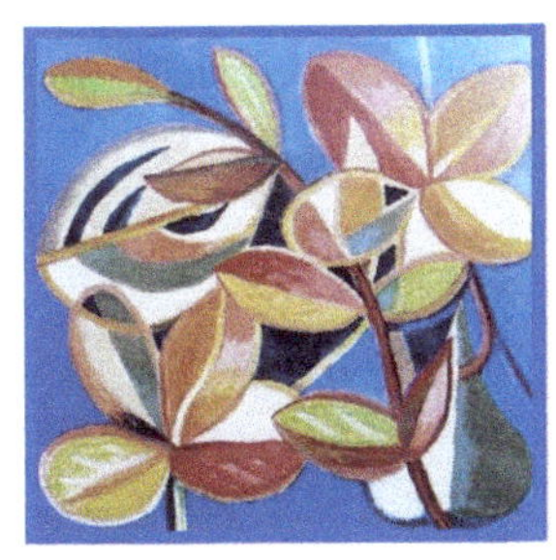

Floral Inspiration

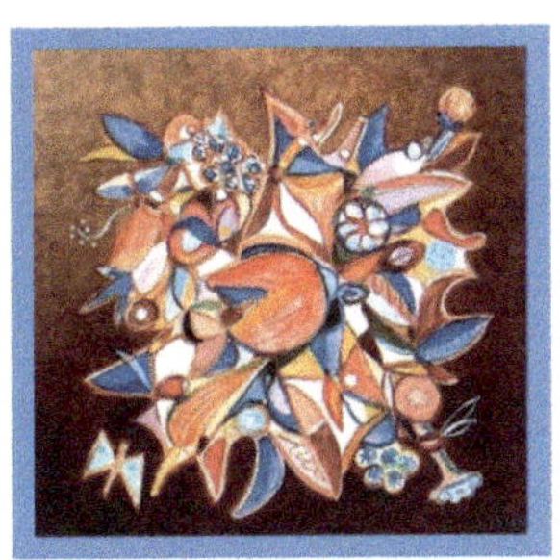

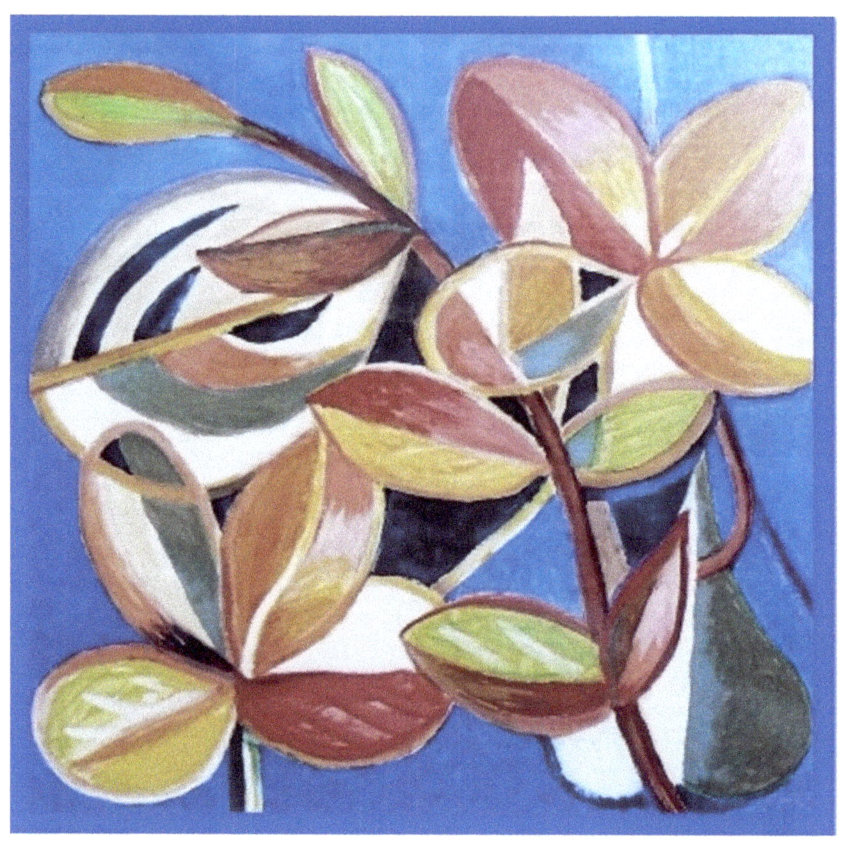

Floral Motive

Acrylic on board, 59 x 58 cm, 2006

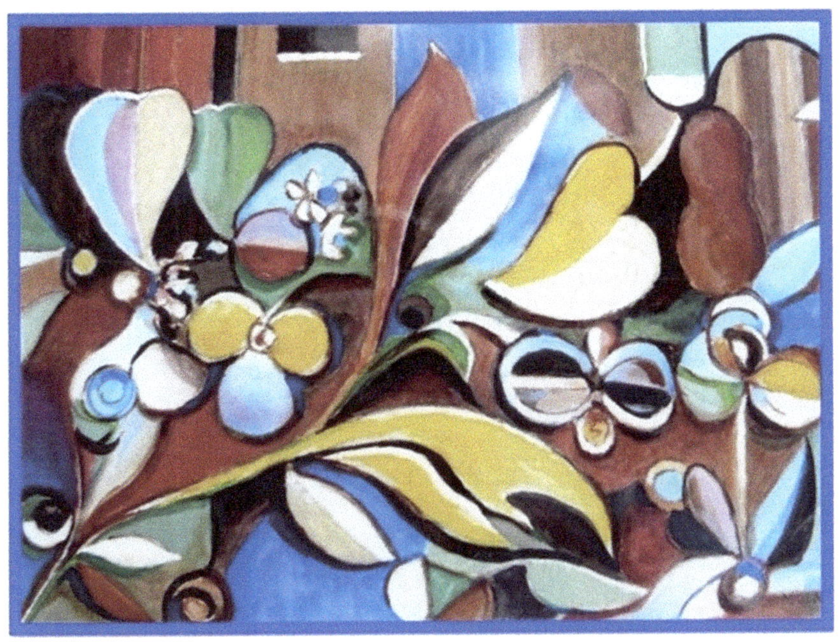

Floriade

Acrylic on board, 41 x 57 cm, 2002

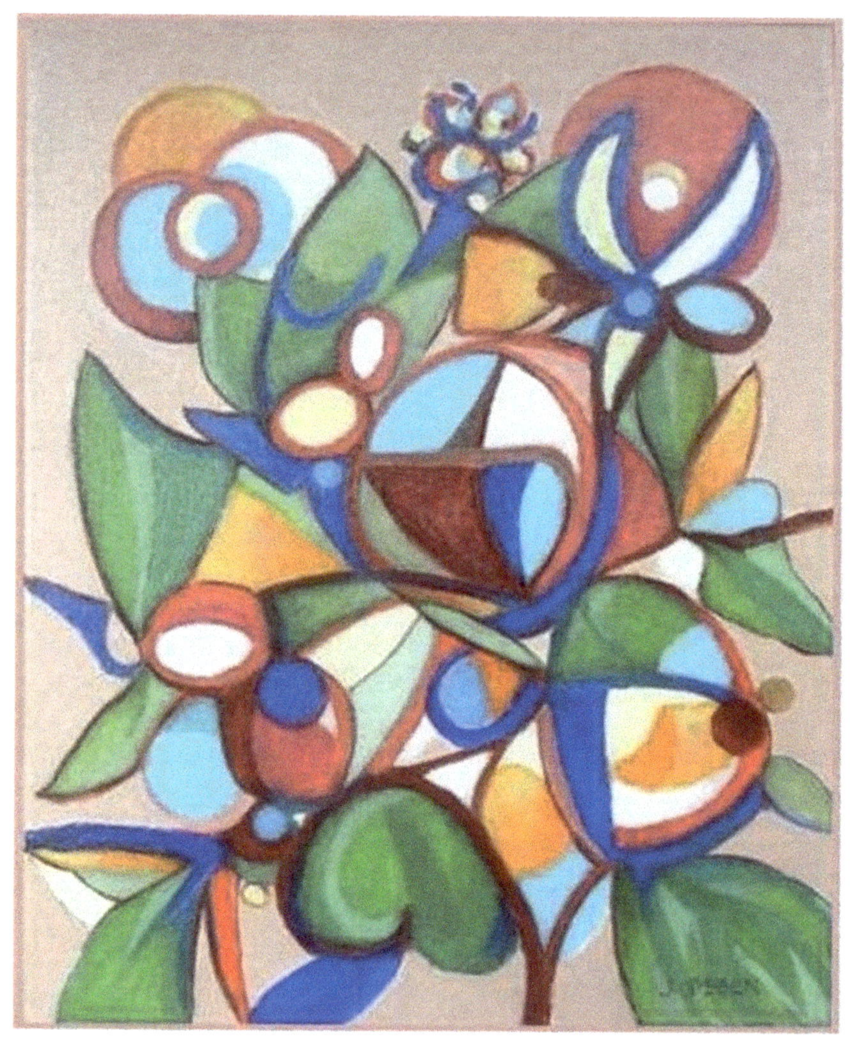

A Nice Day

Oil on canvas, 50 x 40 cm, 2011

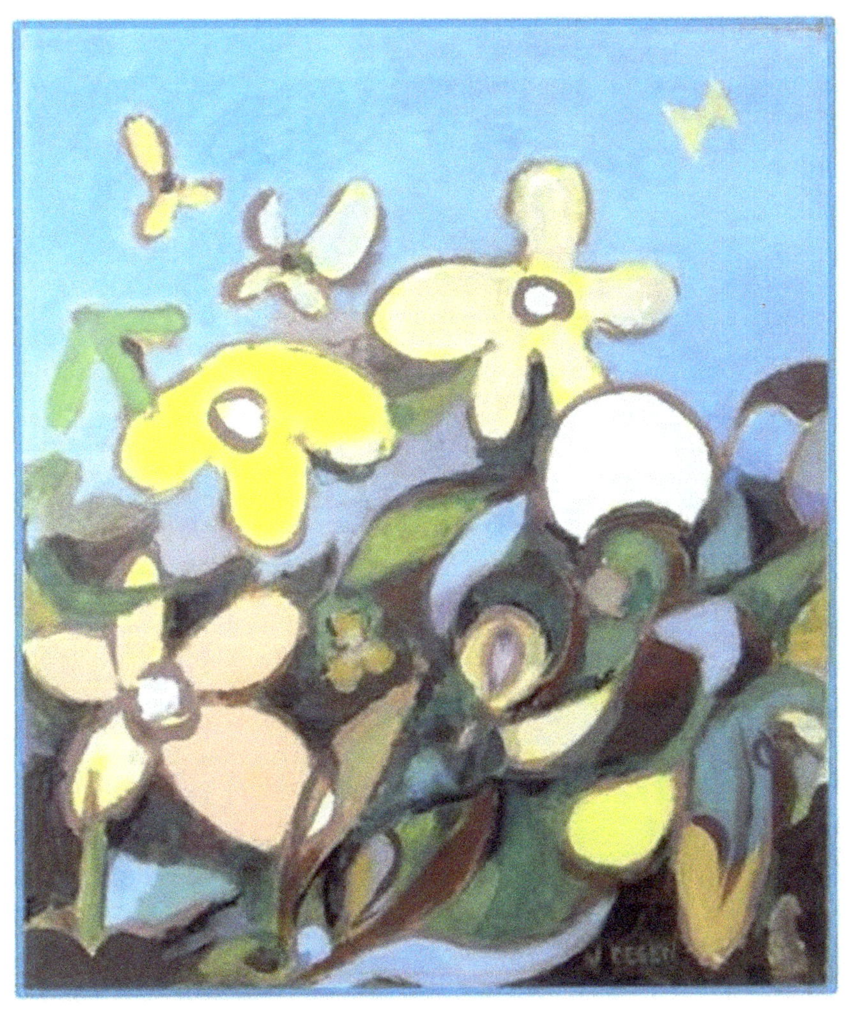

End of Day

Acrylic on board, 51 x 42 cm, 2011

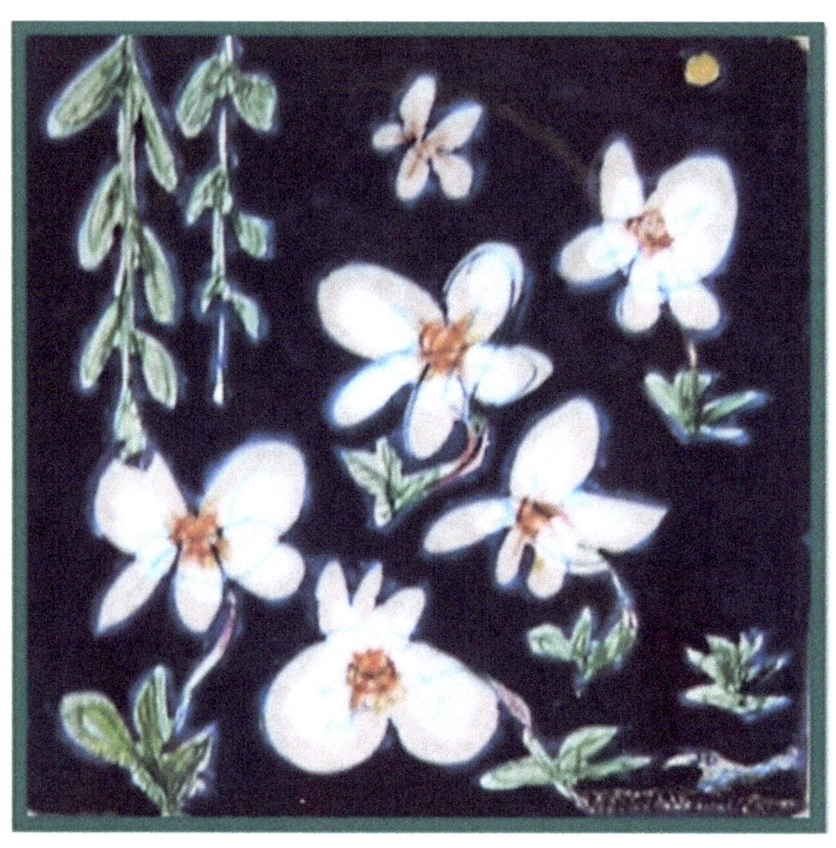

Flowering

Acrylic on paper, 28 x 28 cm, 2006

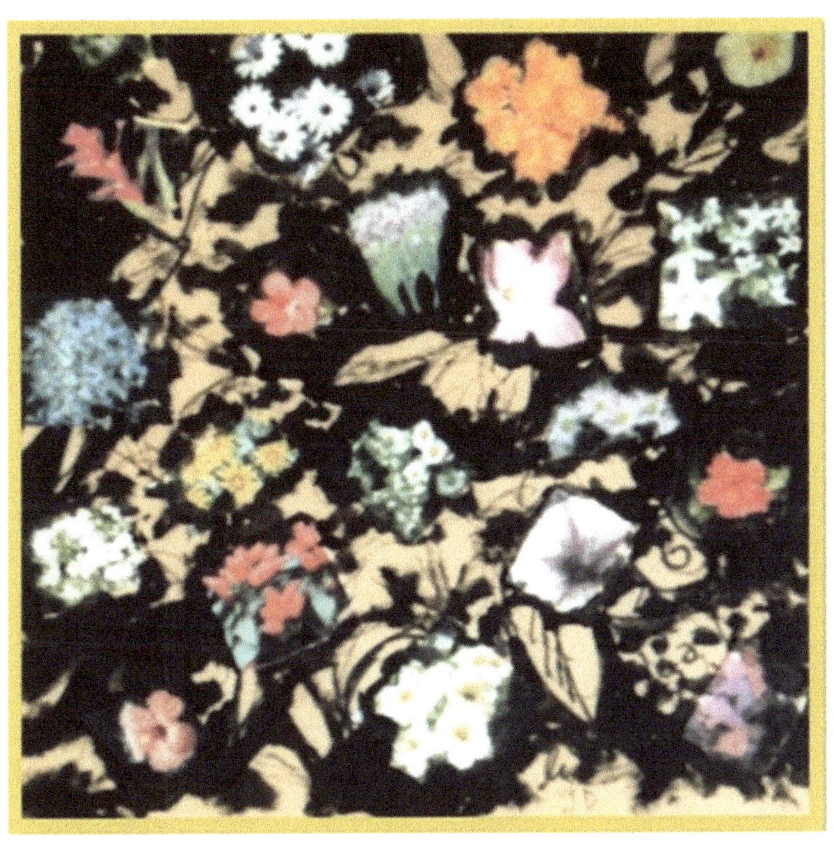

Flowerage

Collage and acrylic on paper, 27 x 26 cm, 2008

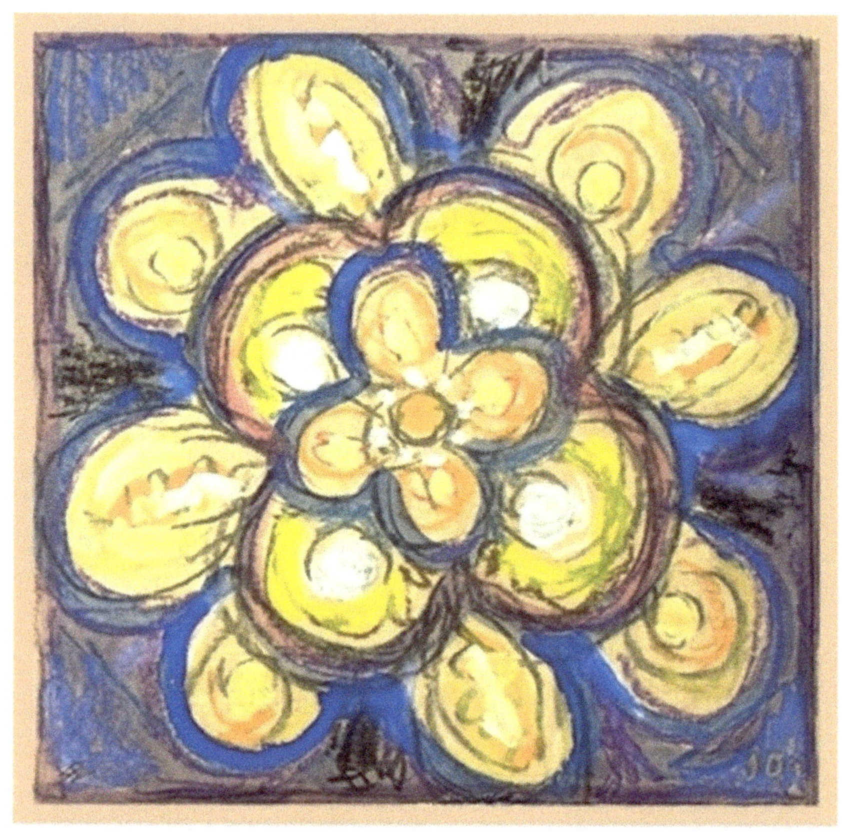

Golden Flower

Mixed media on paper, 28 x 28 cm, 2010

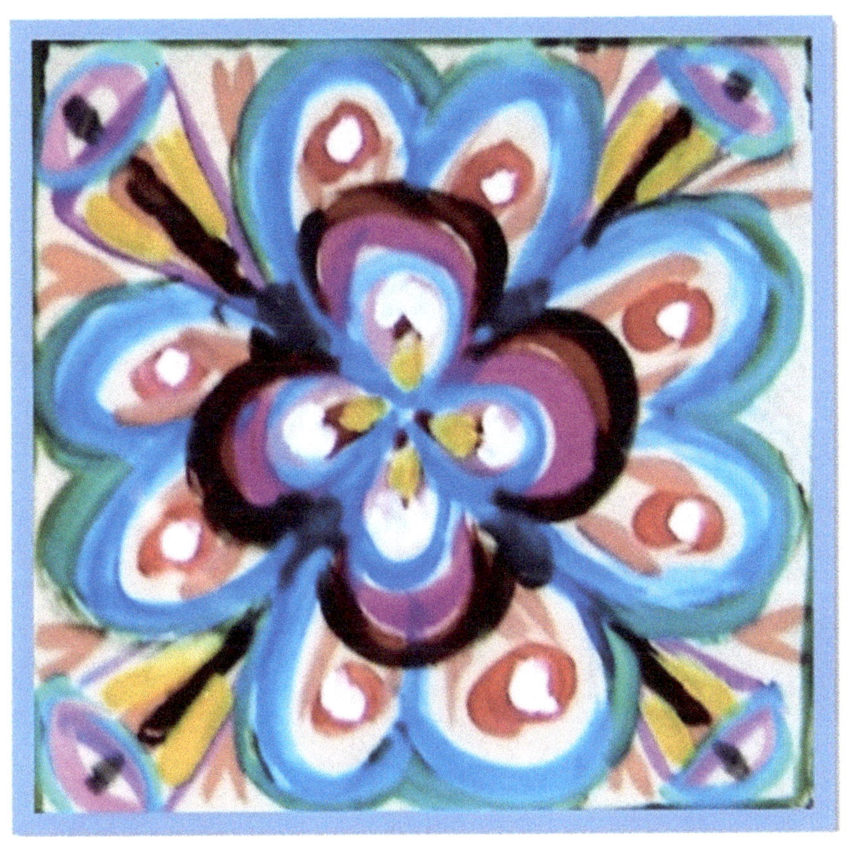

Petals

Acrylic on paper, 27 x 27 cm, 2006

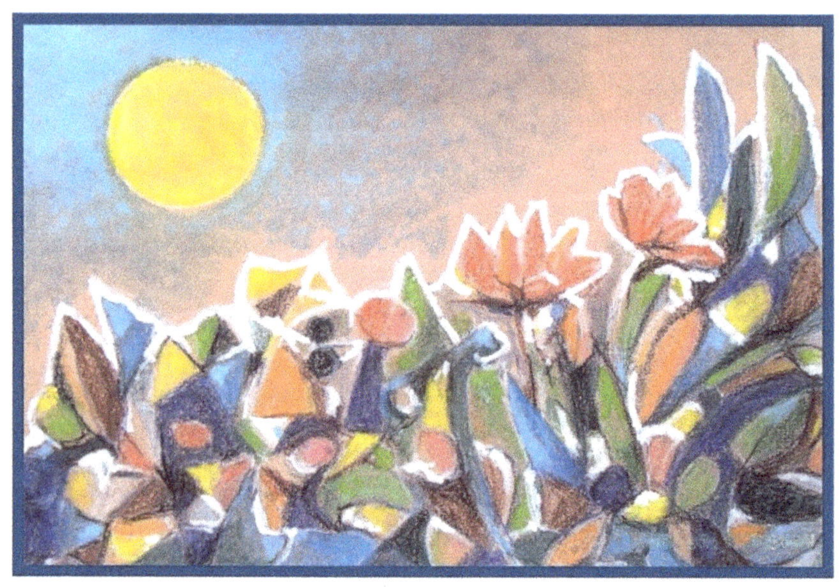

Garden

Acrylic and pastel on paper, 28 x 39 cm, 2009

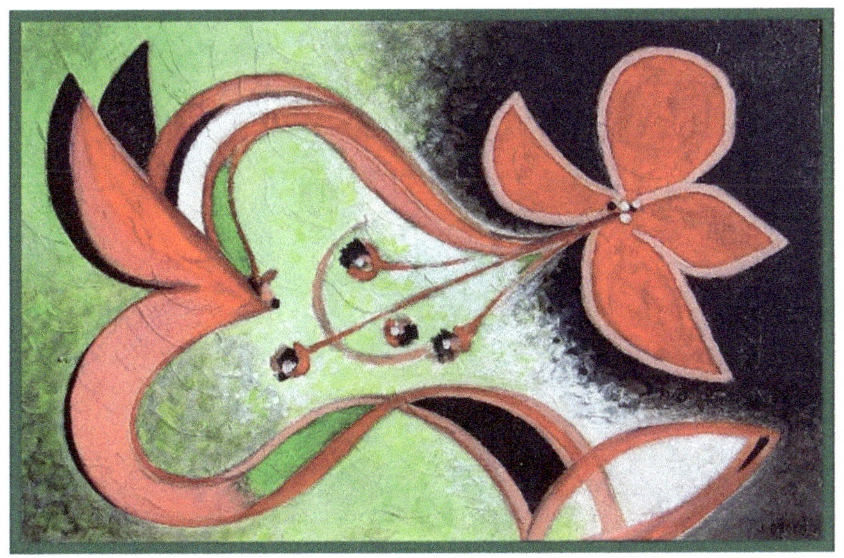

In the Garden

Acrylic on board, 60 x 90 cm, 2009

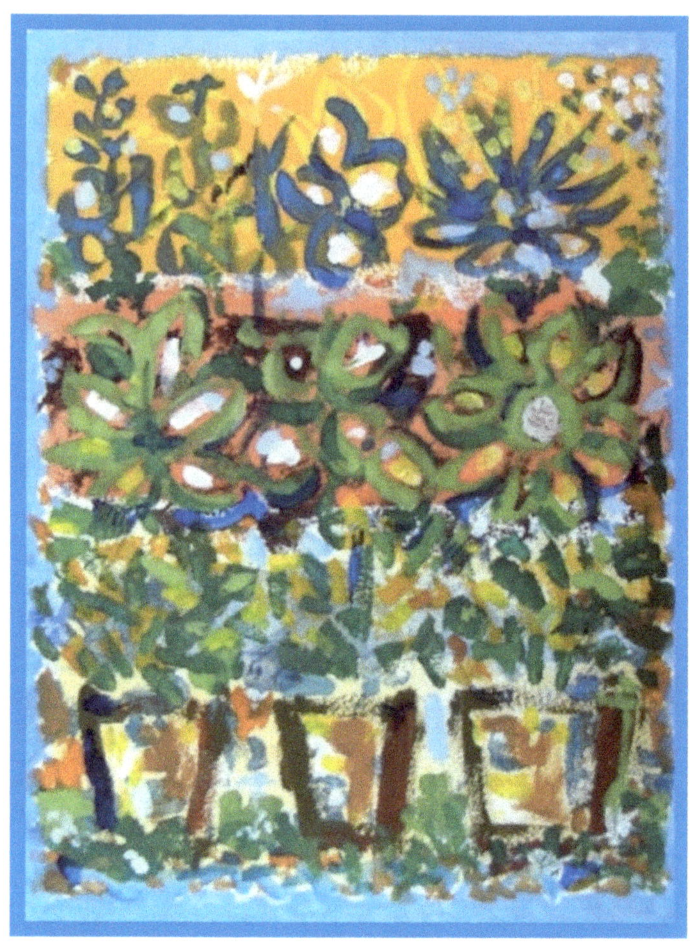

Garden Setting

Acrylic on paper, 38 x 28 cm, 2009

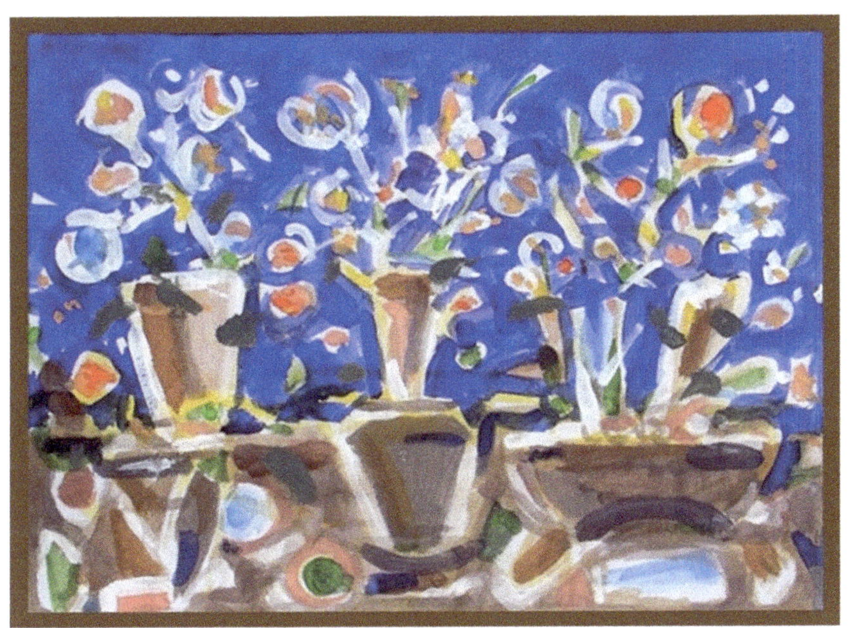

Flower Pots

Acrylic on paper, 26 x 32 cm, 2009

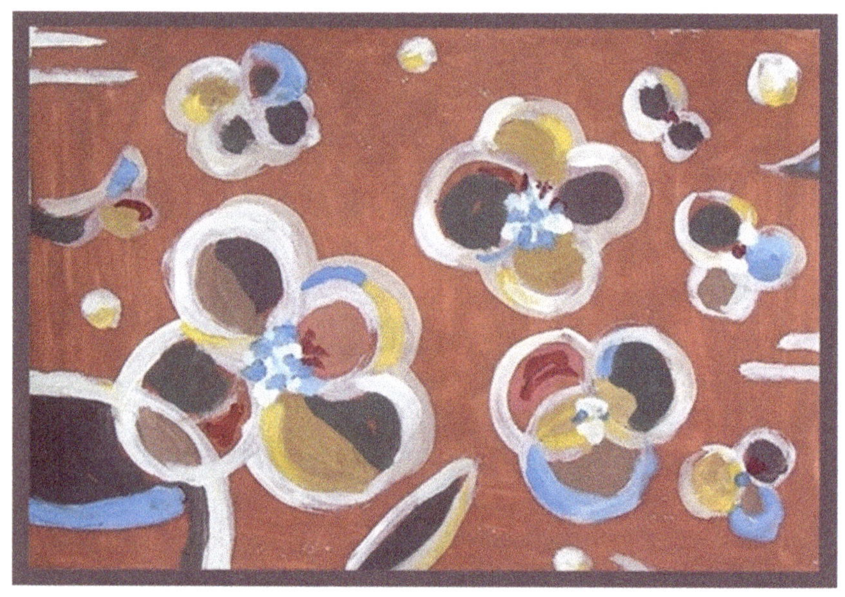

Four, Three, Two, One

Acrylic on paper, 24 x 30 cm, 2010

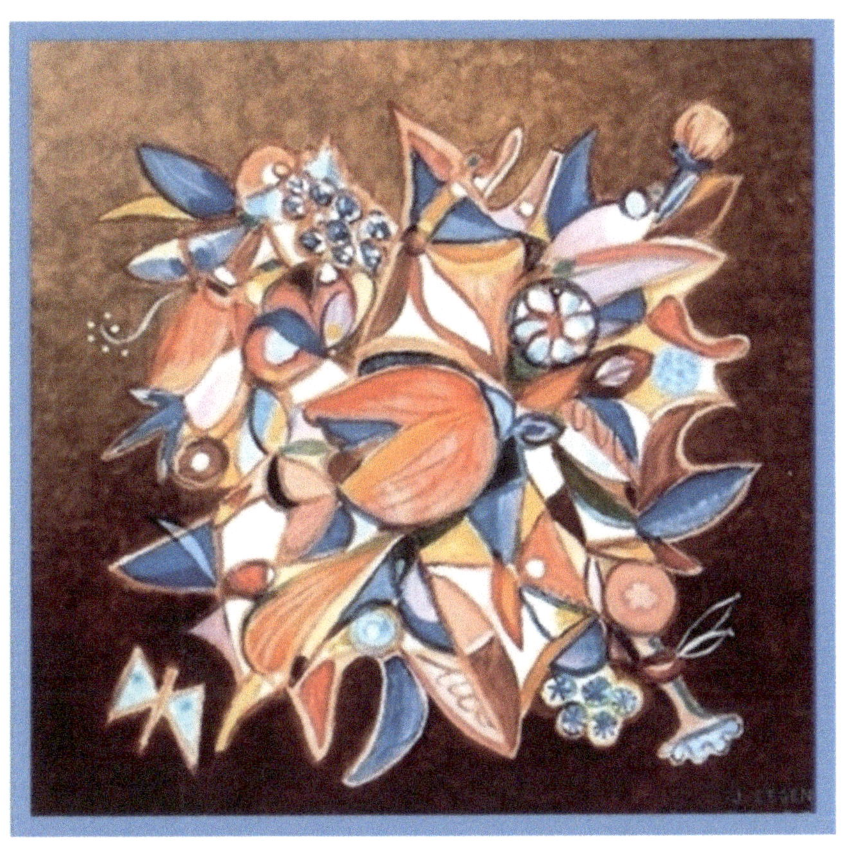

Emblem

Oil on board, 55 x 55 cm, 2001

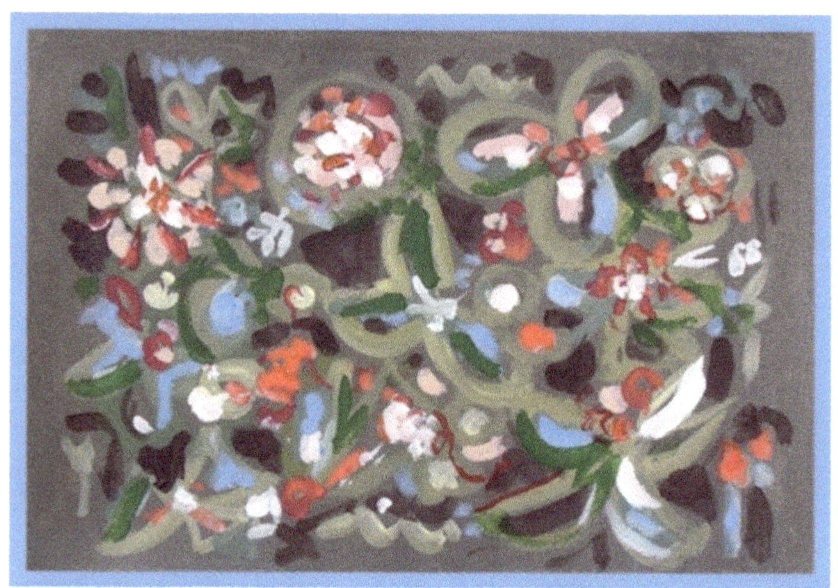

Flower Time

Acrylic on paper, 22 x 28 cm, 2010

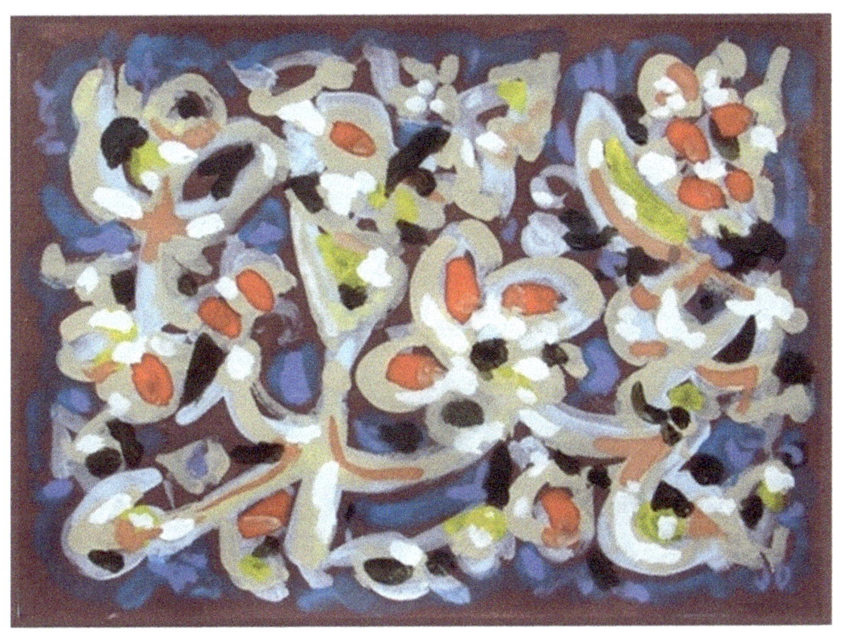

Flowers at Night

Acrylic on paper, 29 x 38 cm, 2009

Growth itself has the germ of happiness.
(Pearl S. Buck)

How beautifully leaves grow old.
How full of light and color are their last days.
(George Burns)

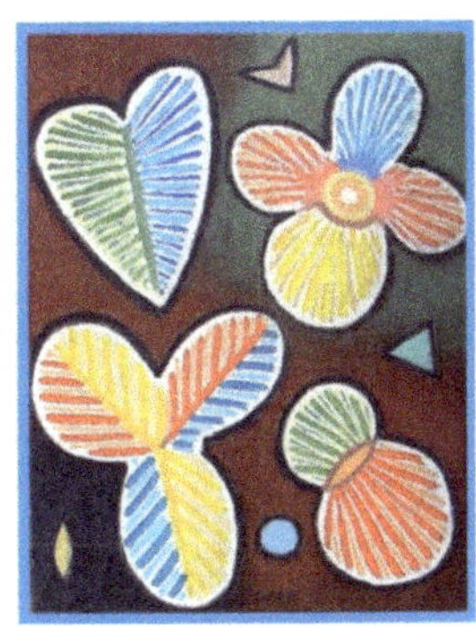

Growth and Leafage

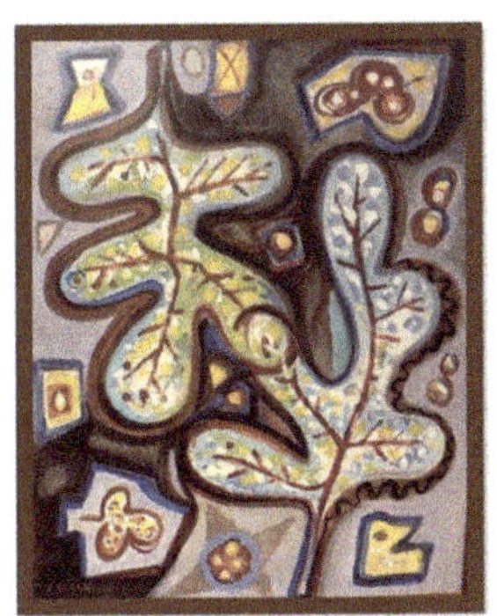

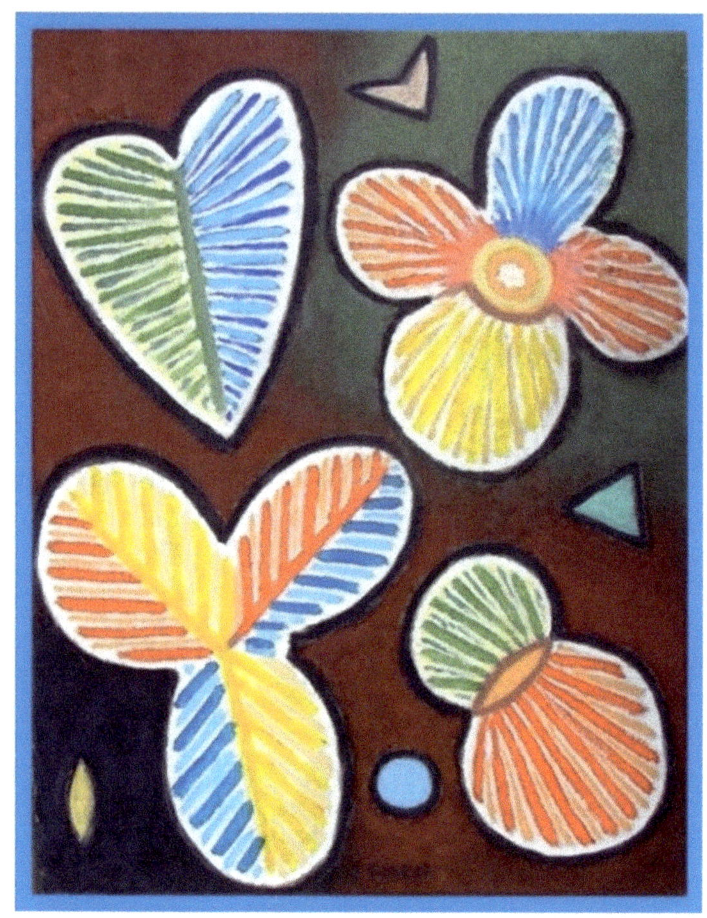

One, Two, Three, Four

Oil on board, 61 x 46 cm, 2009

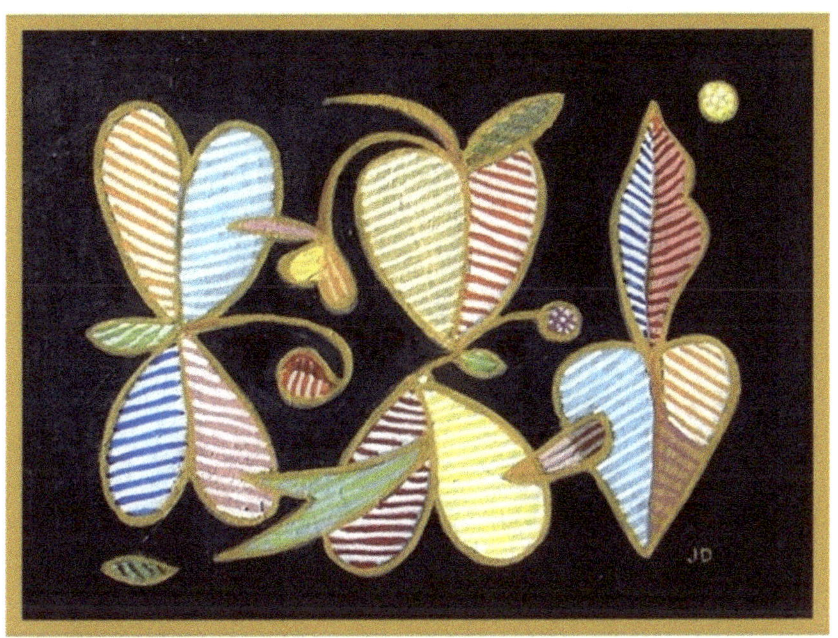

Garden Fantasy

Acrylic on canvas, 27 x 35 cm, 2010

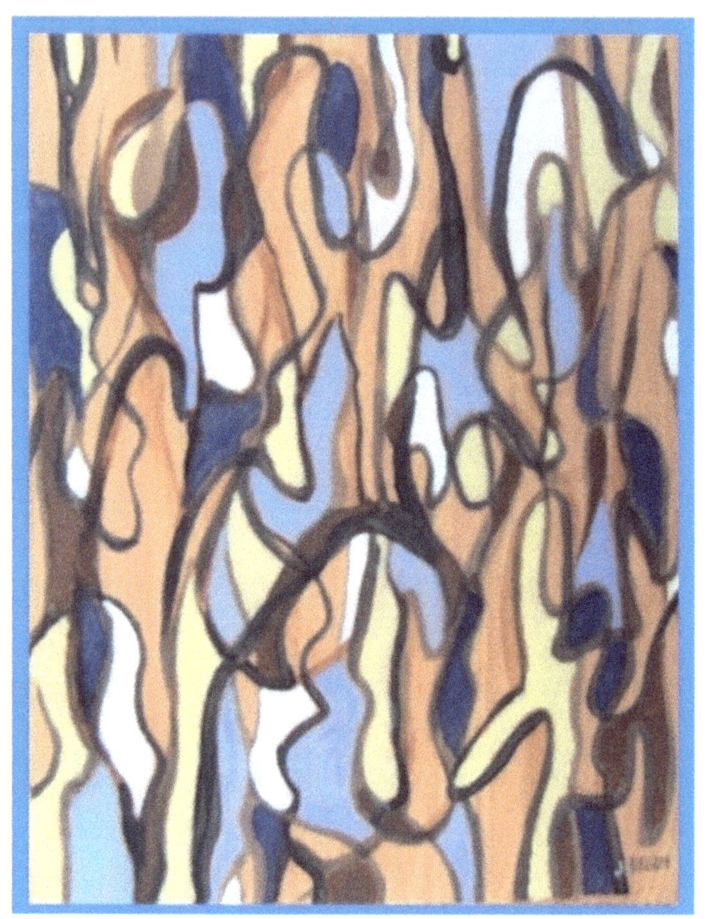

Growth

Acrylic on paper, 38 x 28 cm, 2009

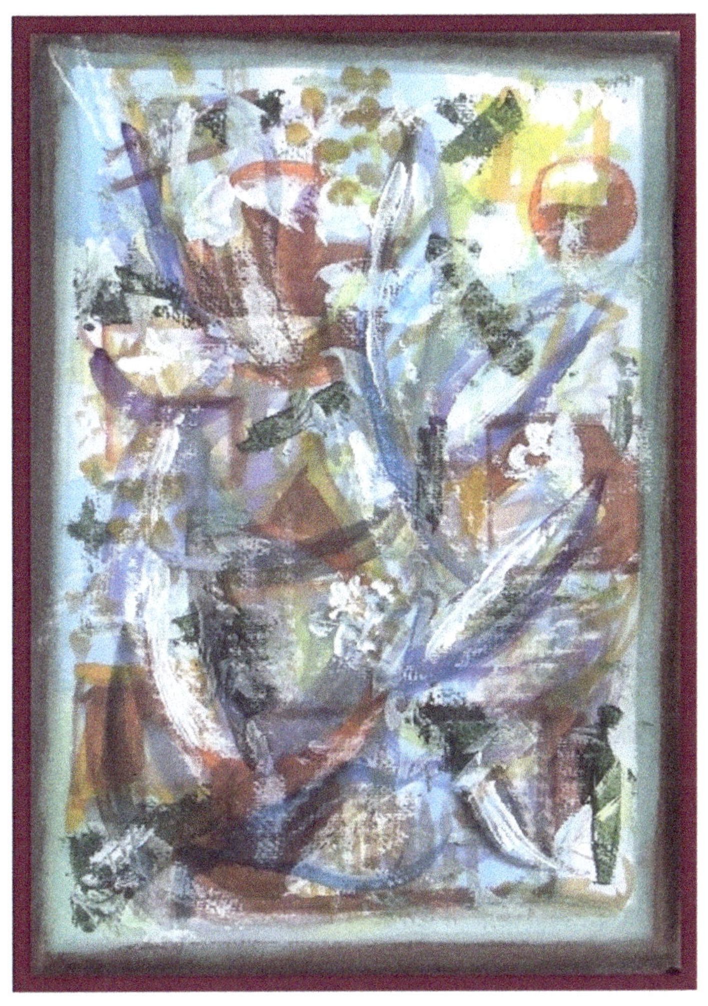

Undergrowth

Acrylic on paper, 40 x 28 cm, 2009

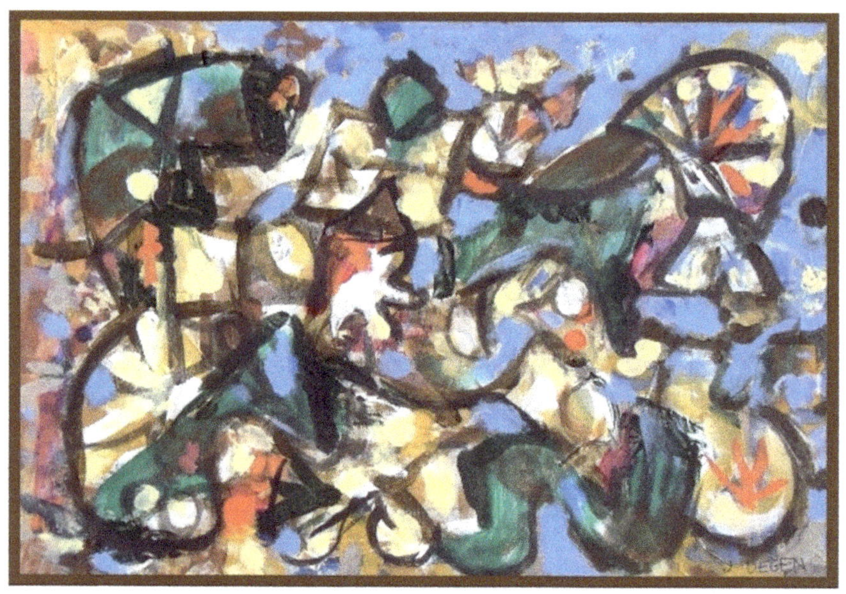

Coloured Growth

Acrylic on board, 30 x 42 cm, 2009

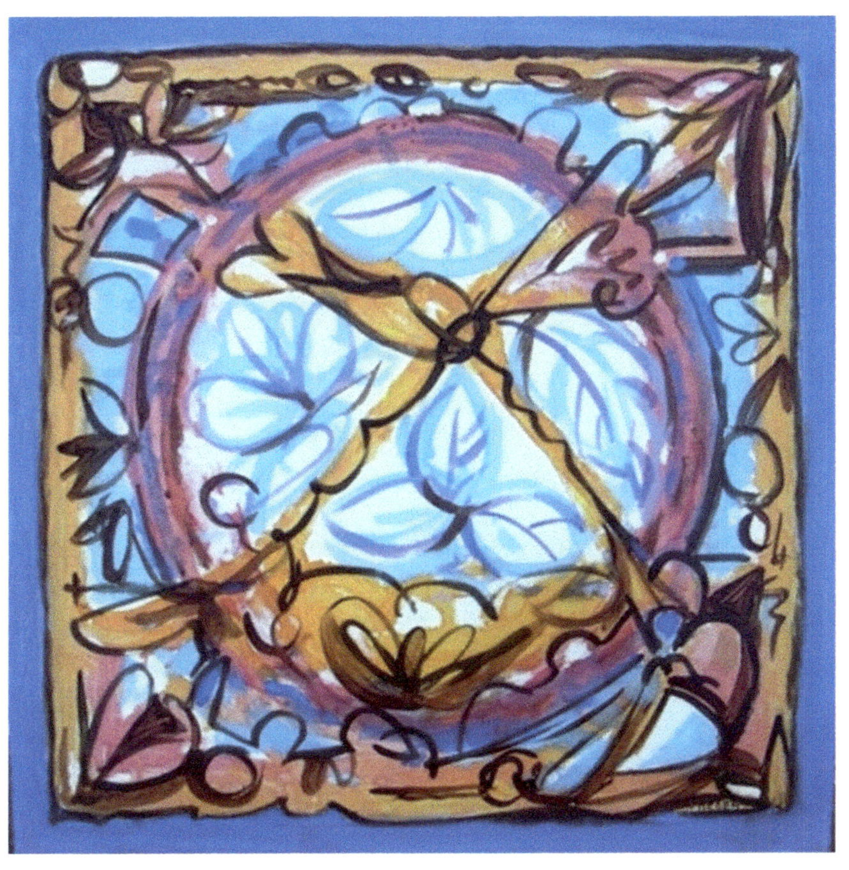

Leaves in a Circle

Acrylic on board, 60 x 59 cm, 2008

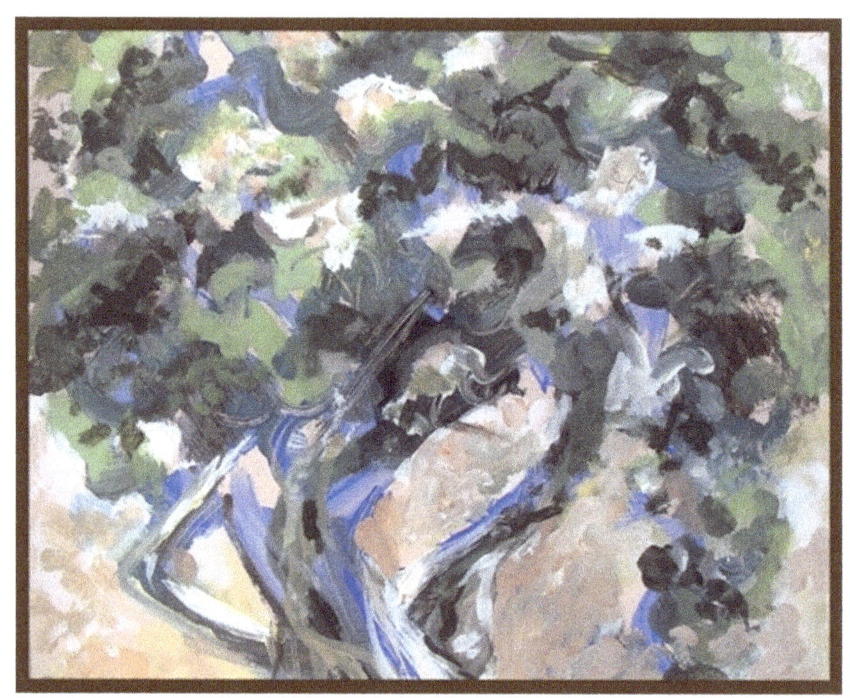

Fairy Tree

Acrylic on card, 42 x 30 cm, 2009

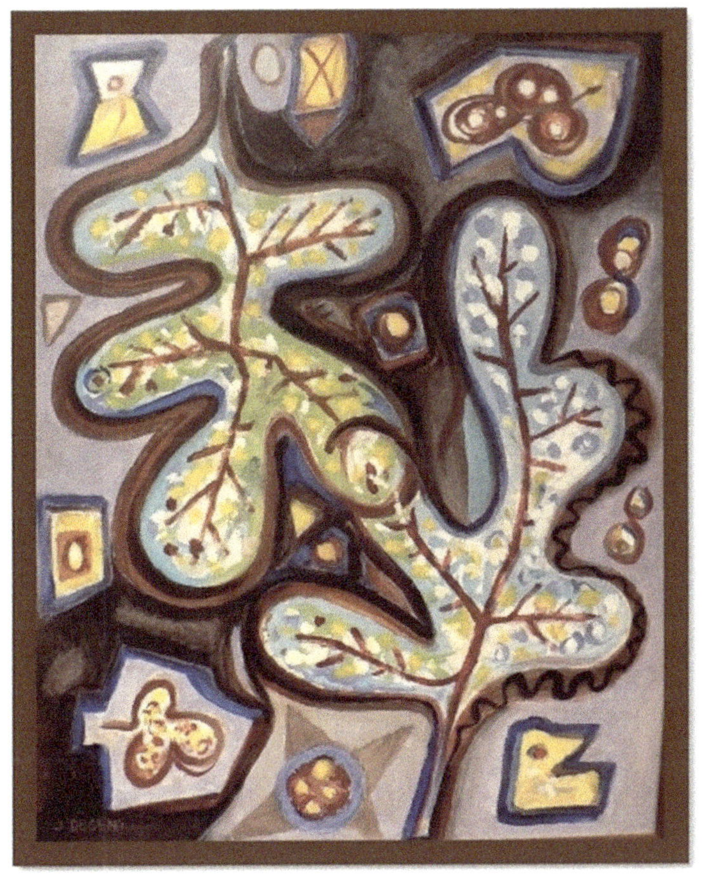

Supplicating Leaves

Oil on board, 75 x 59 cm, 2005

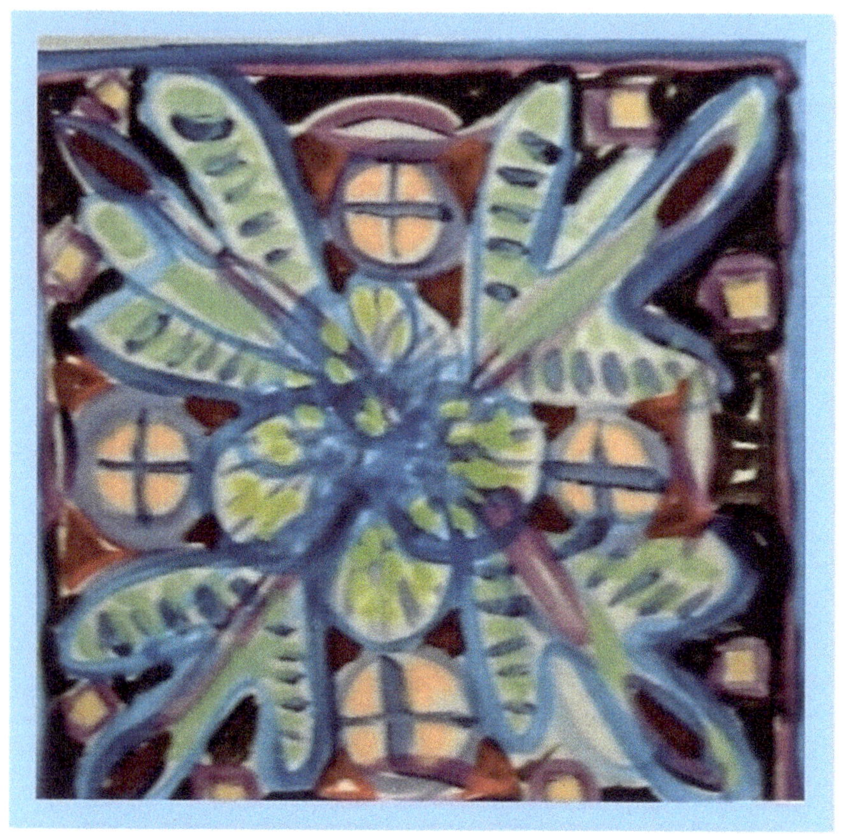

Leafage

Acrylic on paper, 28 x 28 cm, 2005

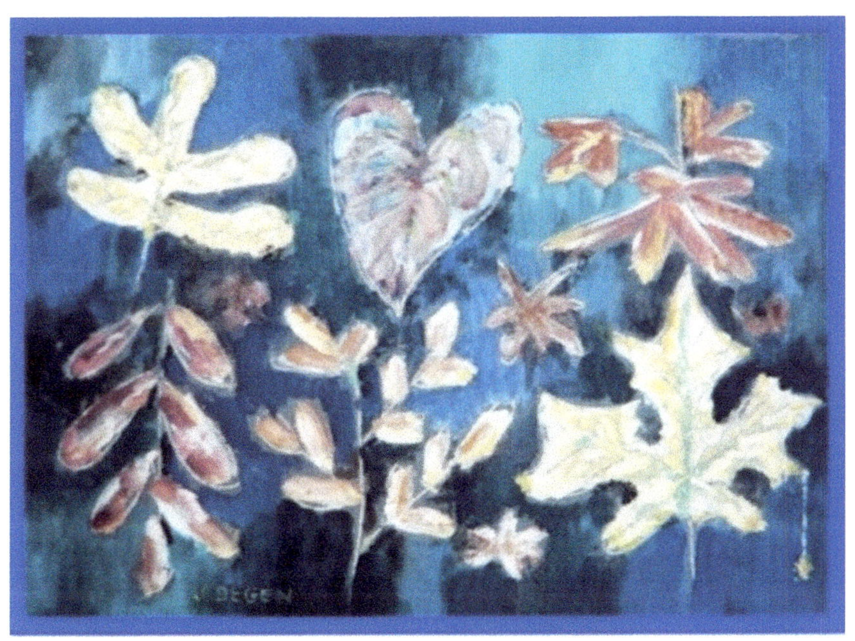

Foliage

Acrylic on paper, 28 x 38 cm, 2003

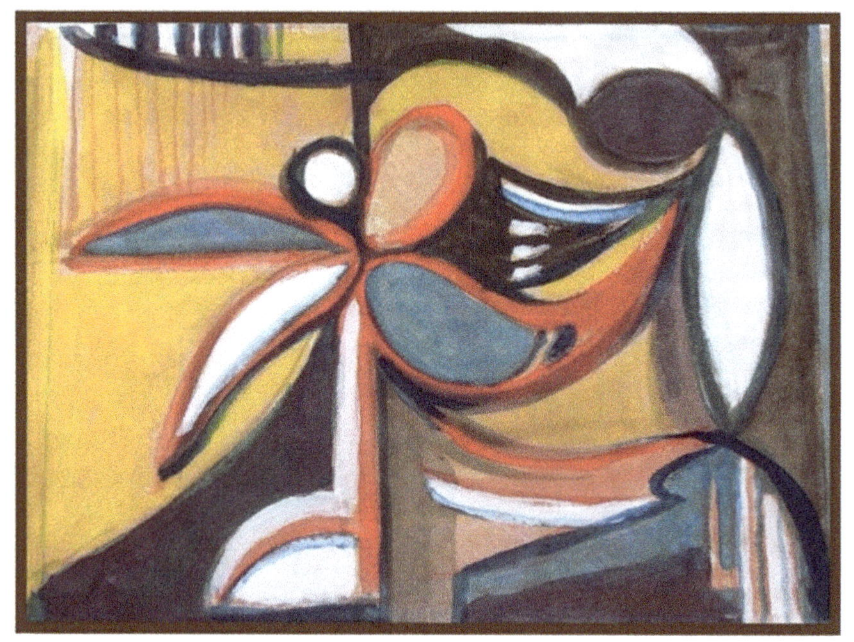

Garden Exotica

Acrylic on paper, 27 x 34 cm, 2009

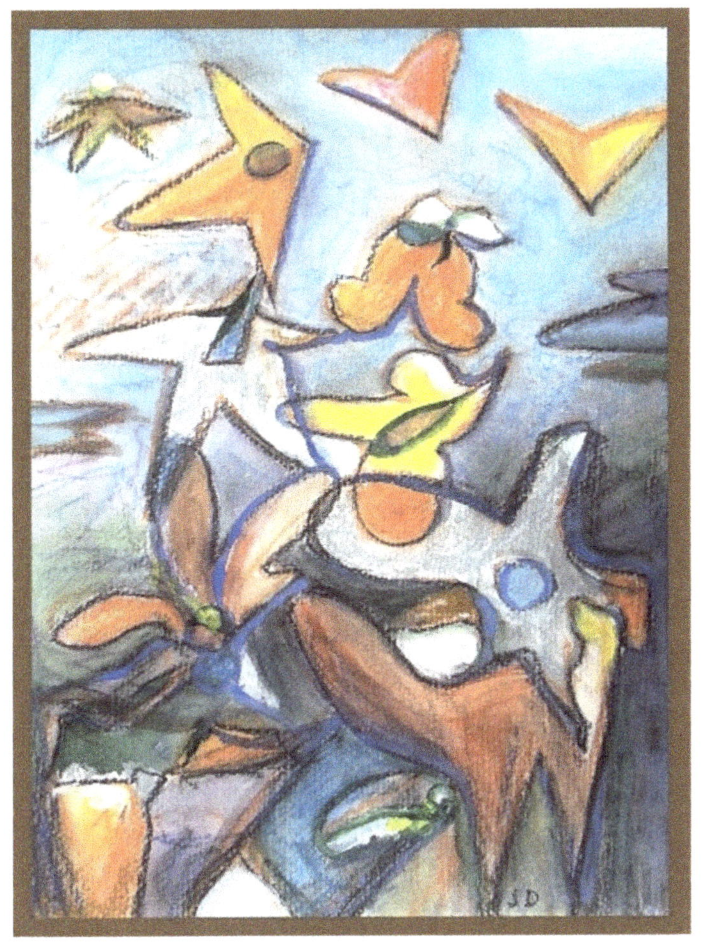

Autumn Celebration

Mixed media on paper, 40 x 30 cm, 2009

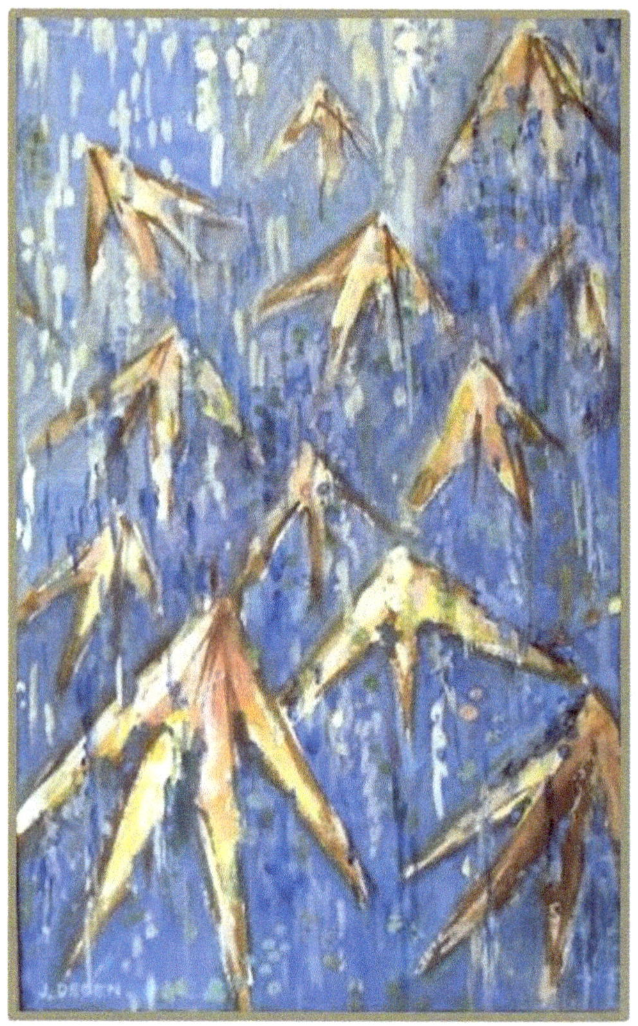

Autumn

Acrylic on paper, 35 x 50 cm, 2011

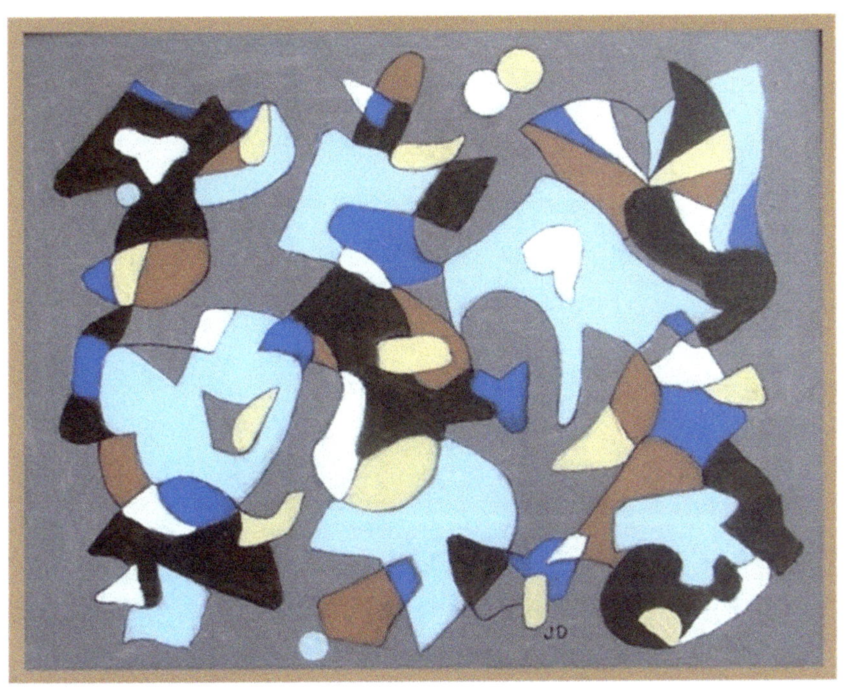

Autumn Memories

Acrylic on board, 38 x 47 cm, 2009

Animals are such agreeable friends -
they ask no questions,
they pass no criticisms.
(George Eliot)

In order to keep a true perspective of one's
importance,
everyone should have a dog that will worship him
and a cat that will ignore him.
(Dereke Bruce)

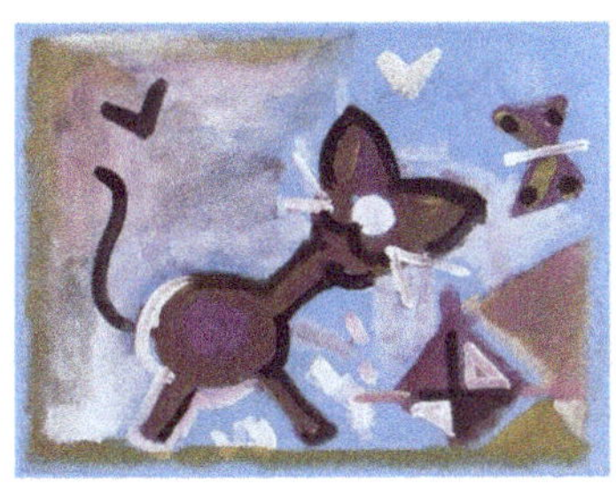

Living Creatures

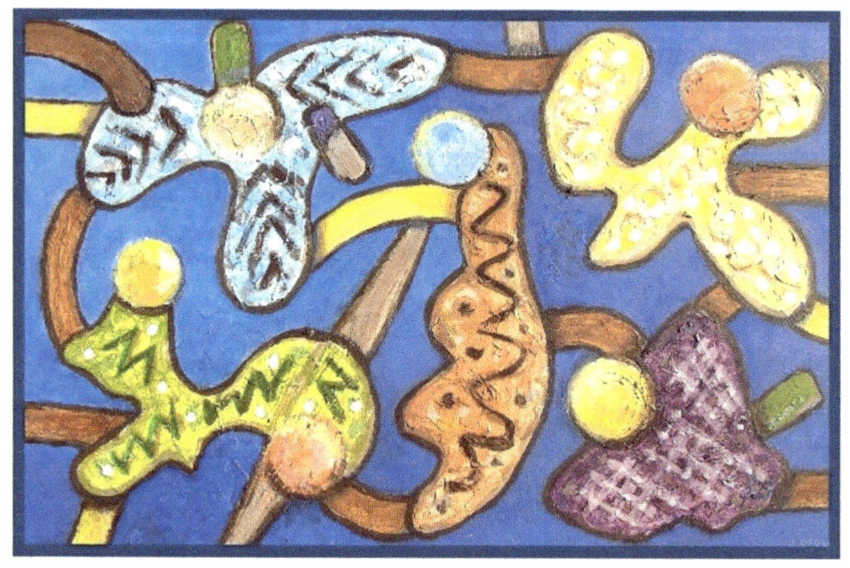

In the Stream

Acrylic on board, 61 x 91 cm, 2009

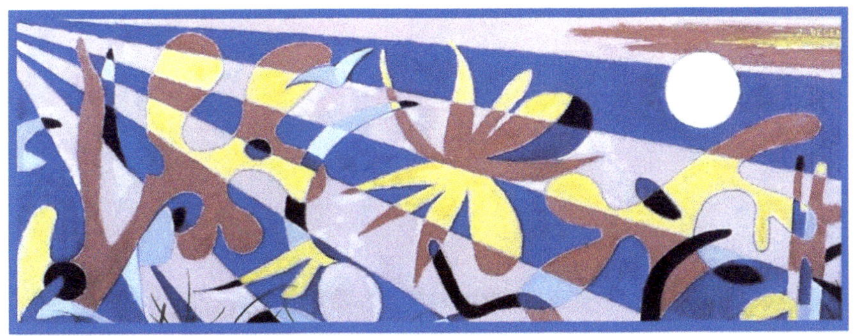

Bayside

Oil on board, 29 x 75 cm, 2003

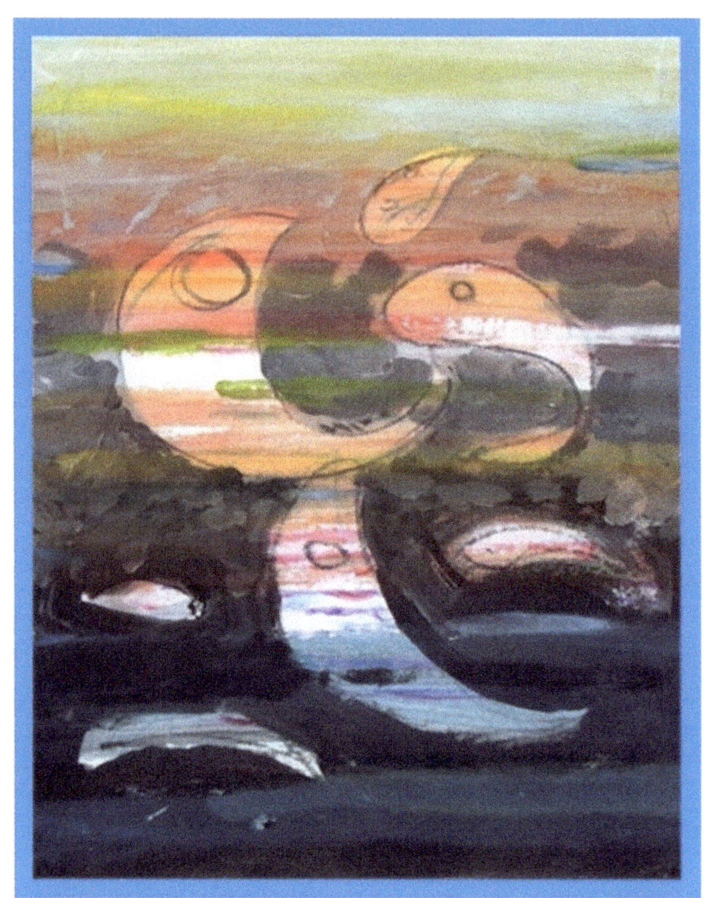

Marine Party

Acrylic on paper, 26 x 21 cm, 2006

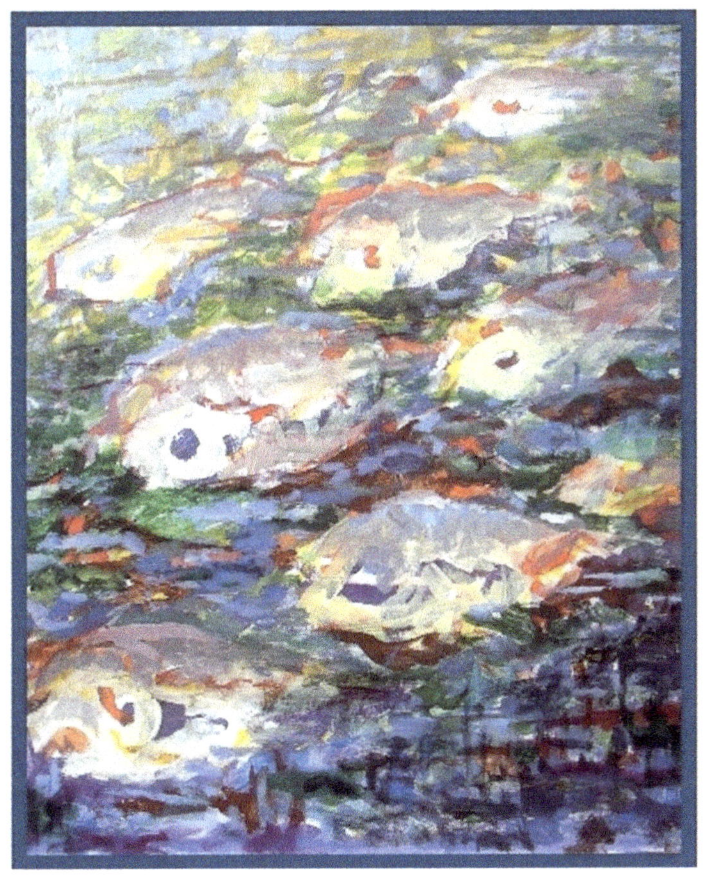

School of Fish

Acrylic on board, 60 x 48 cm, 2009

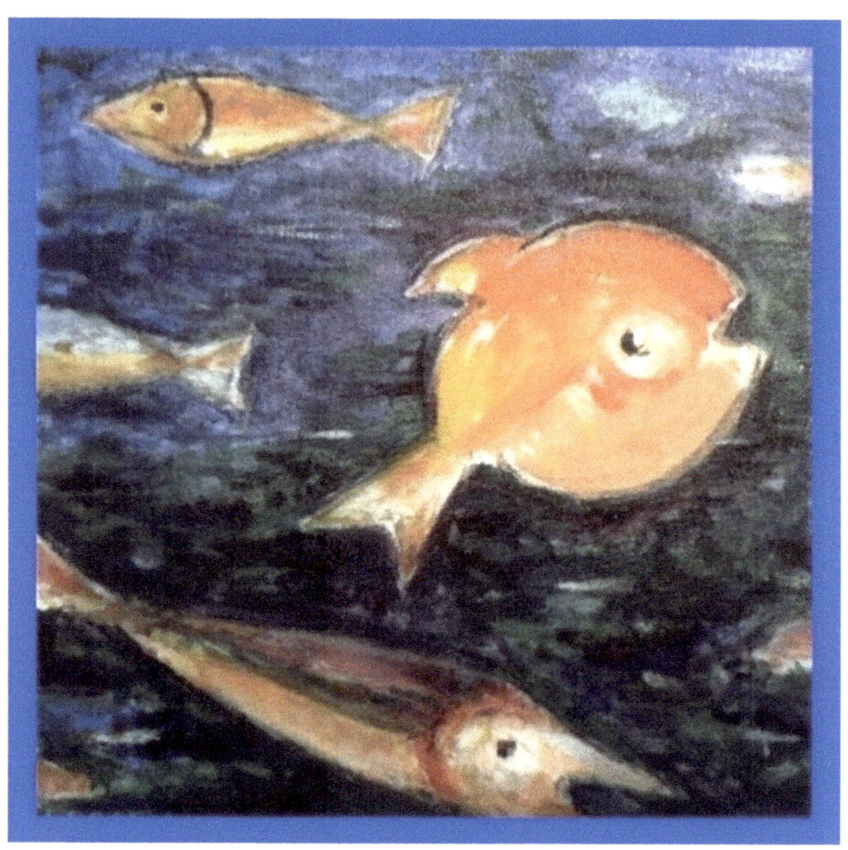

Species Unknown

Acrylic on canvas, 30.5 x 30.5 cm, 2007

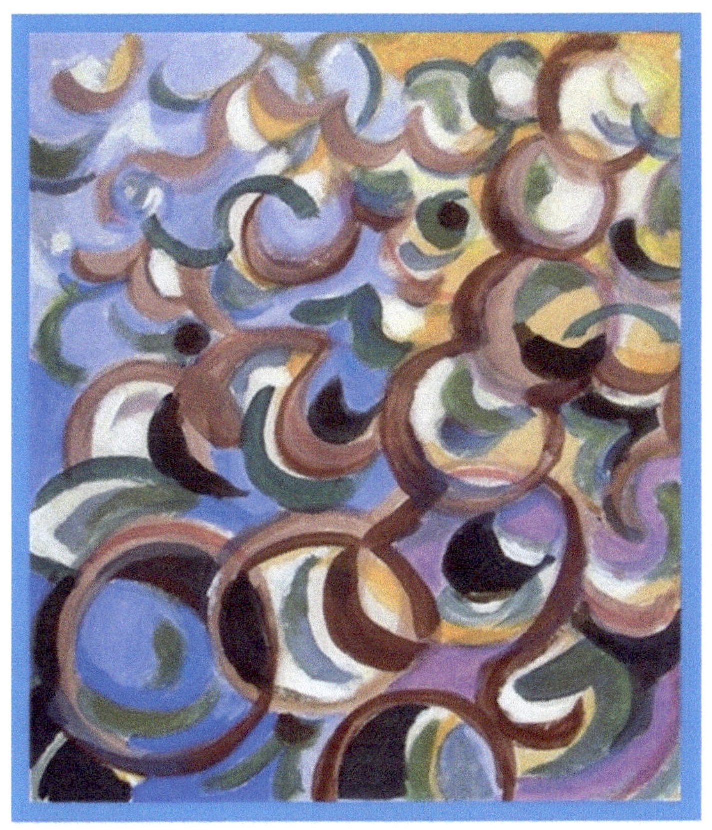

Corals

Acrylic on paper, 30 x 26 cm, 2009

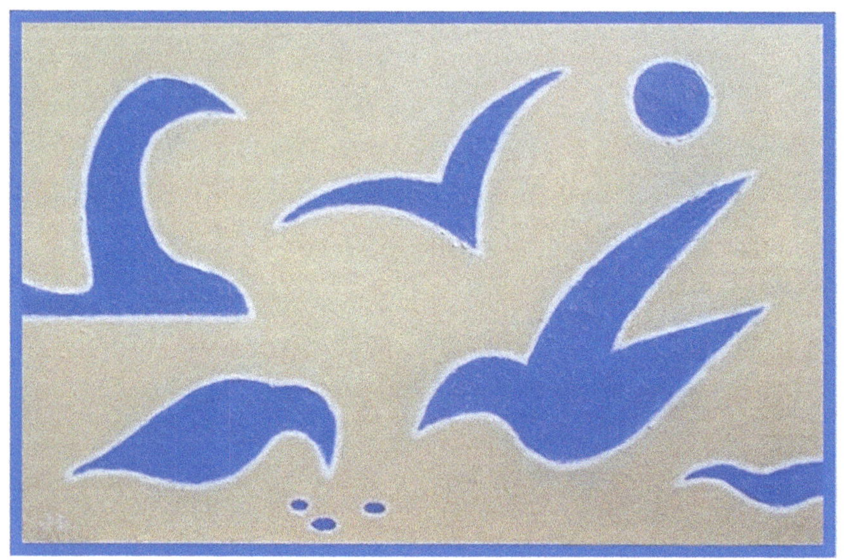

At the Shore

Acrylic on board, 60 x 90 cm, 2009

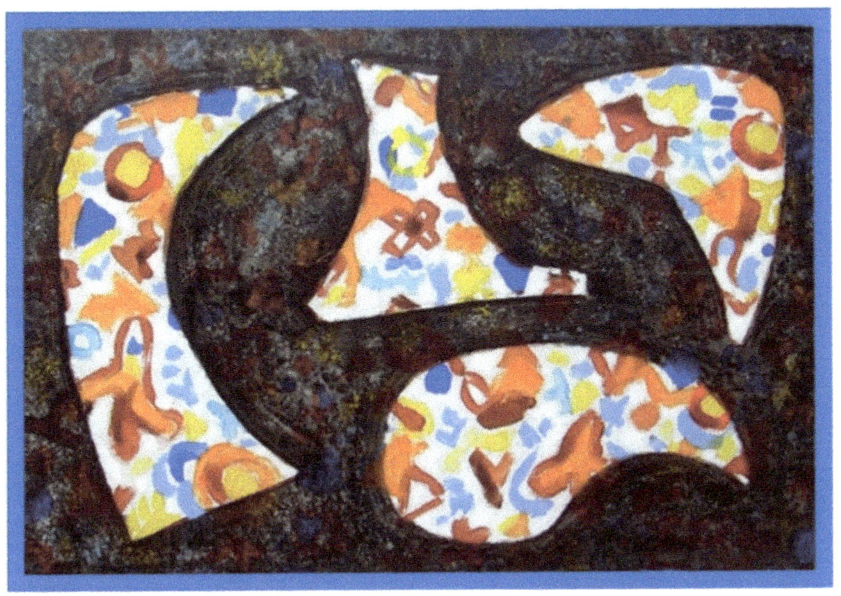

Animalia

Acrylic on board, 46 x 65 cm, 2009

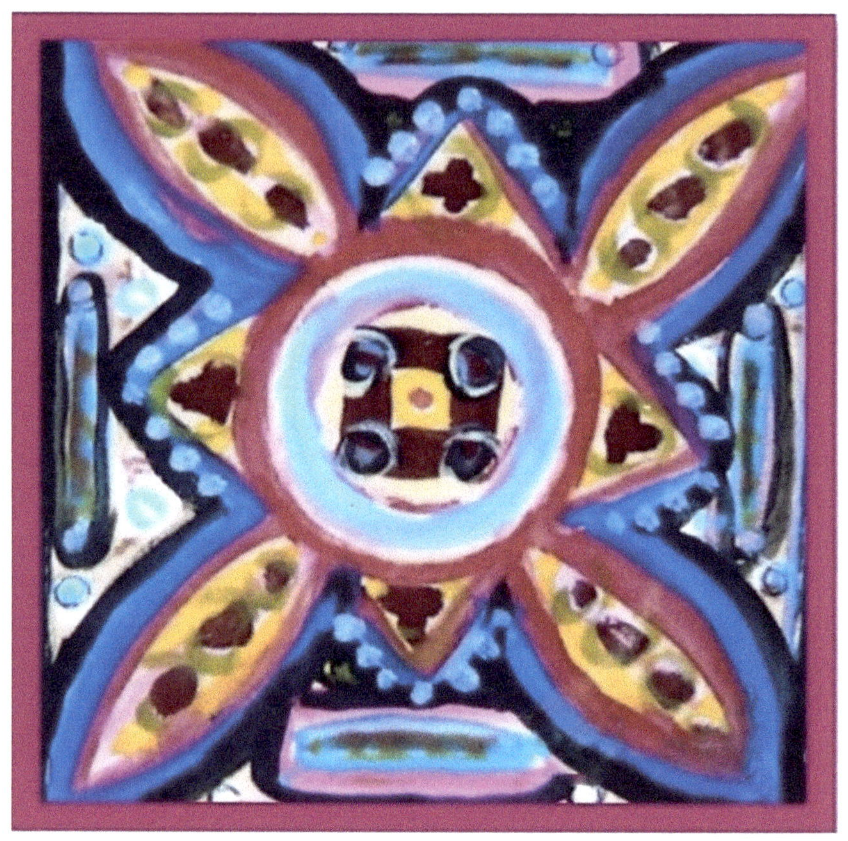

Two Rabbits

Acrylic on paper, 28 x 28 cm, 2004

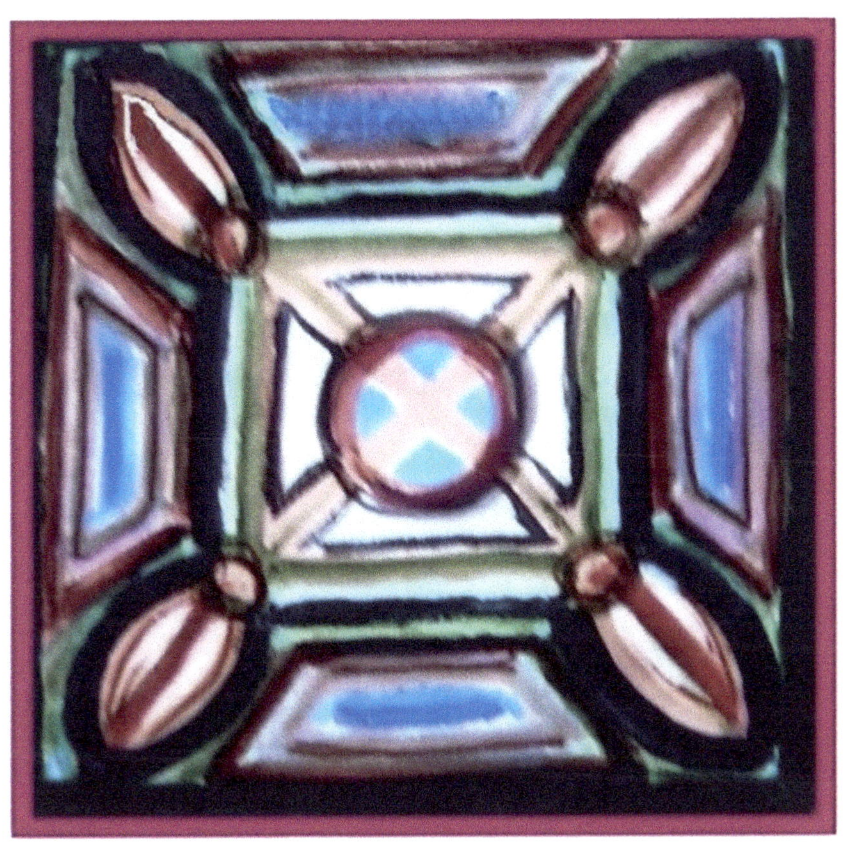

Four Beetles

Acrylic on paper, 28 x 28 cm, 2005

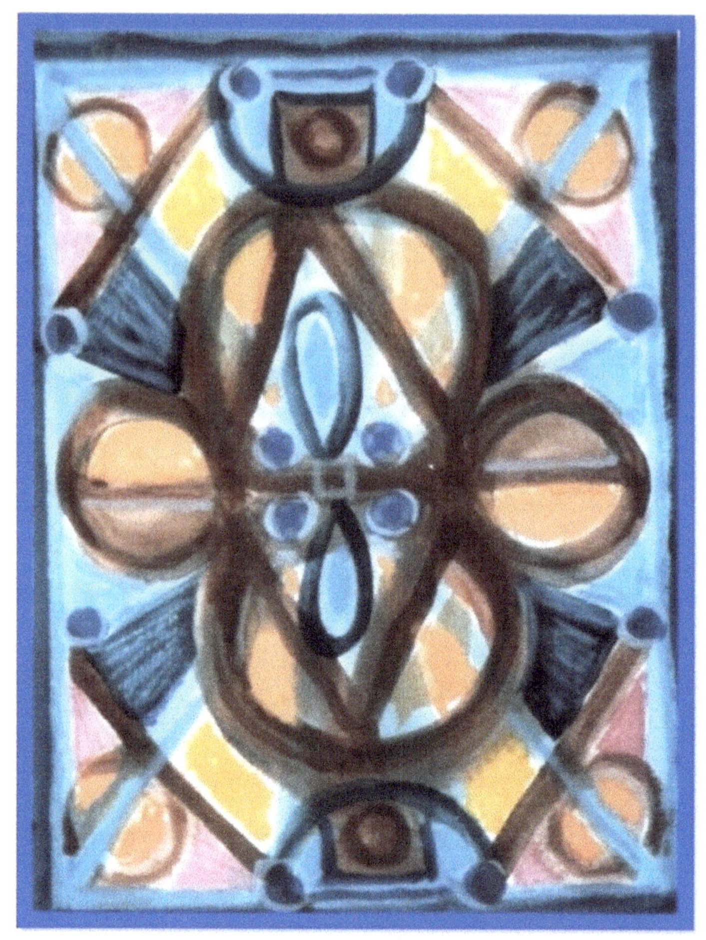

Monkey and Frogs

Acrylic on paper, 36 x 26 cm, 2006

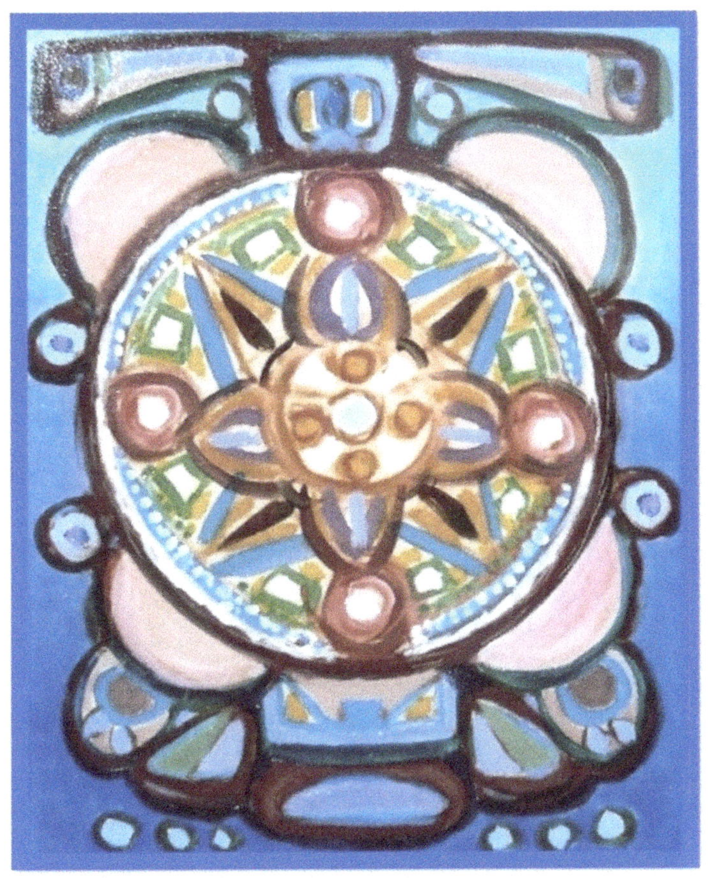

Playful Puppy

Oil on canvas, 45 x 35 cm, 2006

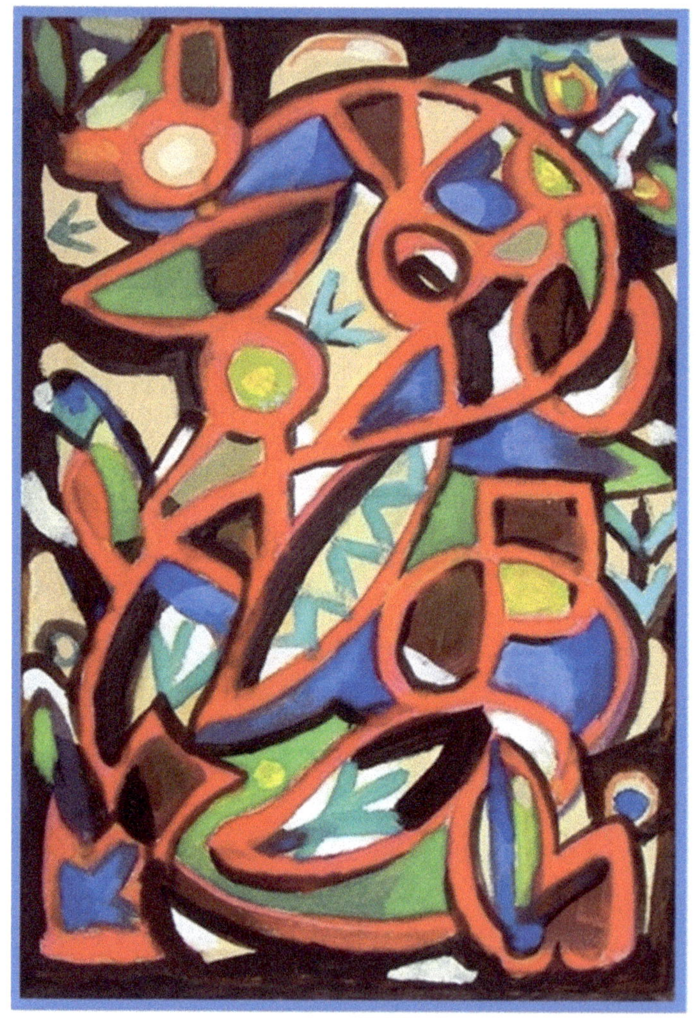

Chick on the Run

Acrylic on paper, 30 x 23 cm, 2006

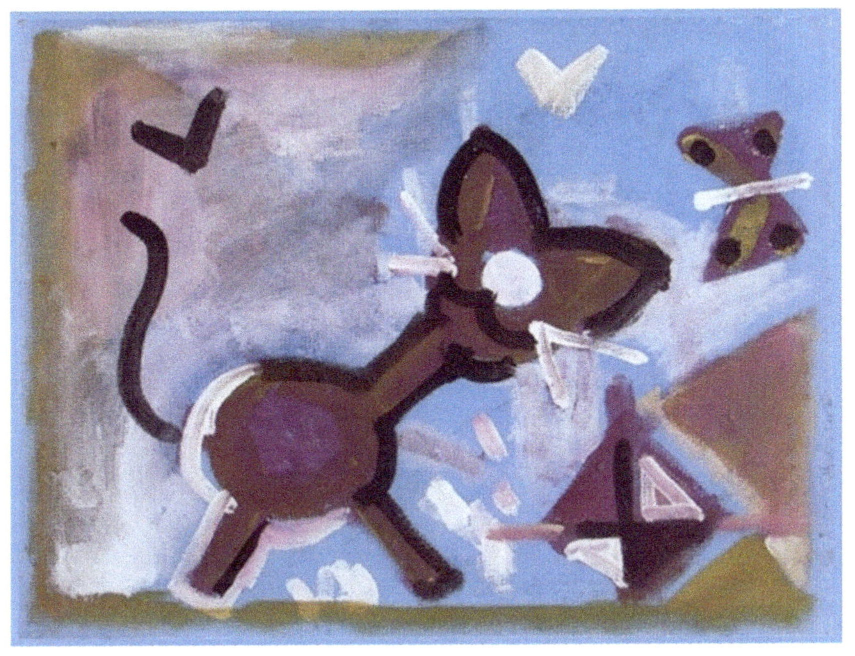

Catch Me If You Can

Acrylic on board, 22 x 28 cm, 2008

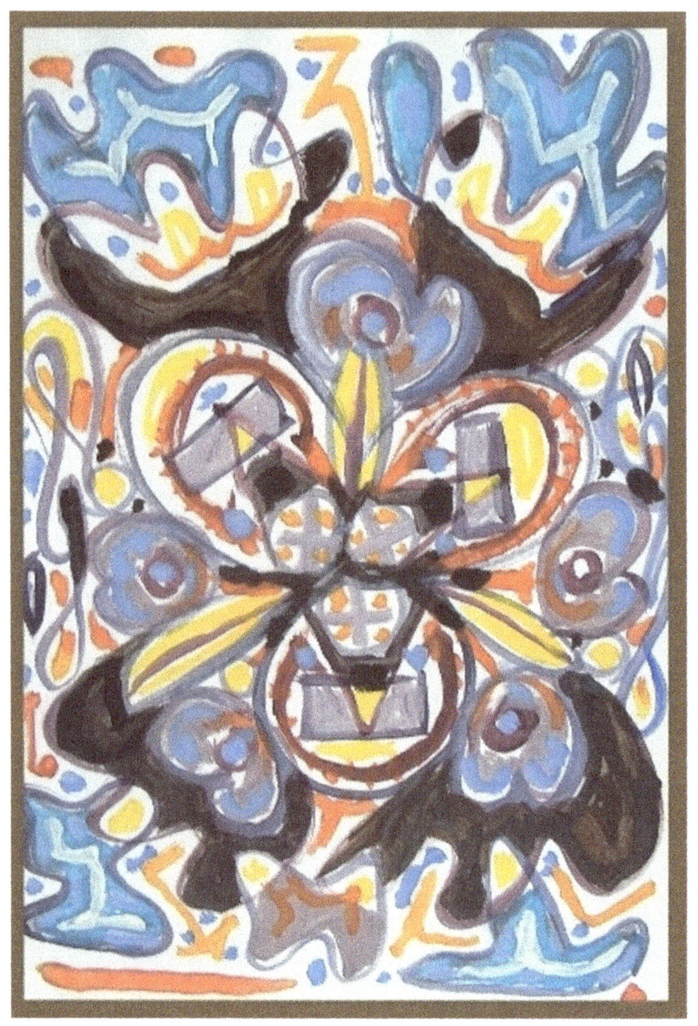

Creature Unidentified

Acrylic on paper, 36 x 25 cm, 2009

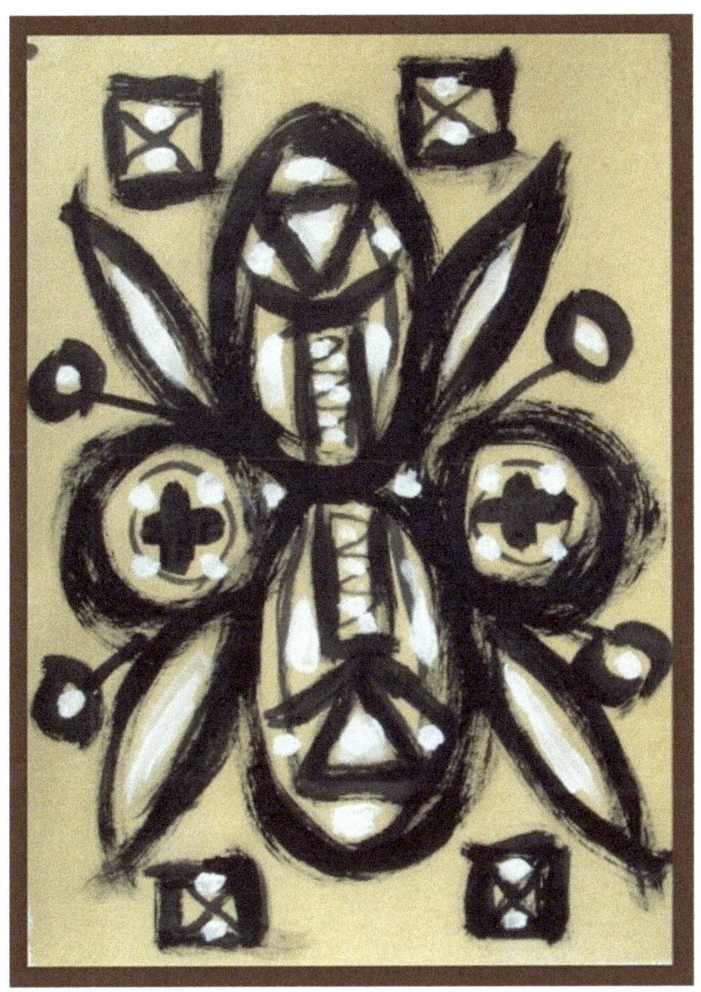

To Bee or Not to Bee

Acrylic on paper, 38 x 26 cm, 2009

Color is all. When color is right, form is right.
Color is everything, color is vibration like music;
everything is vibration.
(Marc Chagall)

Painting is a mosaic of colors
weaved into a seamless whole.
(Igor Babailov)

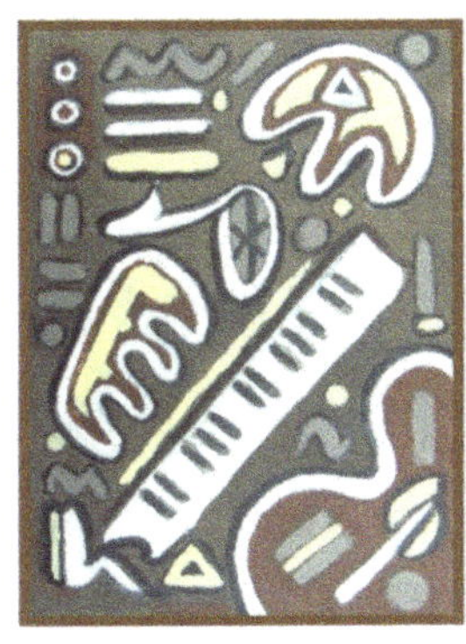

Sound & Colour

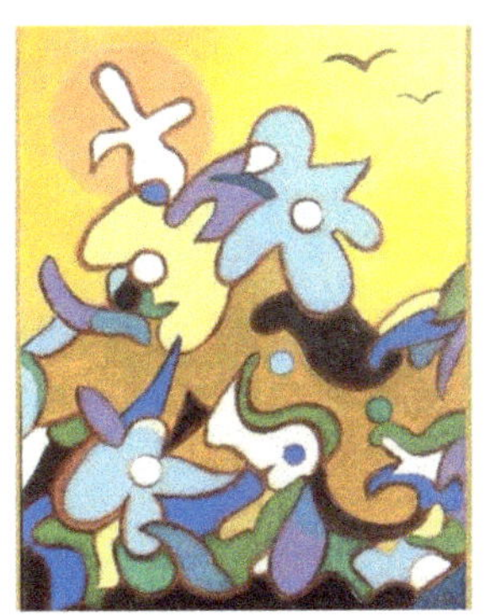

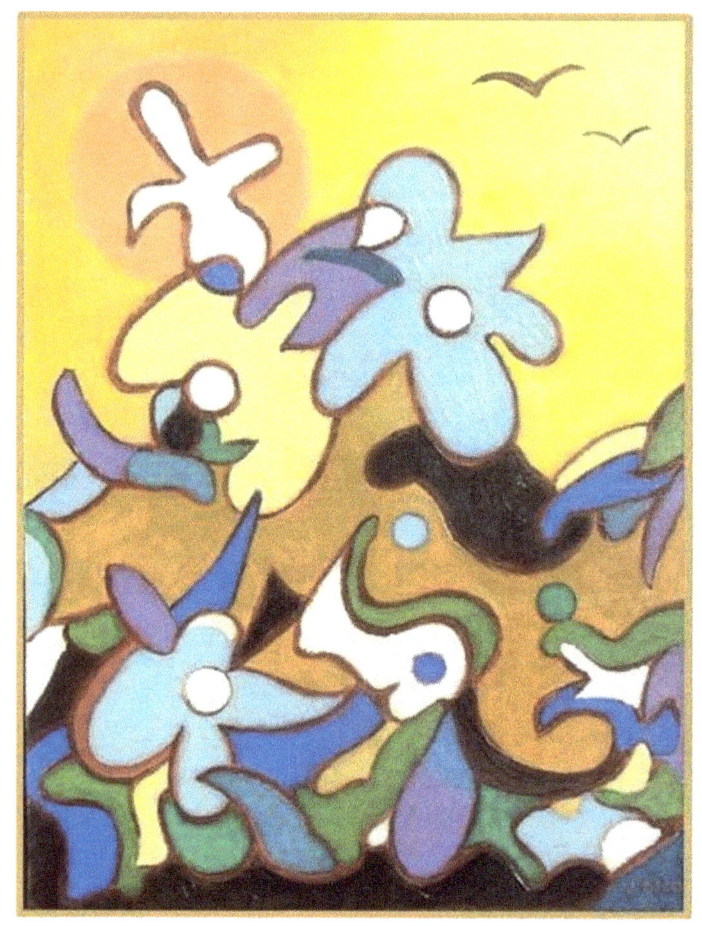

Golden Afternoon

Acrylic on board, 60 x 45 cm, 2011

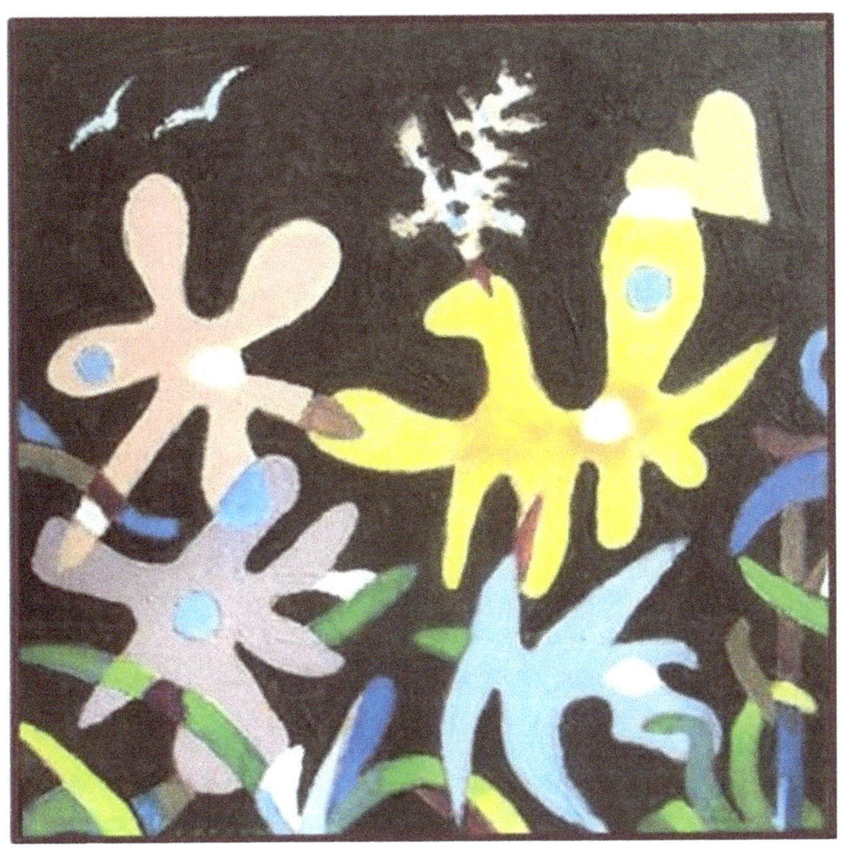

Sound of Colours

Acrylic on canvas, 60 x 60 cm, 2010

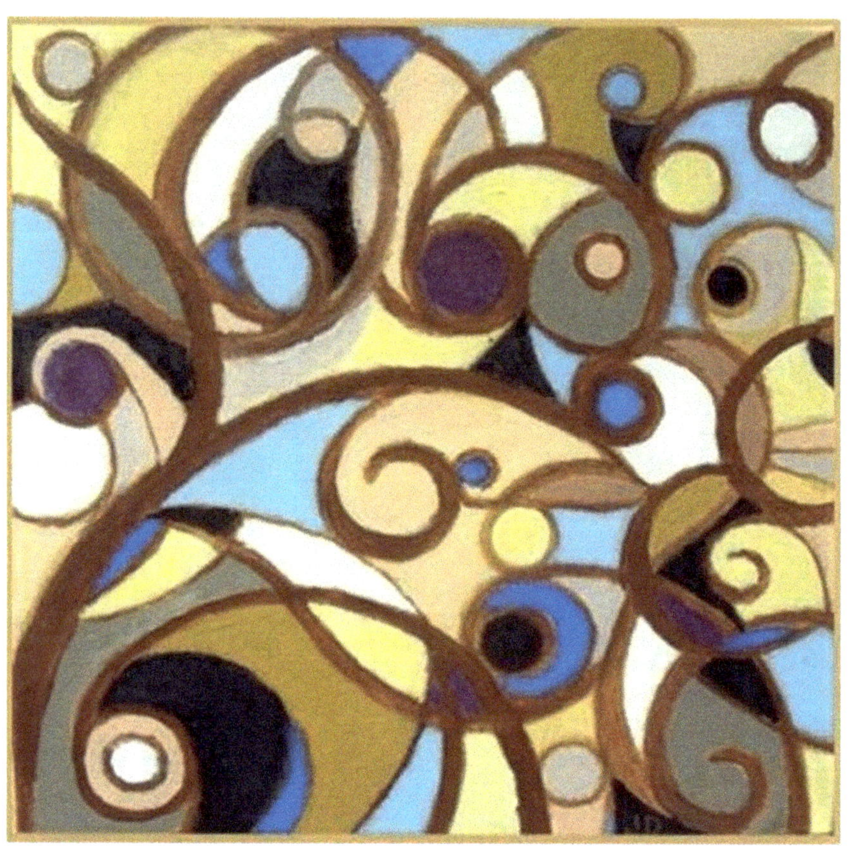

Flow

Acrylic on canvas, 31 x 31 cm, 2010

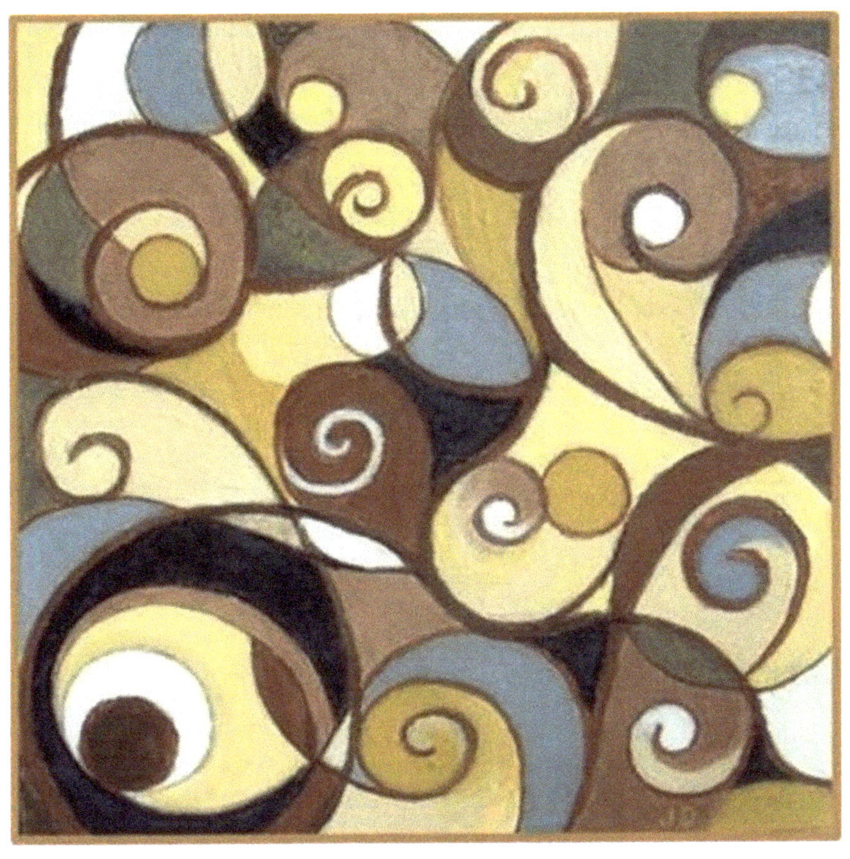

Ripples

Acrylic on canvas, 31 x 31 cm, 2010

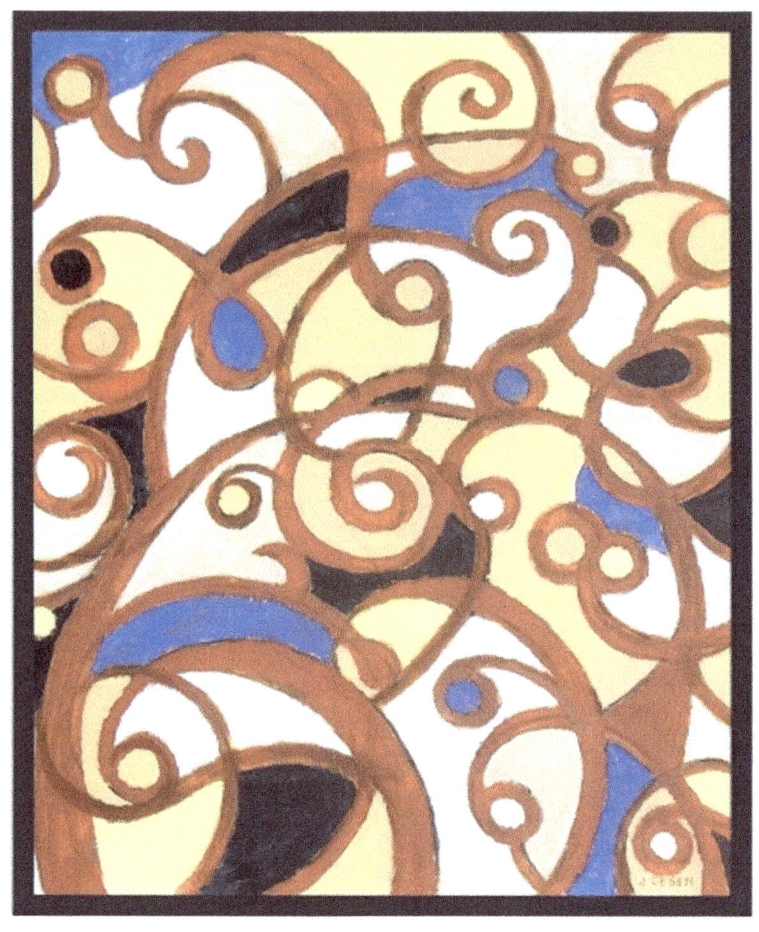

Golden Flow

Acrylic on board, 58 x 43 cm, 2010

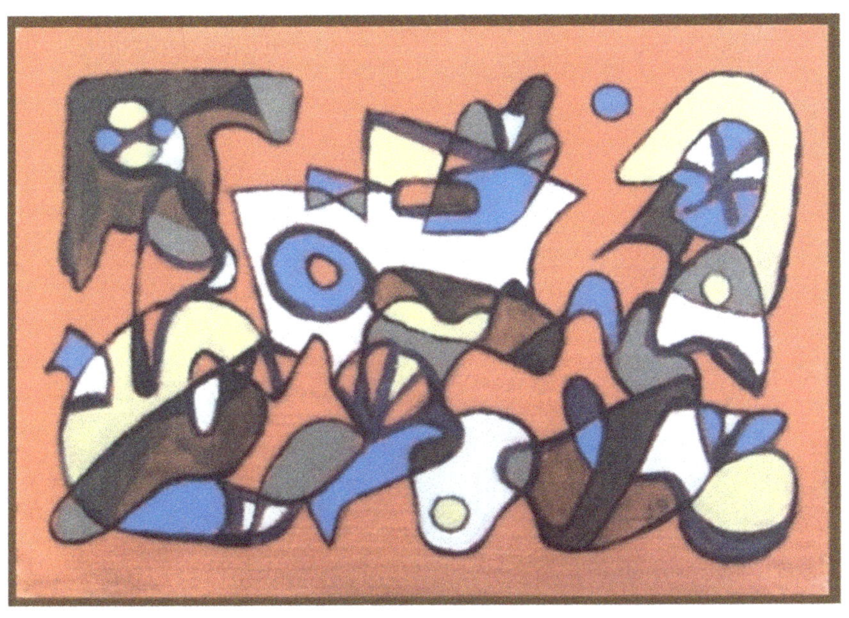

Little Carnival

Acrylic on paper, 28 x 40 cm, 2009

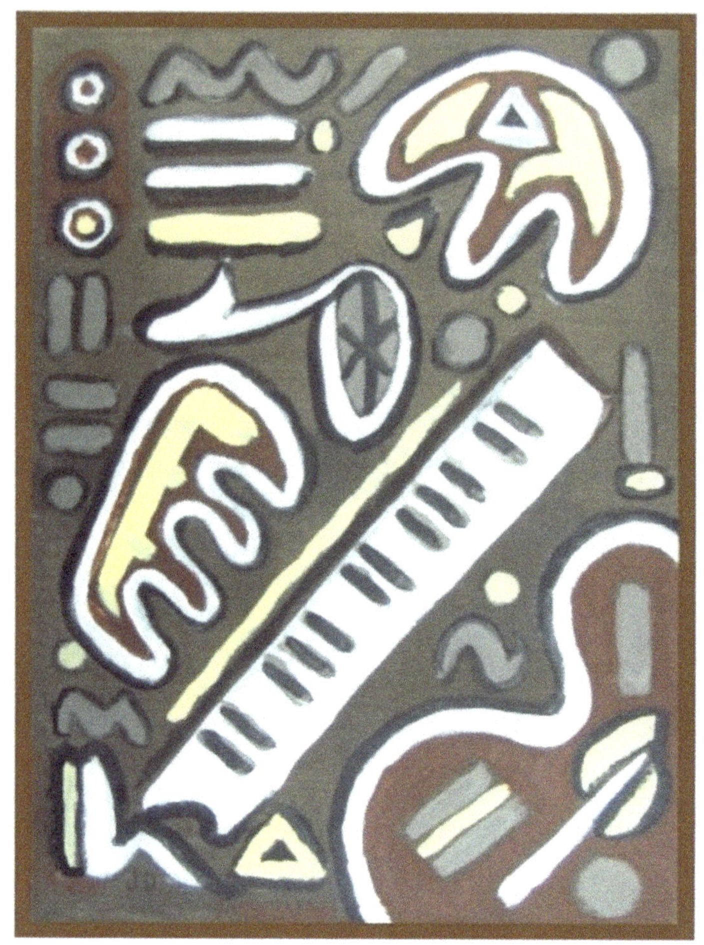

A Little Music

Acrylic on paper, 39 x 28 cm, 2009

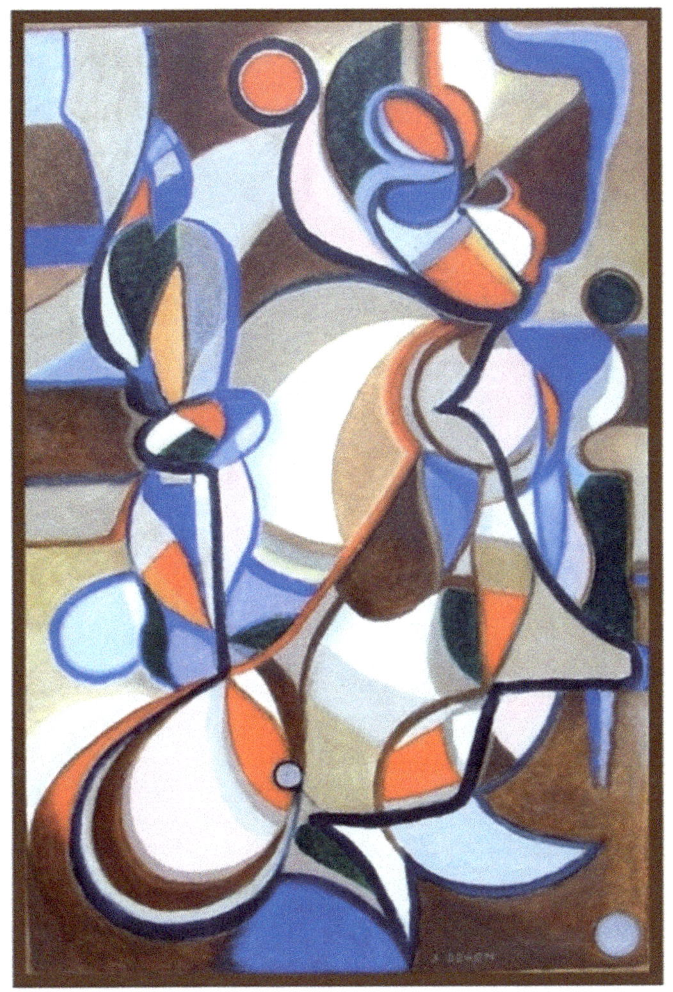

Garden Music

Oil on canvas, 76 x 51 cm, 2005

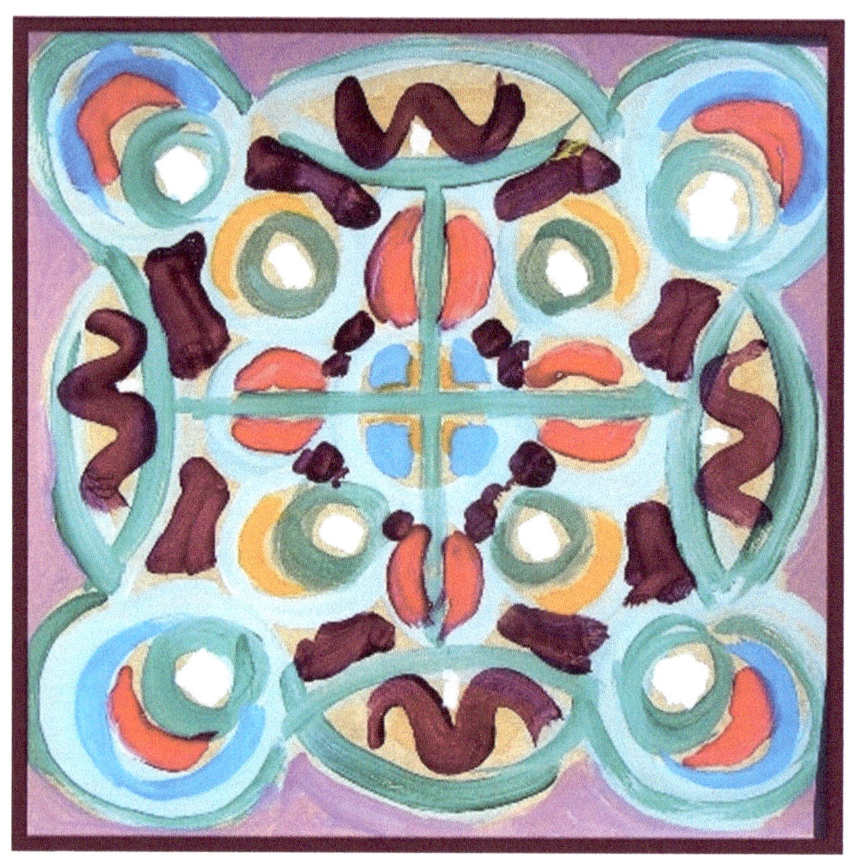

Garden Nook

Acrylic on paper 28 x 28 cm, 2010

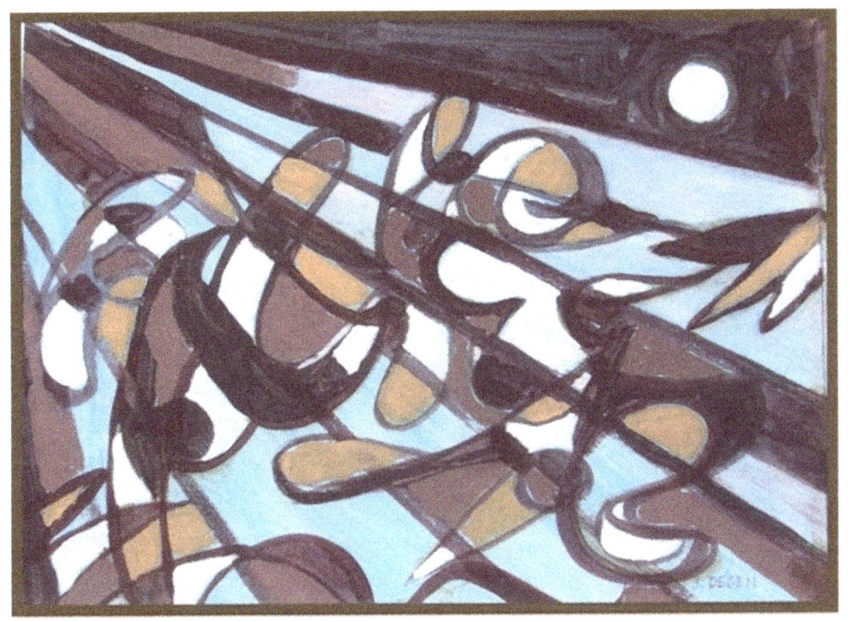

Moon Serenade

Acrylic on paper, 27 x 37 cm, 2009

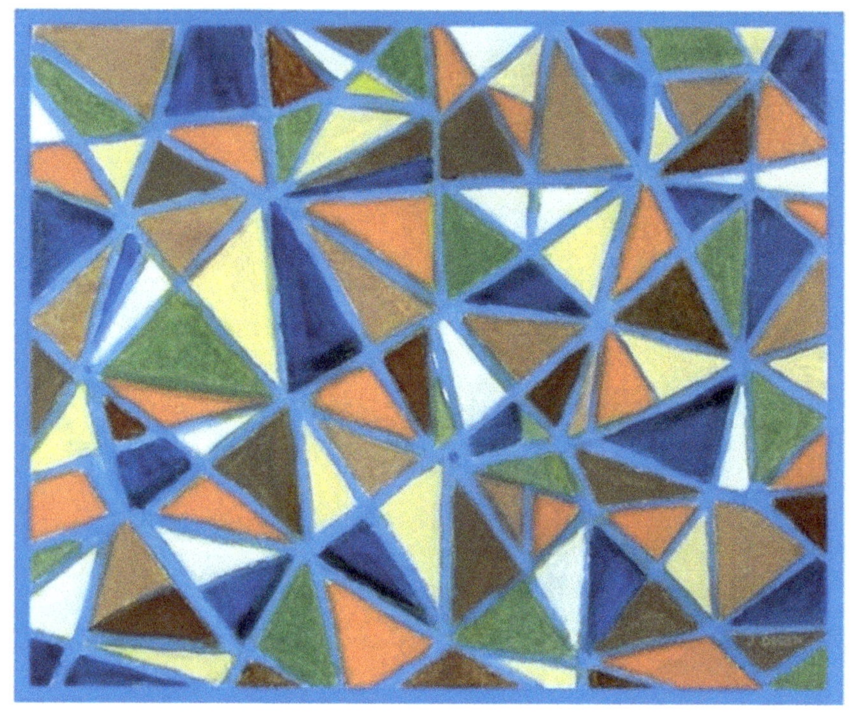

Kaleidoscope

Acrylic on board, 50 x 60 cm, 2009

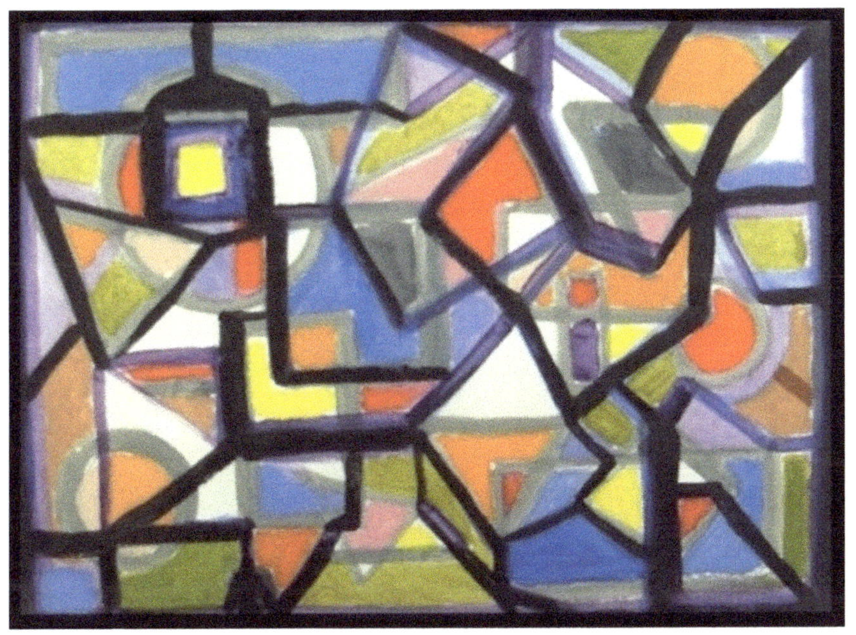

Colour Display

Acrylic on paper, 28 x 38 cm, 2009

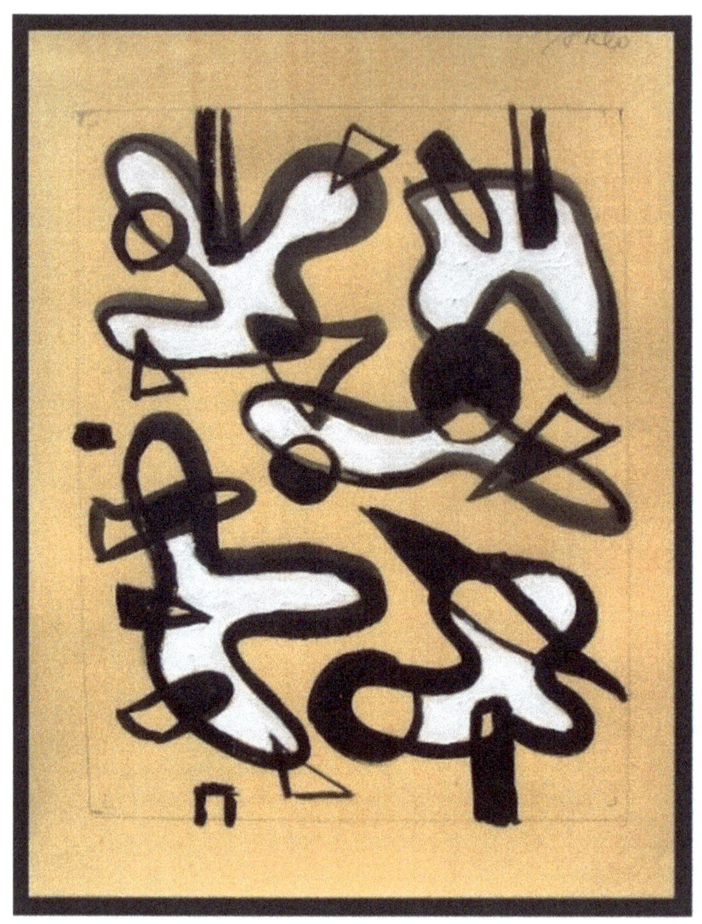

Display in Contrast

Acrylic on paper, 35 x 27 cm, 2009

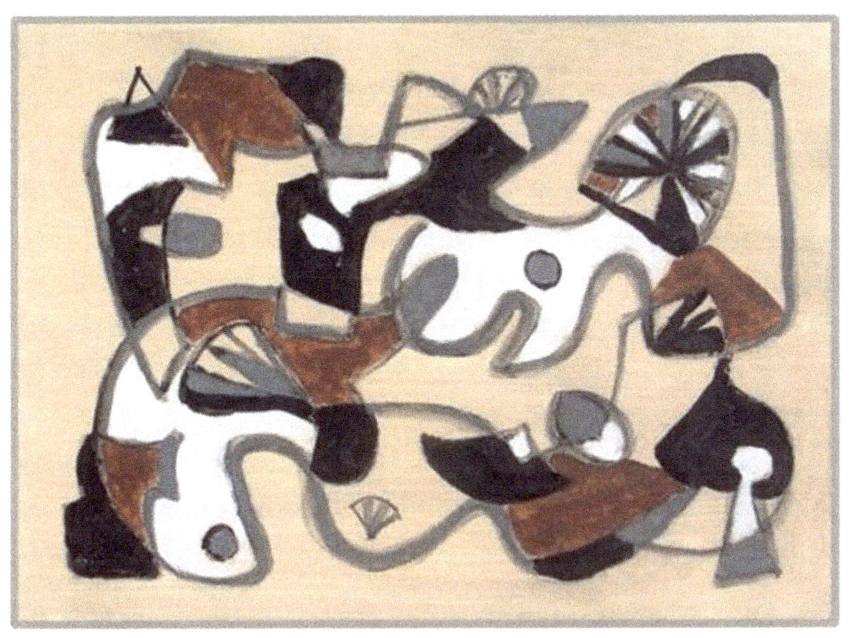

Spanish Encounter

Acrylic on paper, 27 x 36 cm, 2009

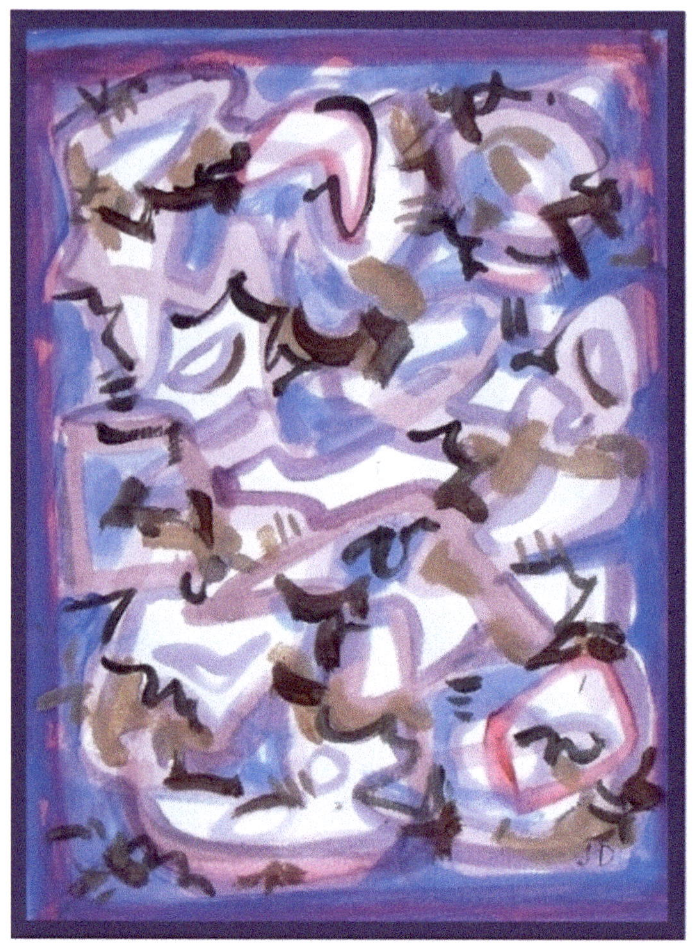

Commotion

Acrylic on paper, 38 x 28 cm, 2009

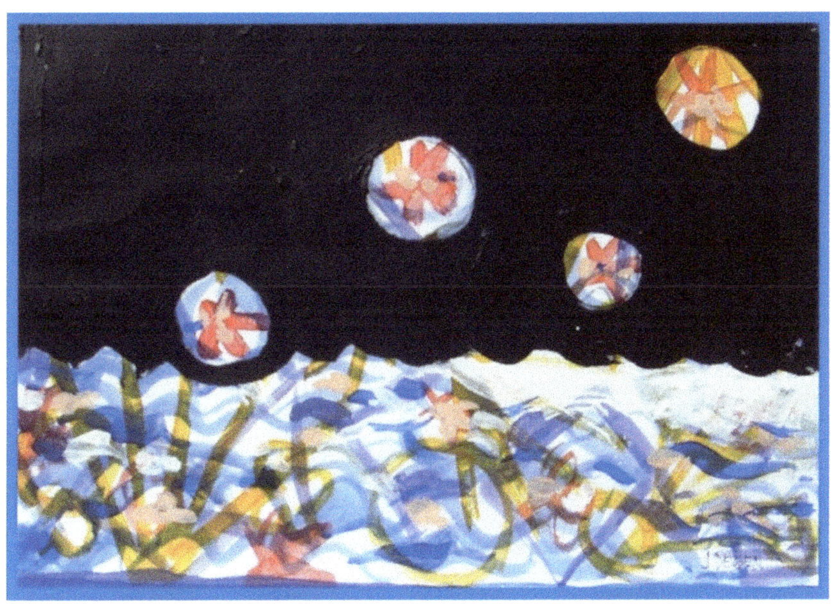

Bubble Bath

Acrylic on paper, 28 x 36 cm, 2009

There are no rules of architecture
for a castle in the clouds.
(G. K. Chesterton)

Cities, like cats, will reveal themselves at night.
(Rupert Brooke)

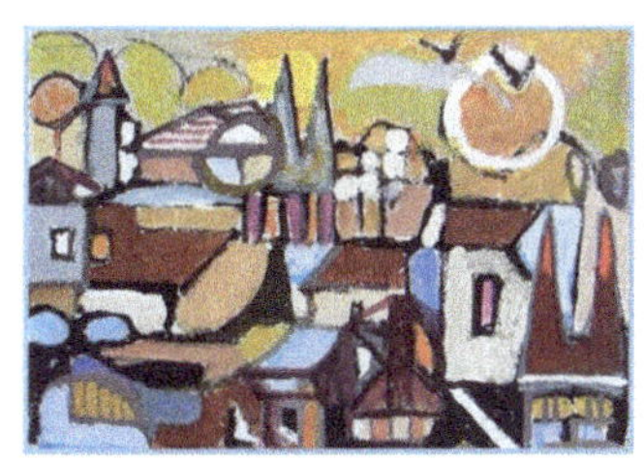

Inspired by Townscapes

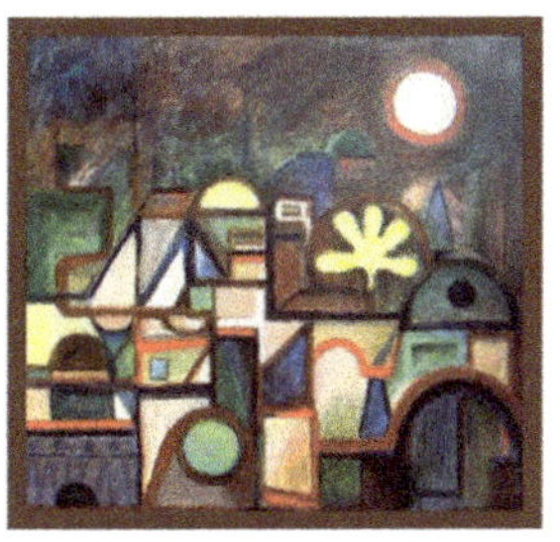

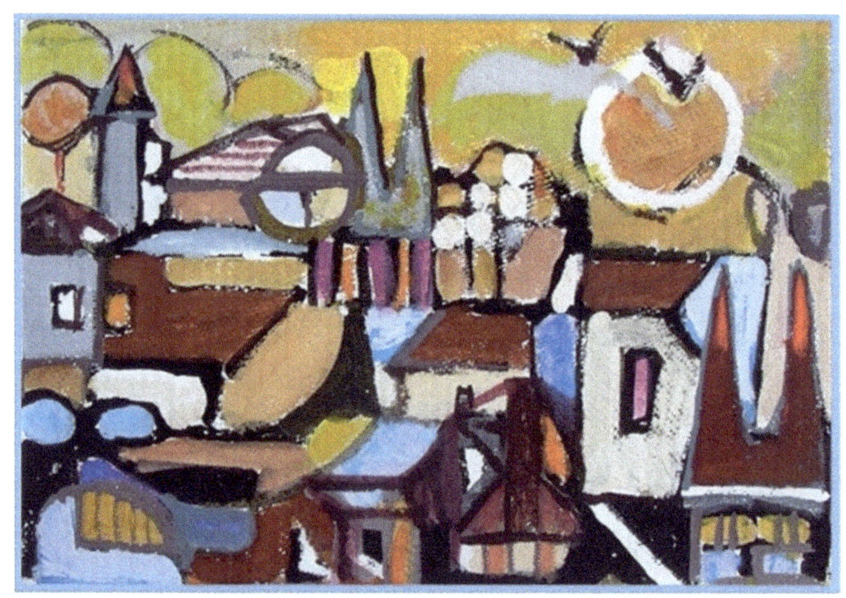

Somewhere in Europe

Acrylic on canvas, 21 x 27 cm, 2005

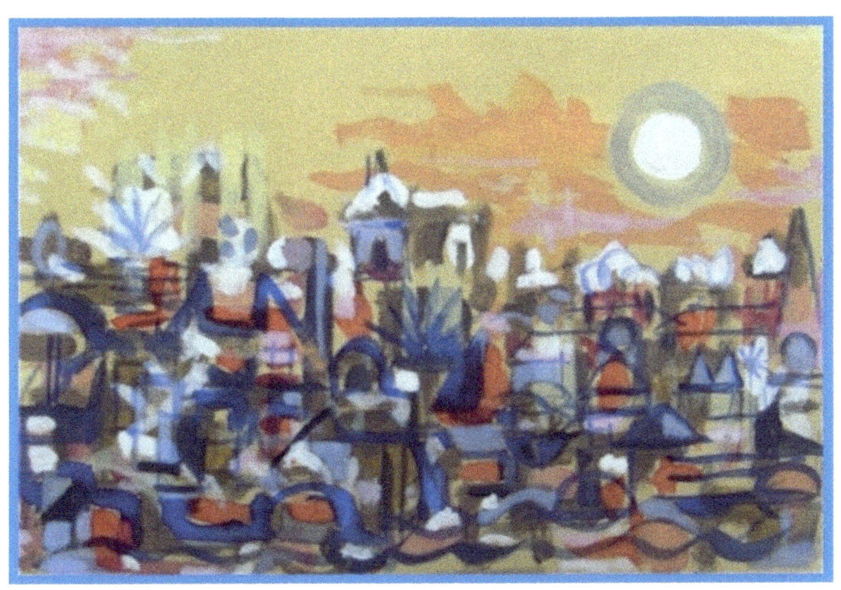

The White Sun

Acrylic on paper, 28 x 40 cm, 2009

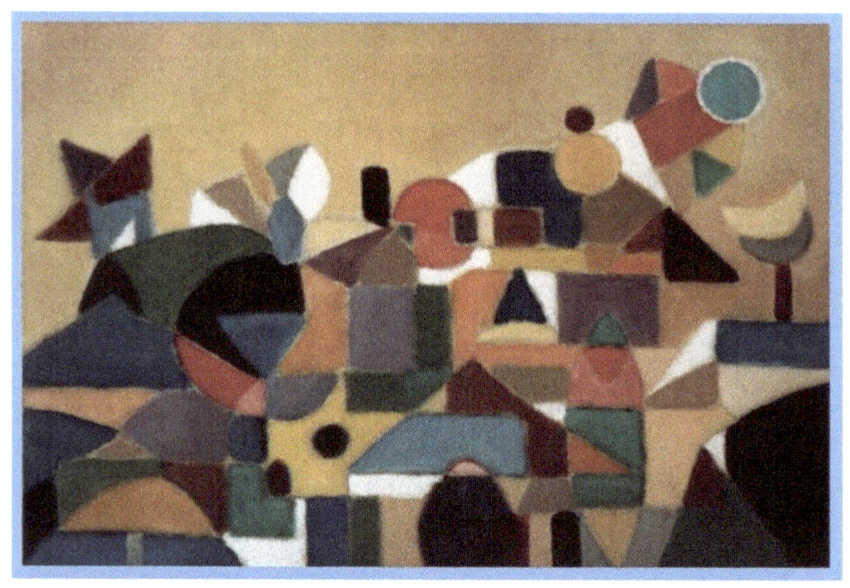

Coloured Town

Acrylic on paper, 30 x 41 cm, 2004

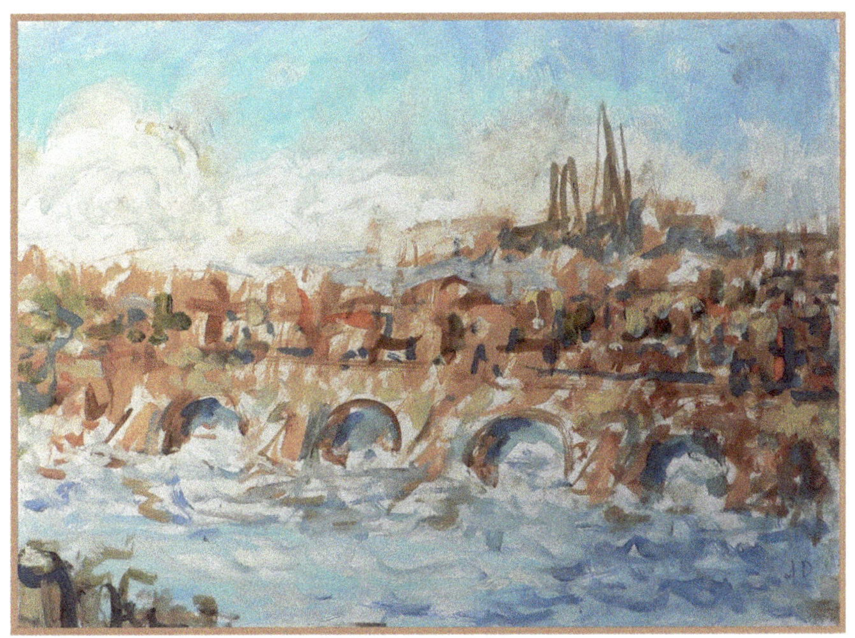

Town in Blue

Oil on paper, 29 x 38 cm, 2006

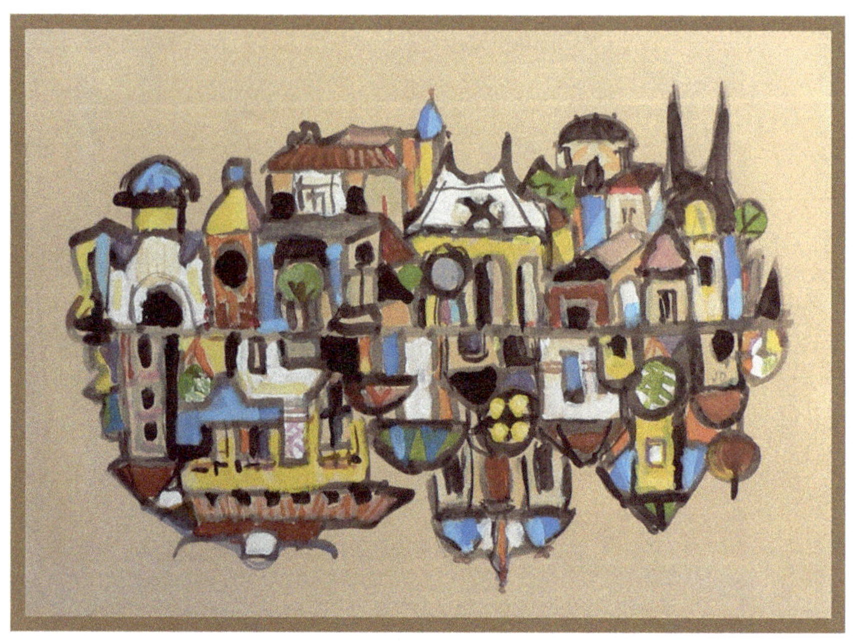

False Mirror

Gouache on paper, 27 x 35 cm, 2006

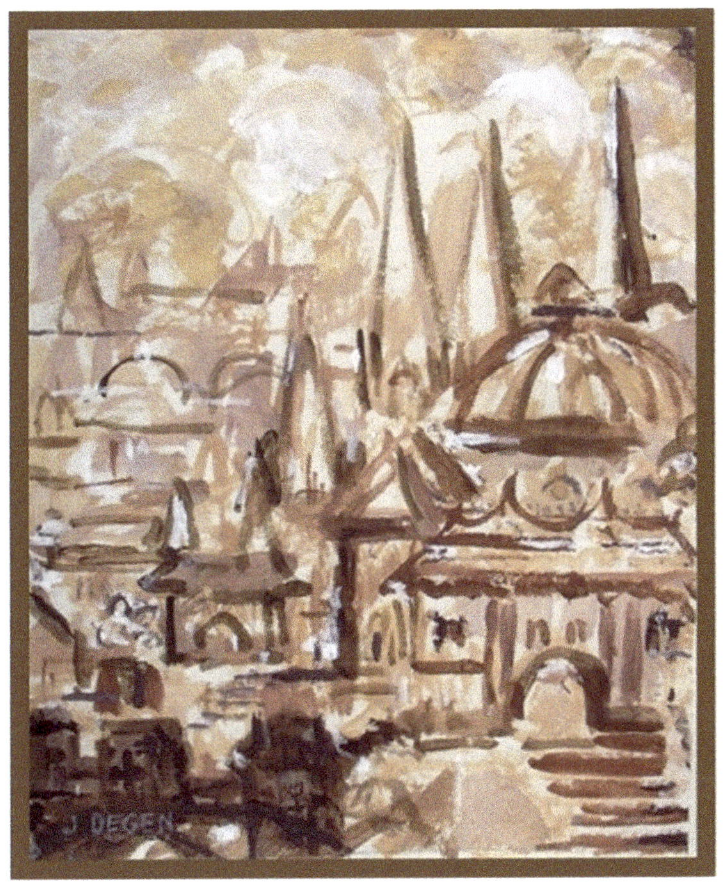

Old Town Fantasy

Acrylic on paper, 28 x 23 cm, 2010

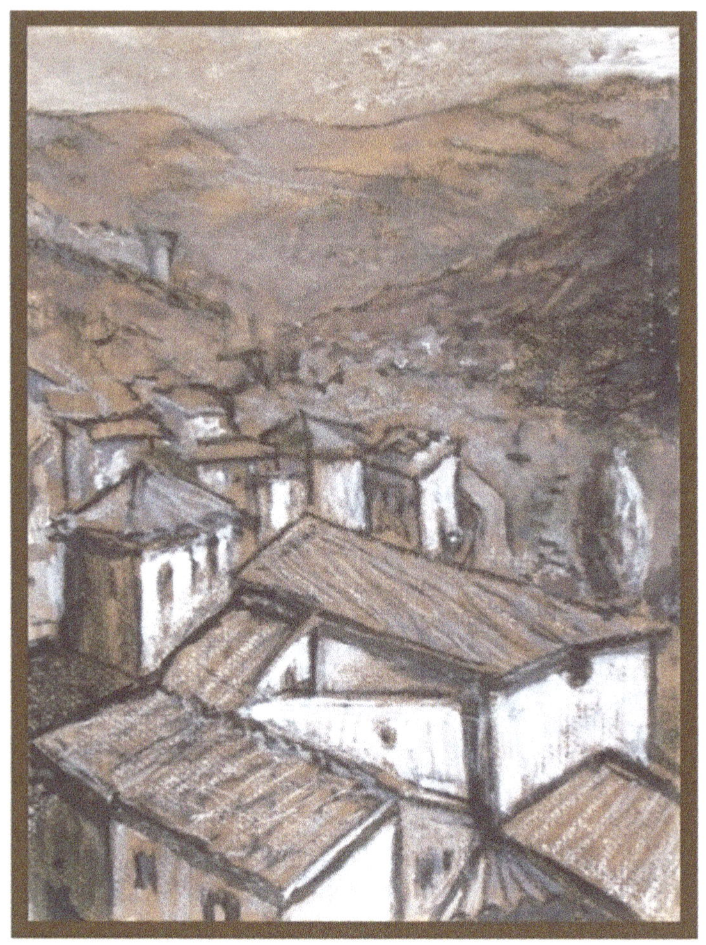

Spanish Village

Acrylic on paper, 38 x 27 cm, 2009

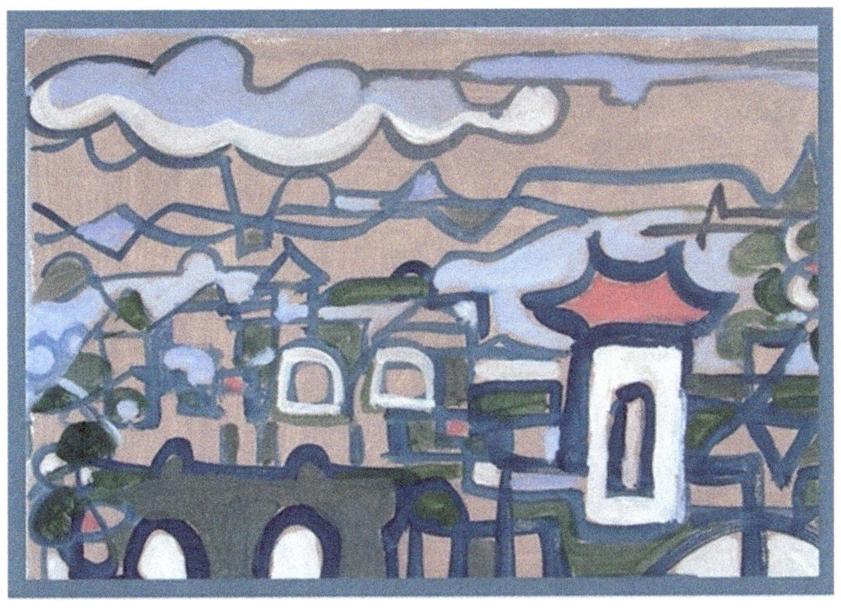

Asian Inspiration

Acrylic on paper, 24 x 31 cm, 2007

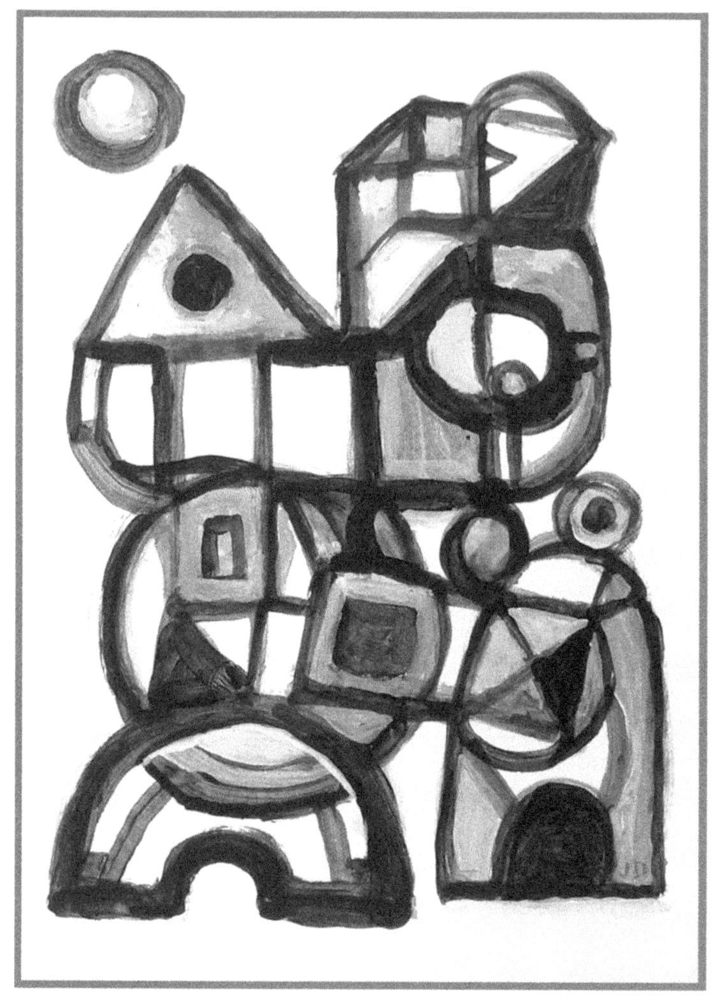

Untidy Town

Acrylic on paper, 35 x 27 cm, 2010

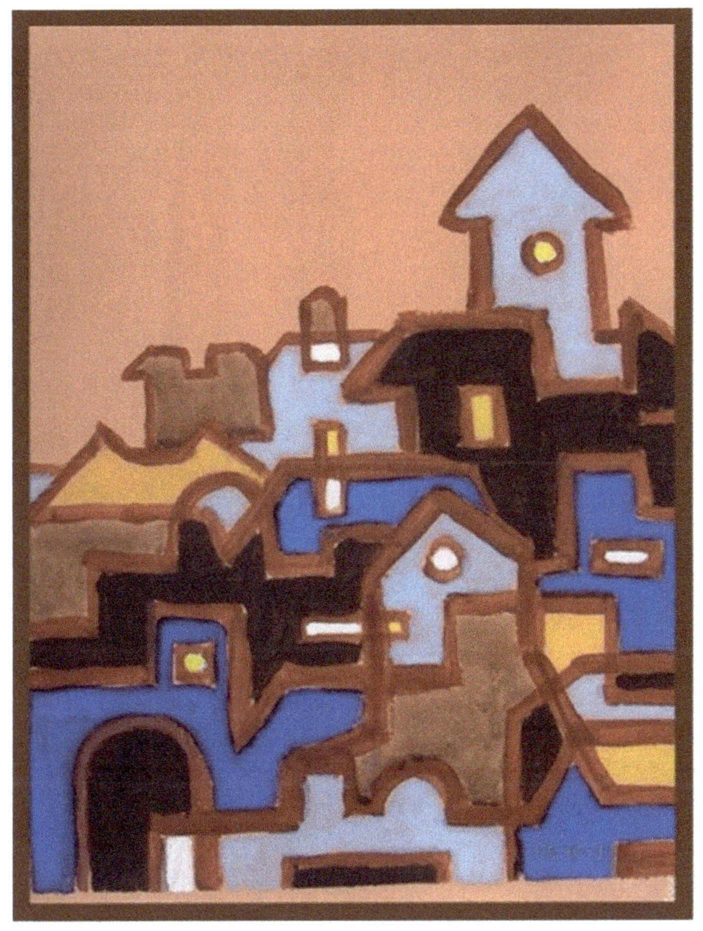

Red Sunset

Acrylic on paper, 28 x 22 cm, 2009

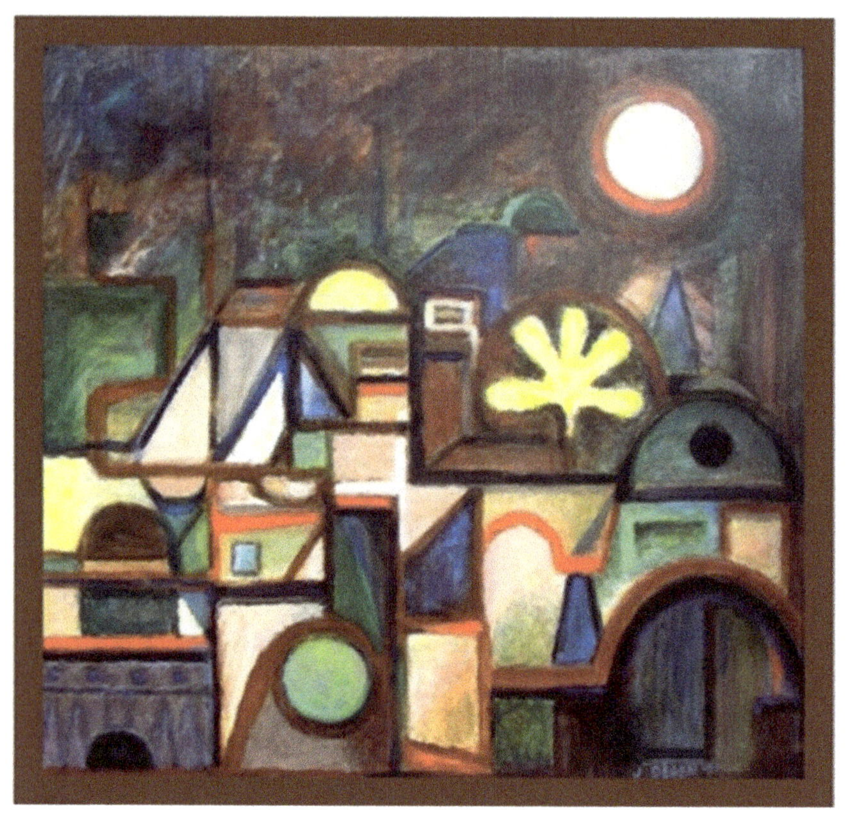

Lights in the Dark

Acrylic on paper, 58 x 59 cm, 2009

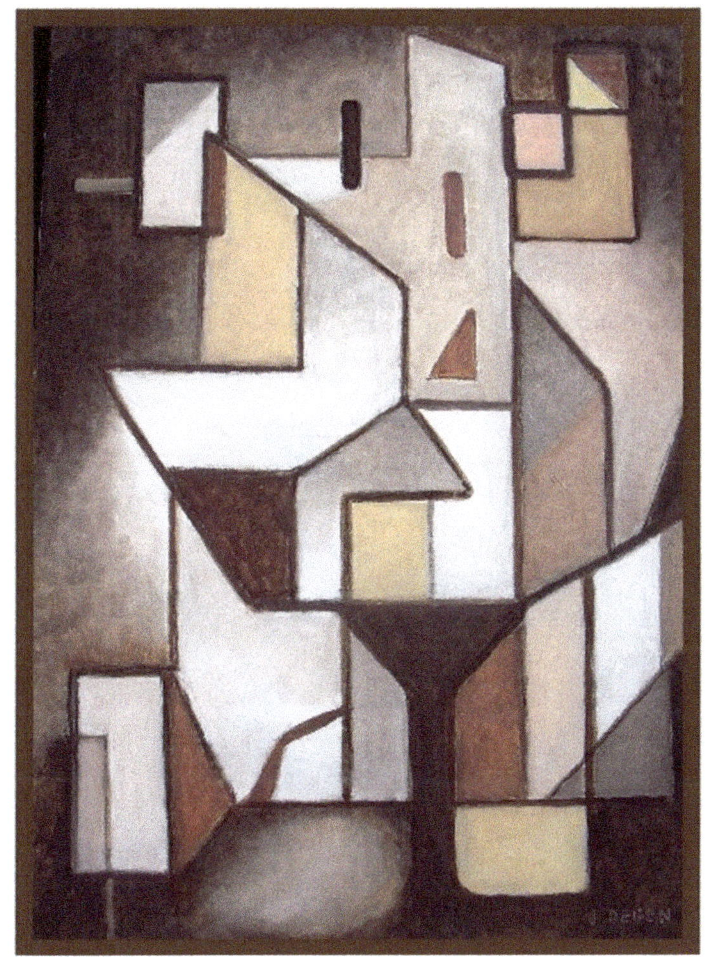

Townscape Dreaming

Oil on canvas, 75 x 51 cm, 2009

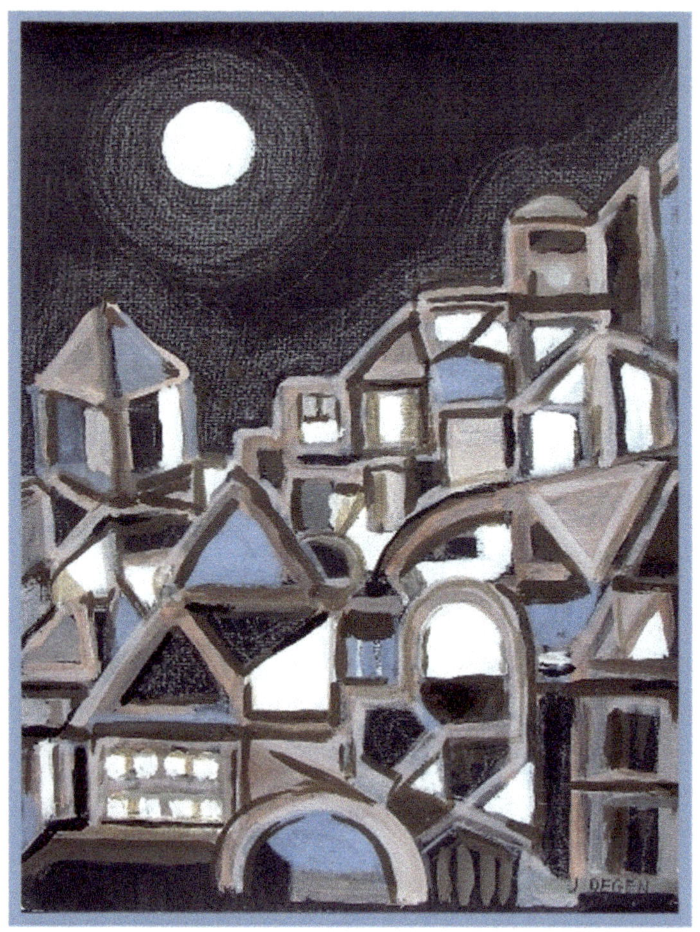

Lit-Up Town

Acrylic on paper, 37 x 27 cm, 2010

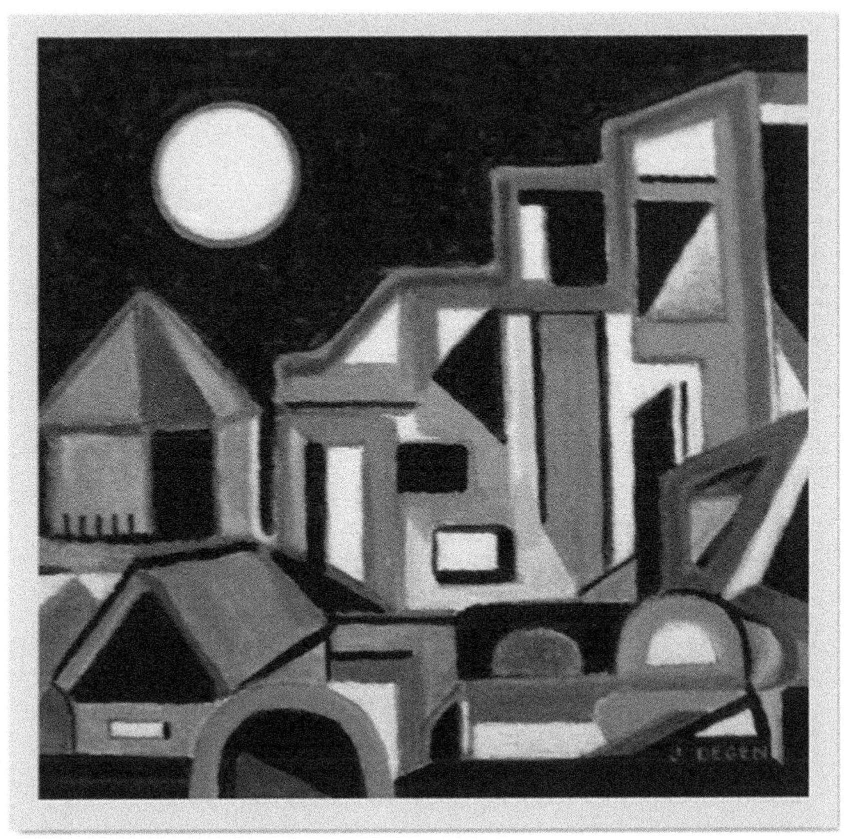

Night Watch

Acrylic on canvas, 30 x 30 cm, 2007

No great artist ever sees things as they really are,
if he did he would cease to be an artist.
(Oscar Wilde)

The longer you look at an object,
the more abstract it becomes,
and, ironically, the more real.
(Lucian Freud)

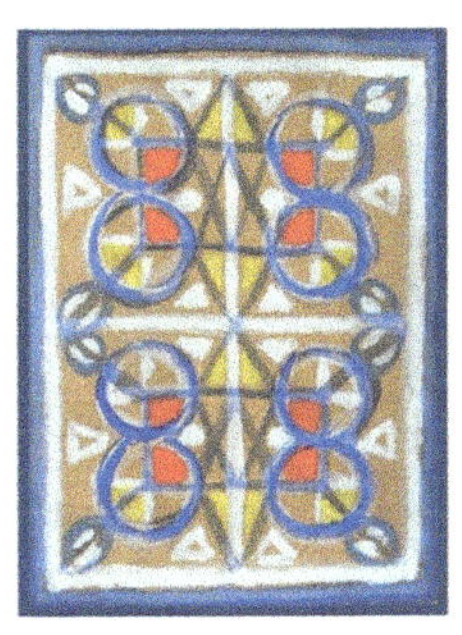

Spatial Expression

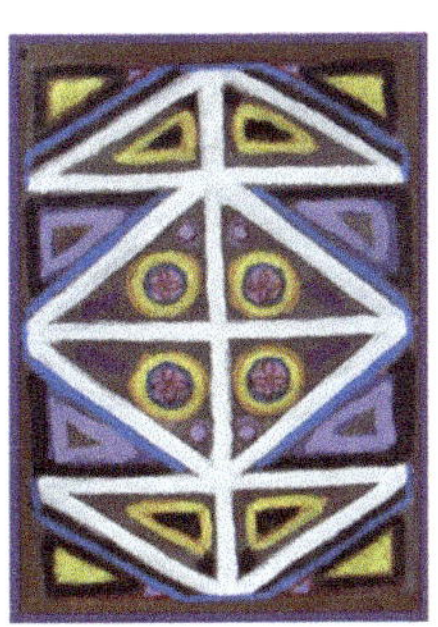

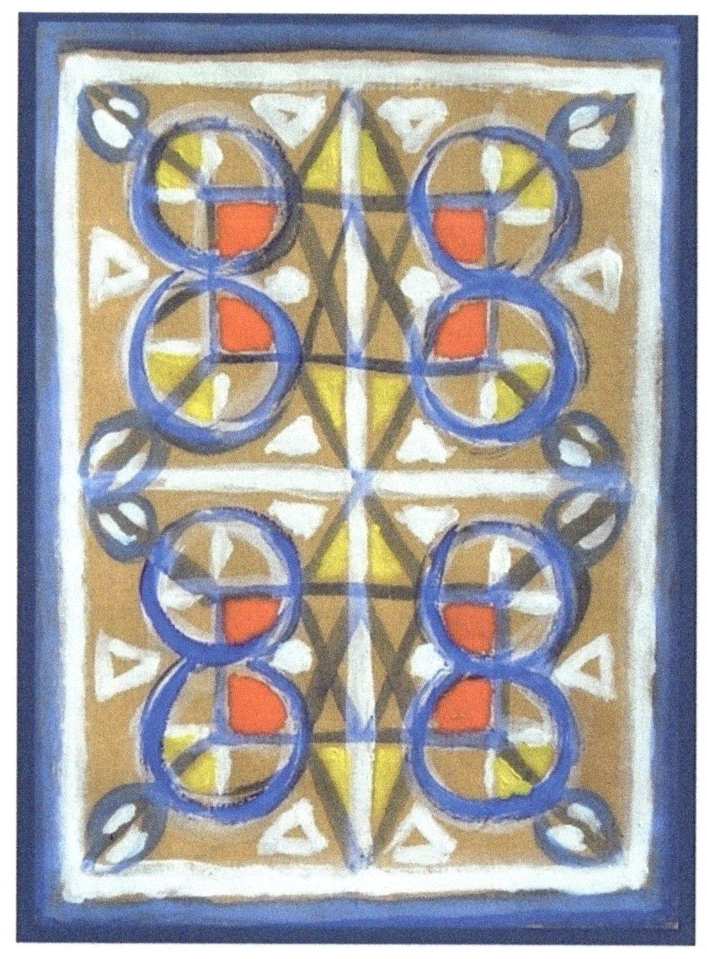

Circles

Acrylic on paper, 38 x 29 cm, 2009

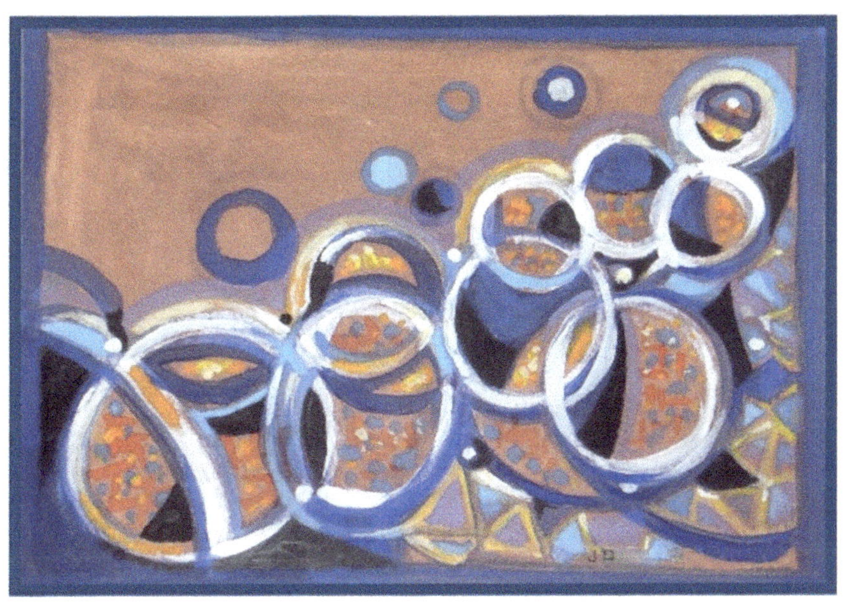

Intersecting Circles

Acrylic on paper, 28 x 38 cm, 2009

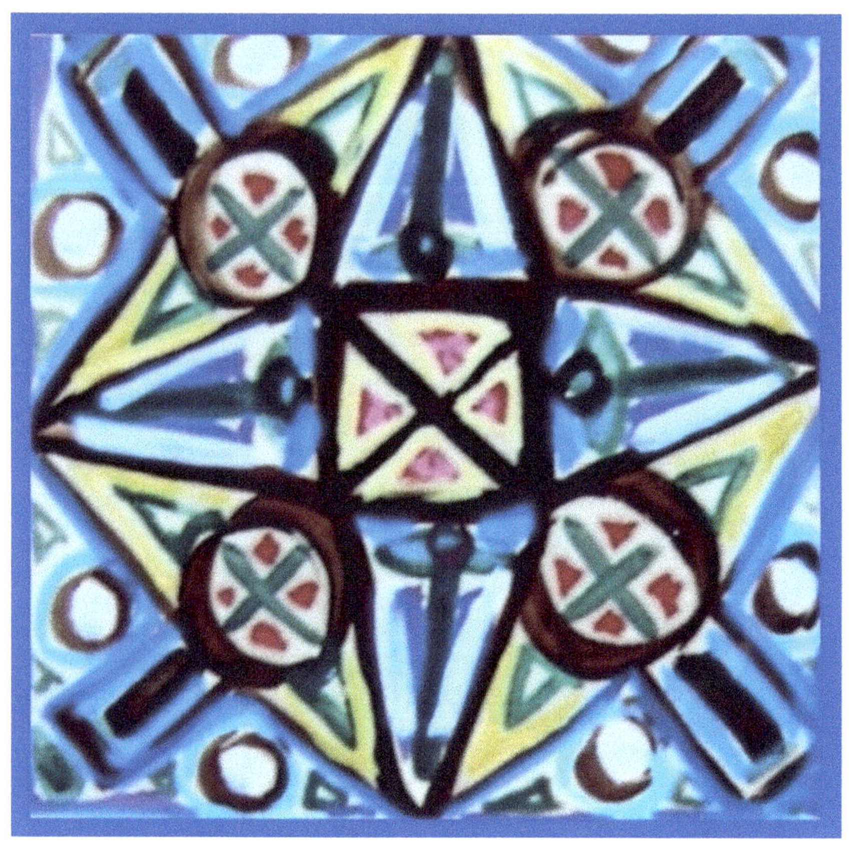

Compass

Acrylic on paper, 28 x 28 cm, 2006

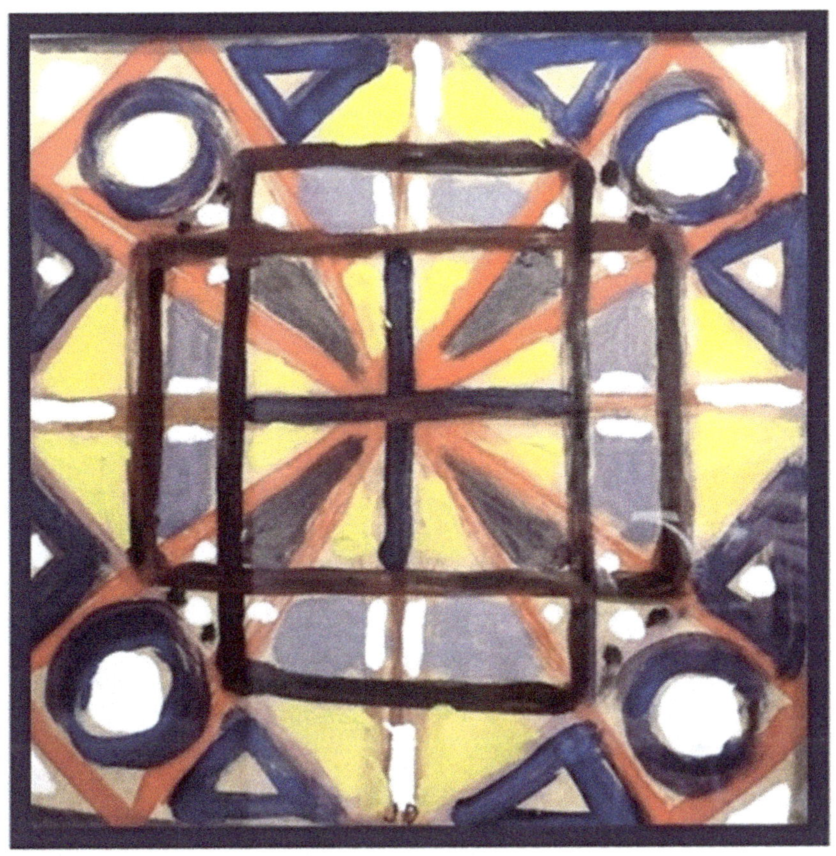

Outlook

Acrylic on paper 28 x 28 cm, 2010

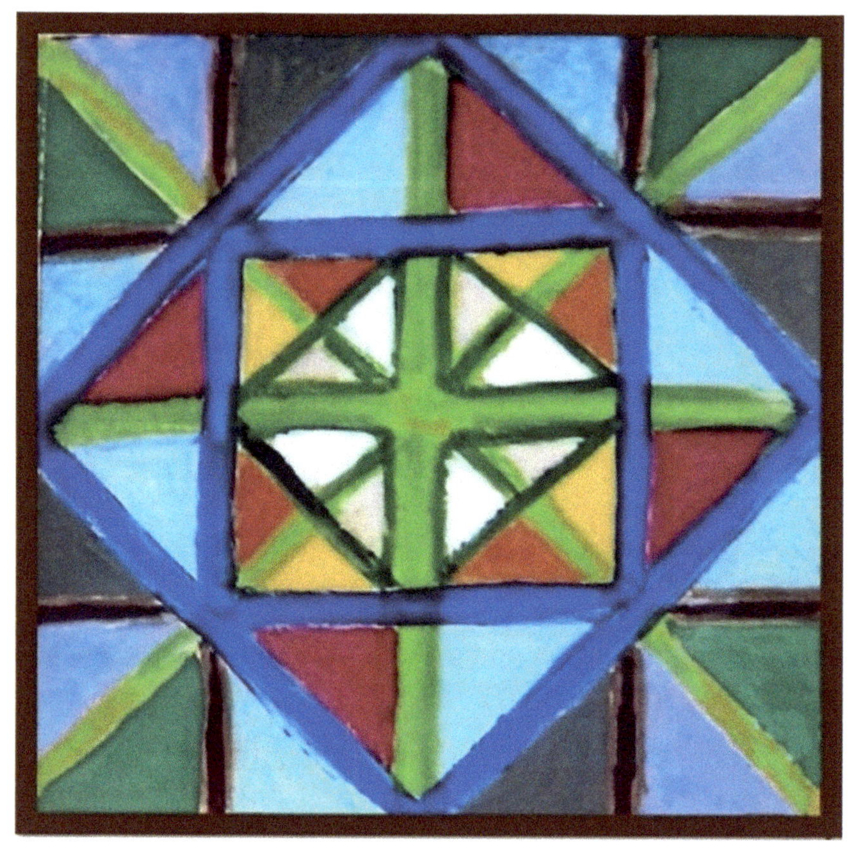

Plain Speaking

Acrylic on paper, 28 x 28 cm, 2007

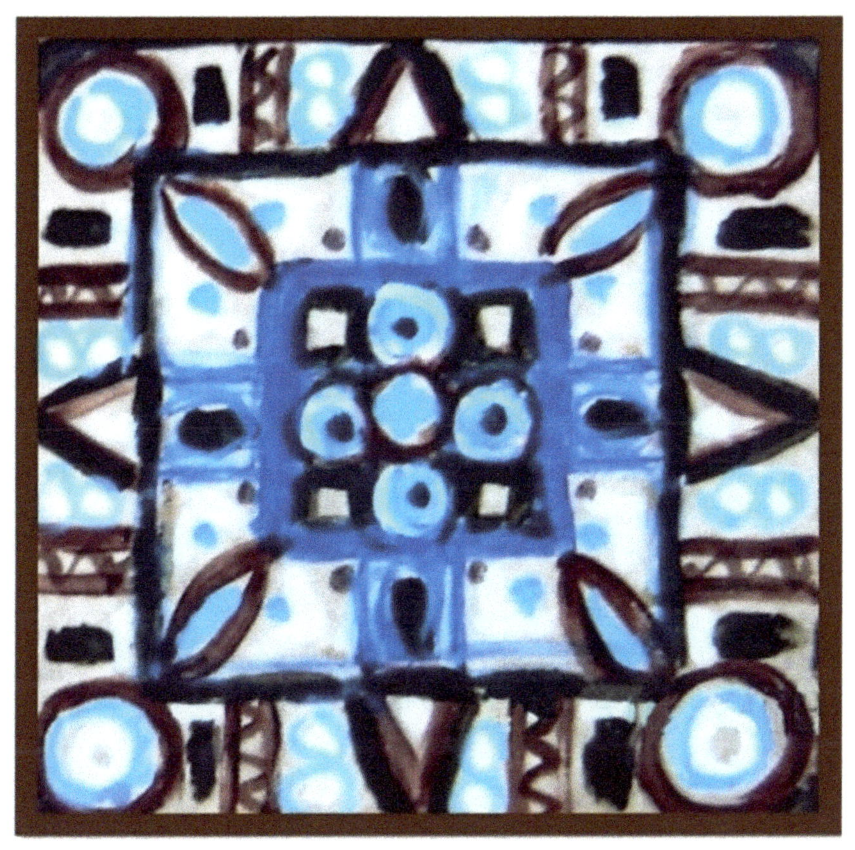

Accents

Acrylic on paper, 28 x 28 cm, 2006

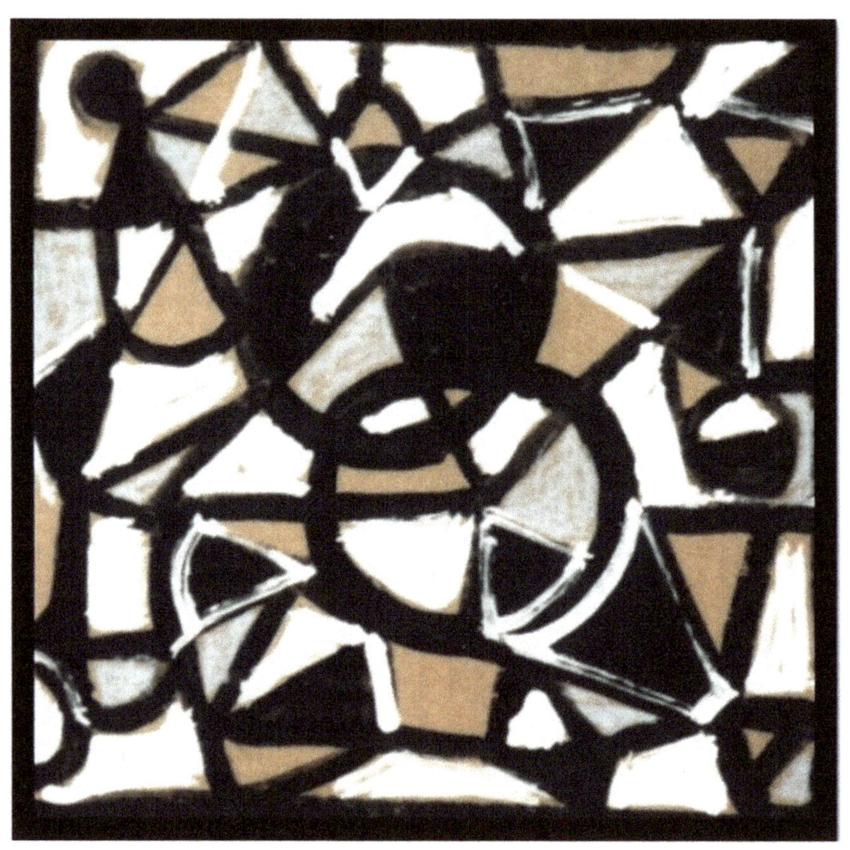

Assembly

Acrylic on paper, 28 x 28 cm, 2002

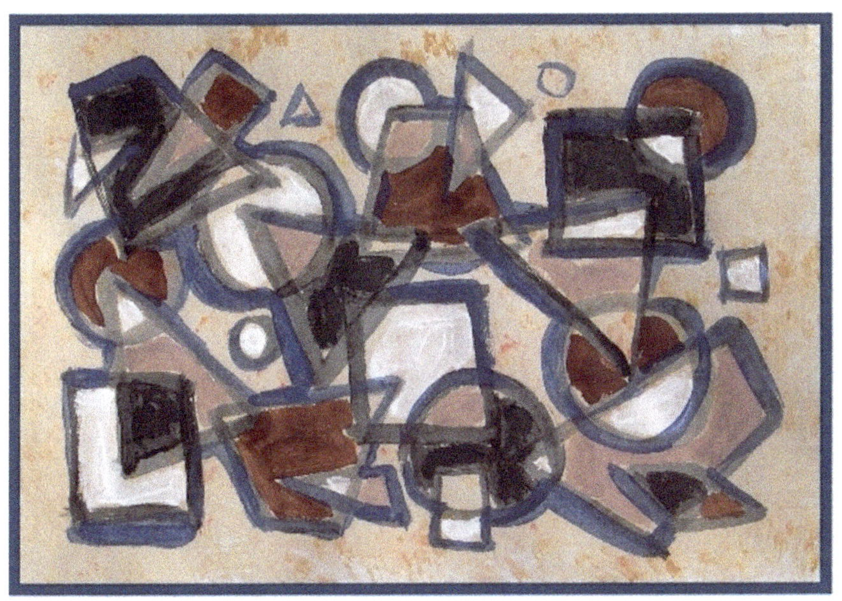

Earthly Improvisation

Acrylic on paper, 28 x 23 cm, 2009

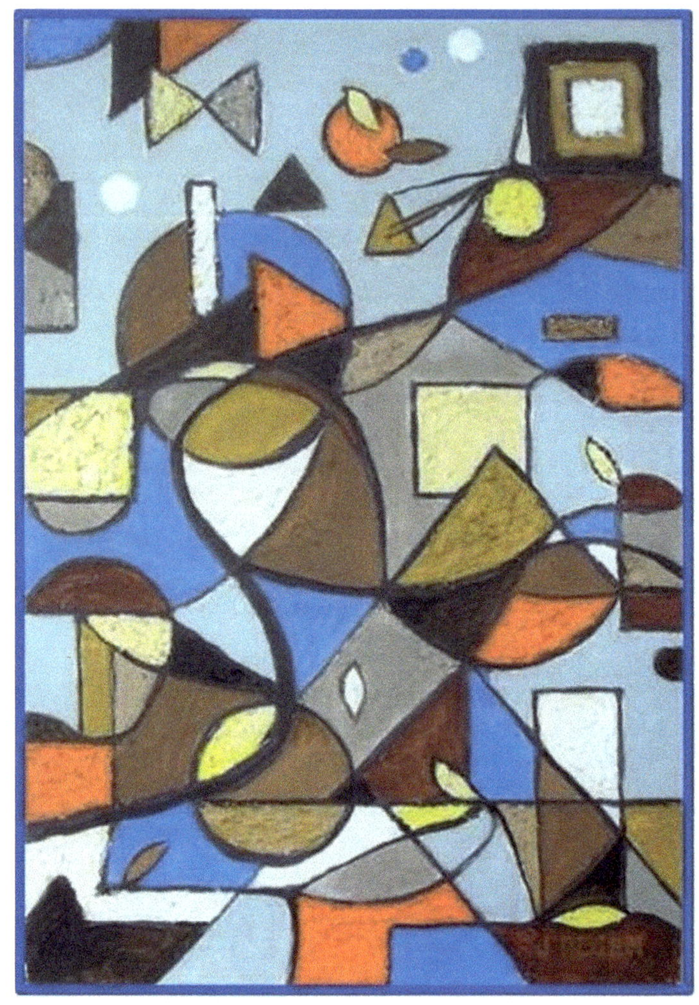

Flying Objects

Acrylic on board, 46 x 31 cm, 2011

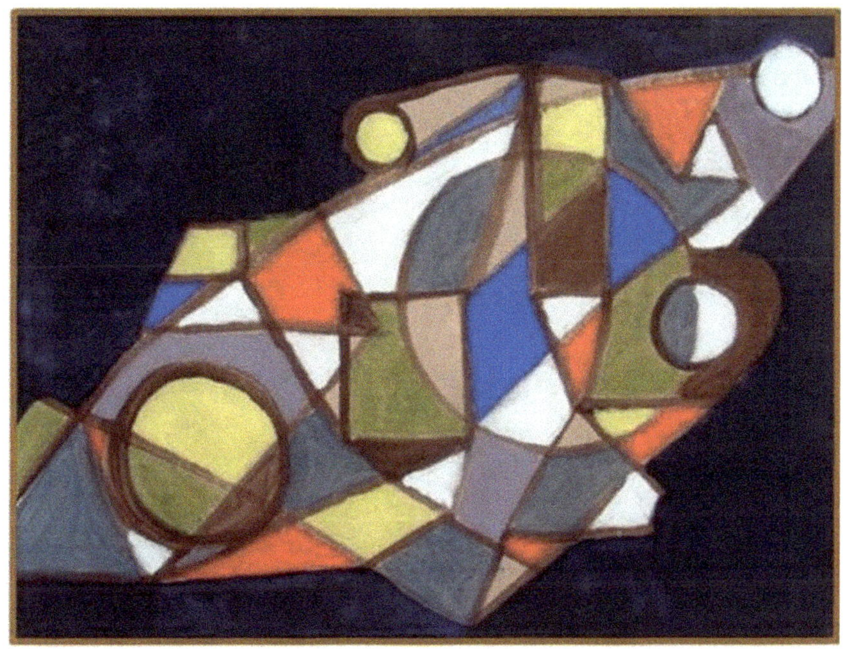

Into Space

Acrylic on paper, 29 x 36 cm, 2009

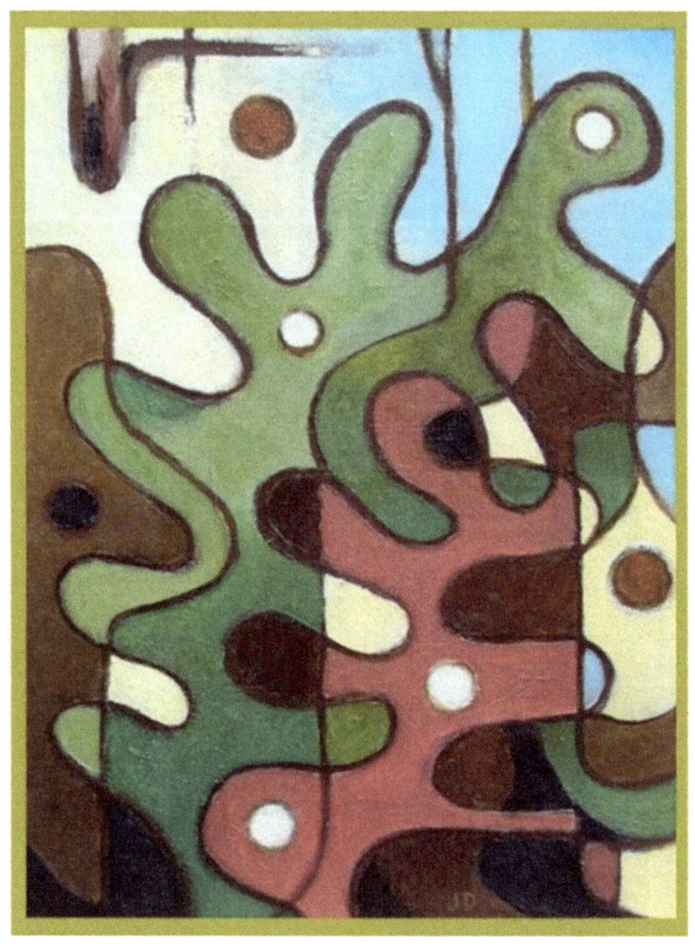

Night and Day 1

Oil on board, 61 x 41 cm, 2009

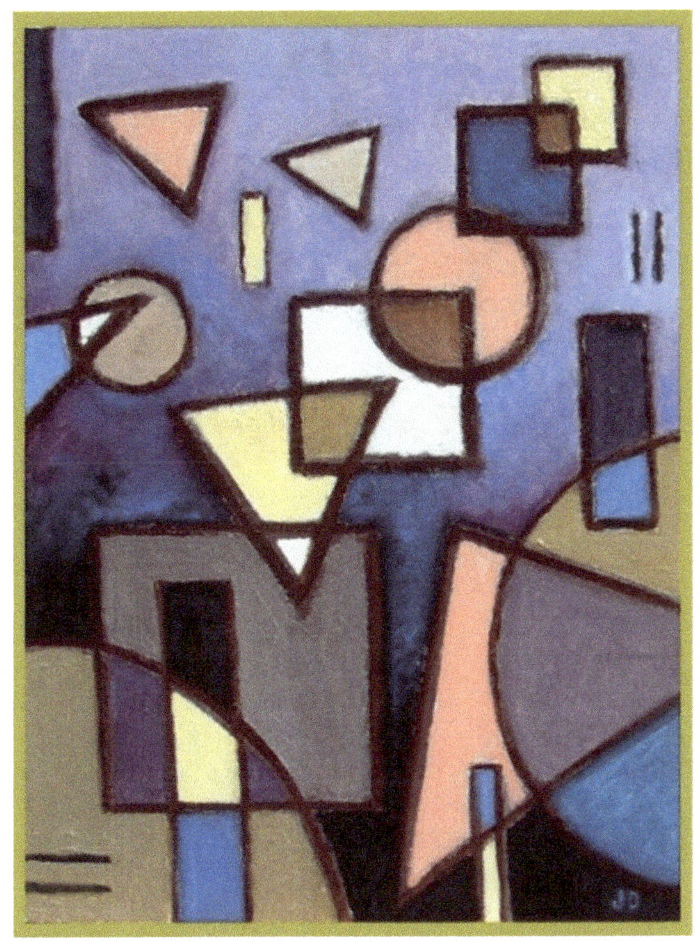

Night and Day 2

Oil on board, 61 x 41 cm, 2009

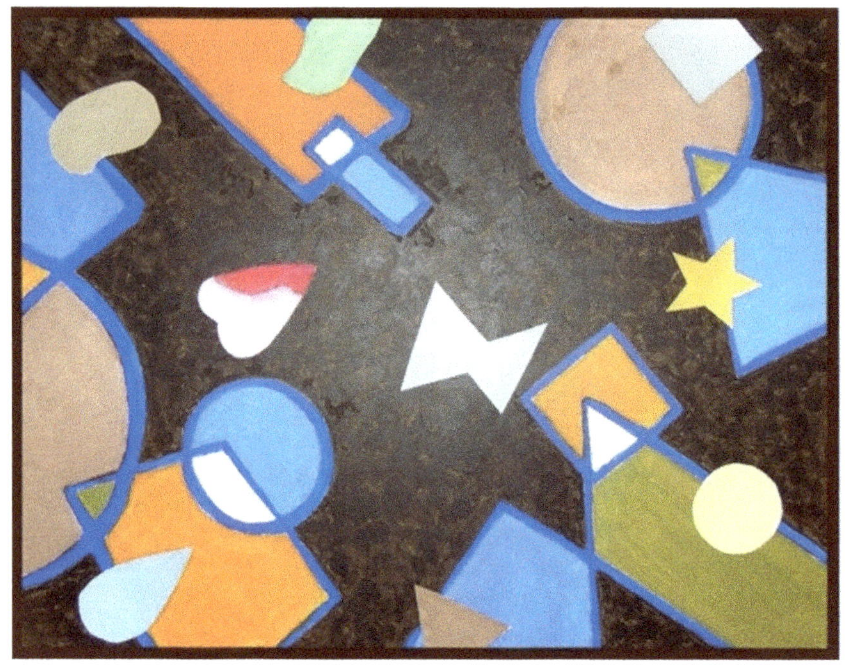

Nocturnalia

Collage, 48 x 61 cm, 2009

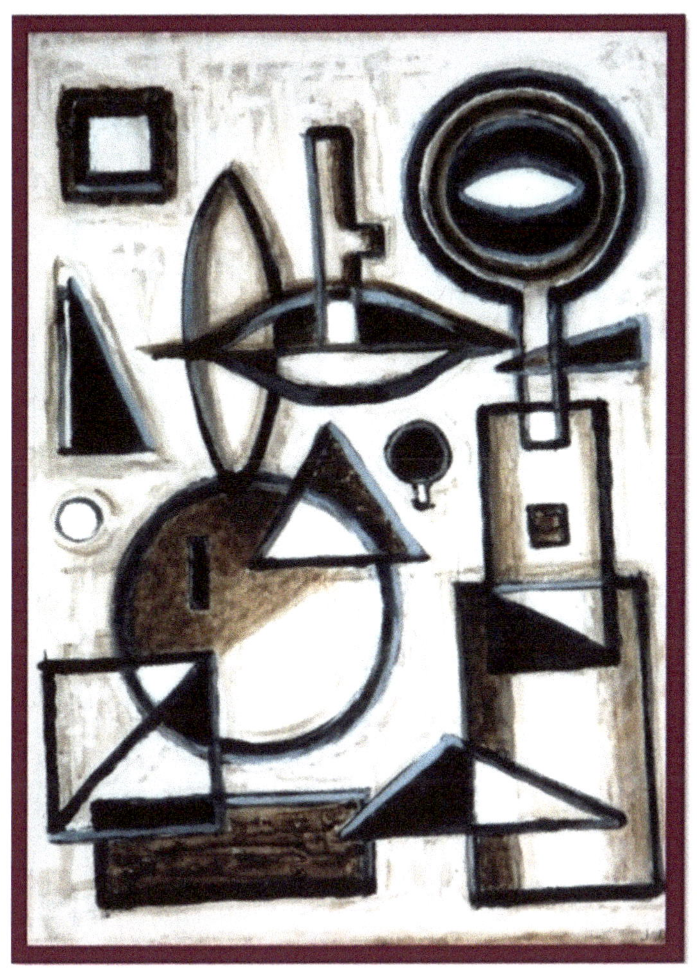

History Unknown

Acrylic on board, 58 x 44 cm, 2009

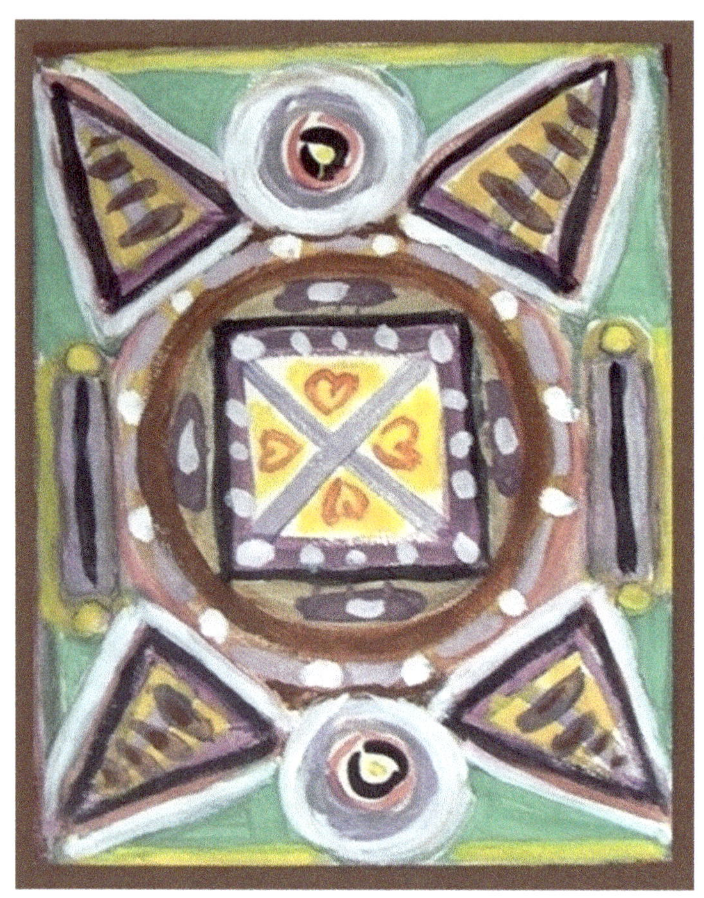

Four Hearts

Acrylic on paper, 37 x 27 cm, 2009

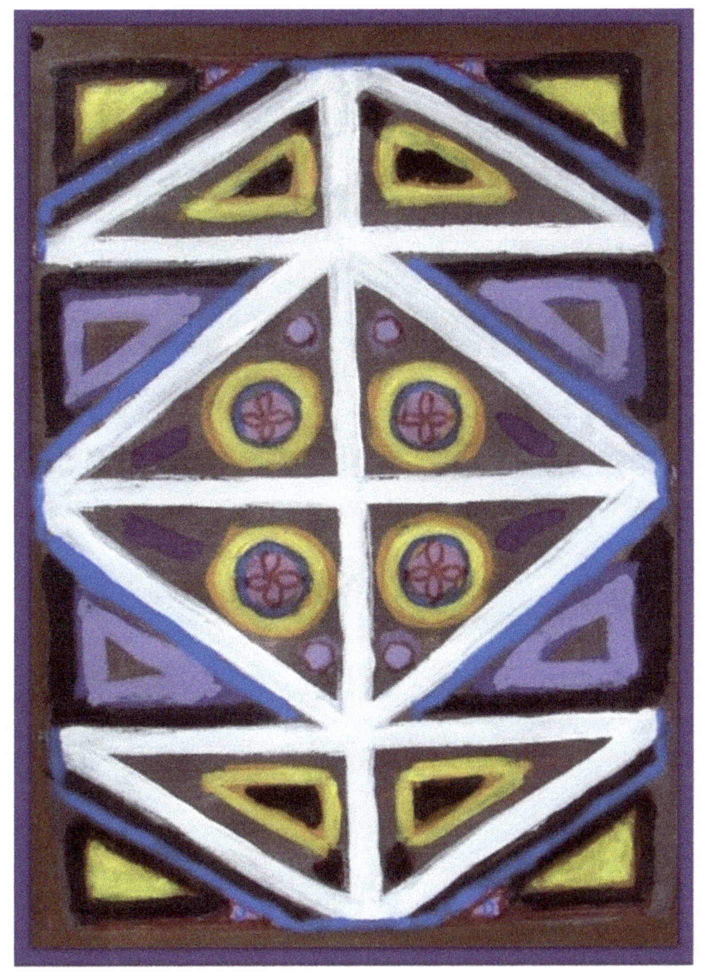

Geometry

Acrylic on paper, 38 x 27 cm, 2009

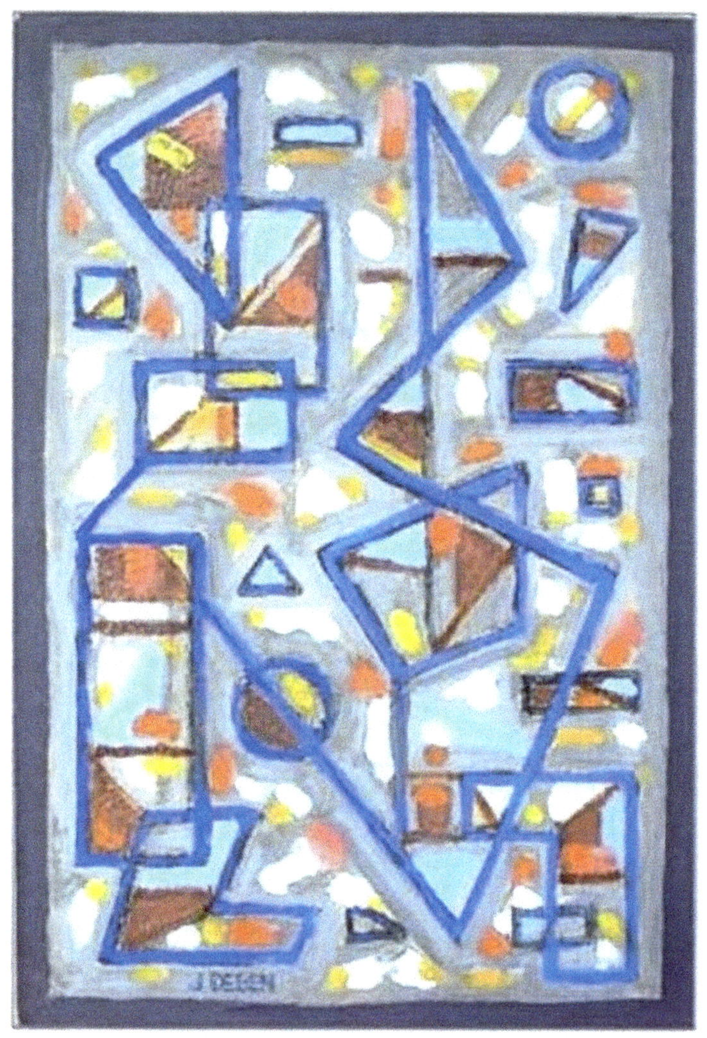

Linkage

Acrylic on board, 45 x 30 cm, 2011

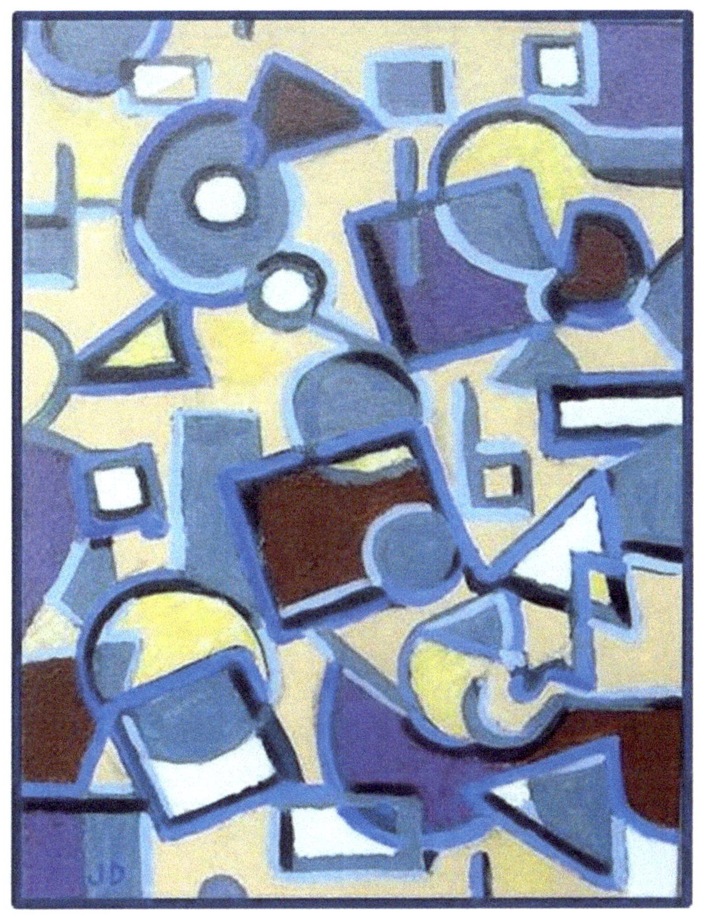

Shapes

Acrylic on canvas, 40 x 30 cm, 2011

Anyone can make the simple complicated.
Creativity is making the complicated simple.
(Charles Mingus)

The most important element in a picture cannot be defined.
(Pierre-Auguste Renoir)

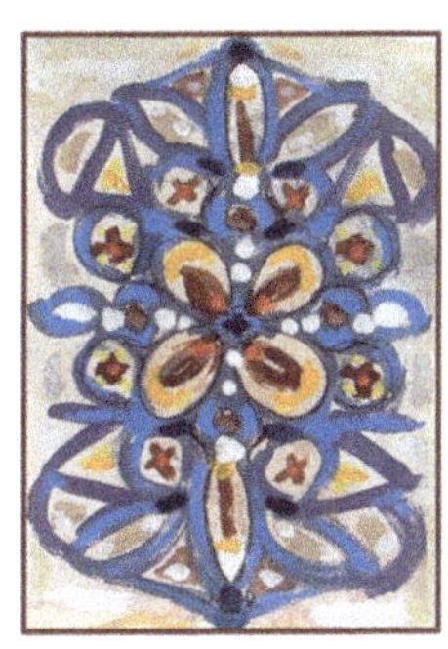

Symmetry & Asymmetry

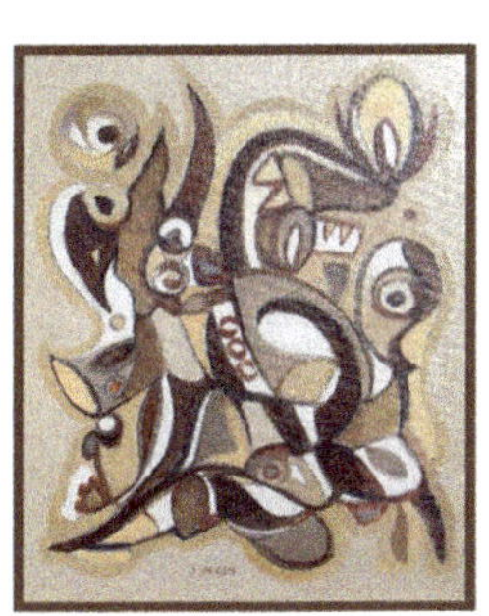

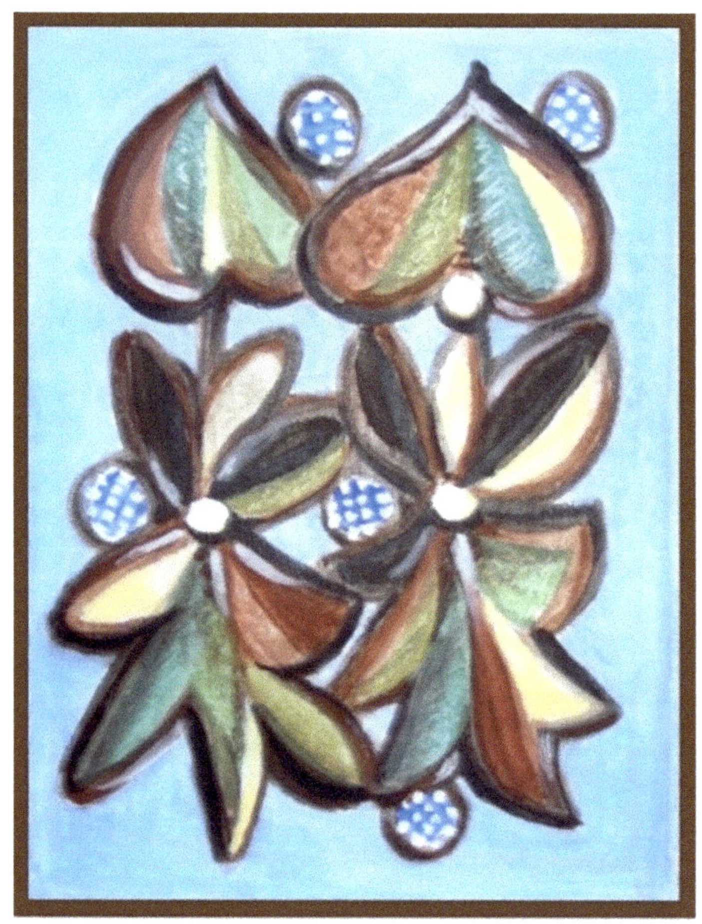

Ornamental

Acrylic on paper, 37 x 27 cm, 2009

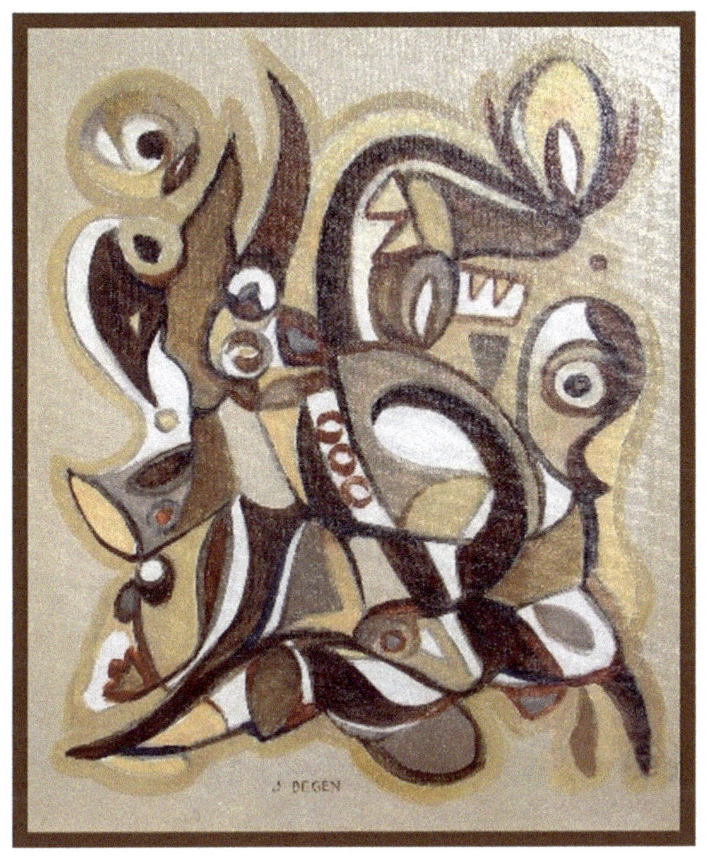

Impromtu

Oil on canvas, 51 x 41 cm, 2009

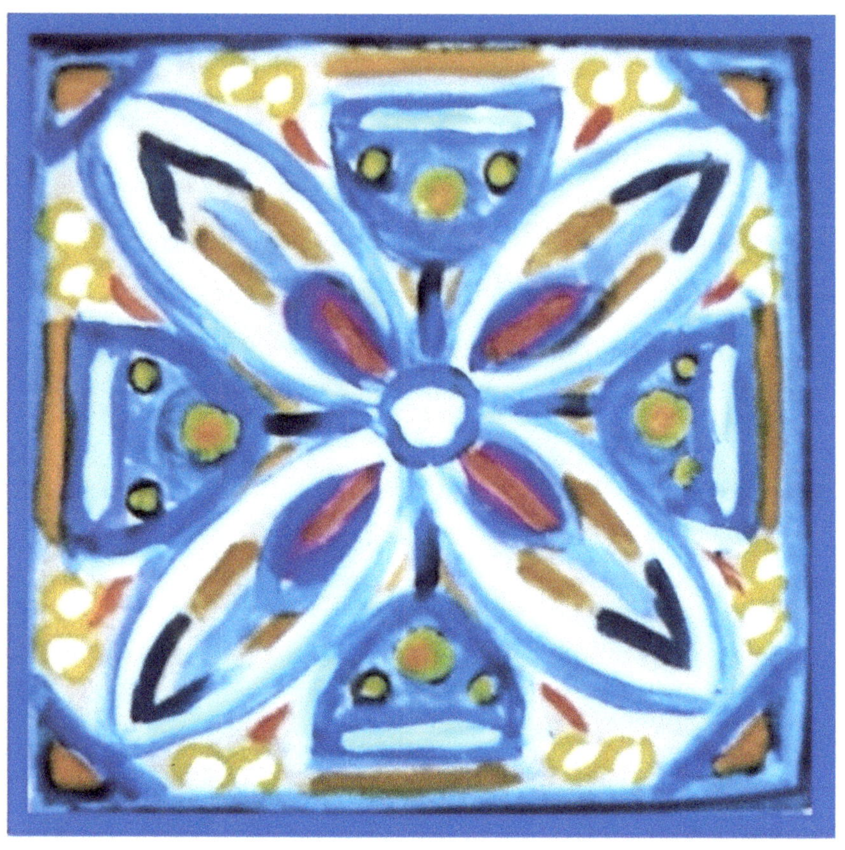

Talisman

Acrylic on paper, 27 x 27 cm, 2007

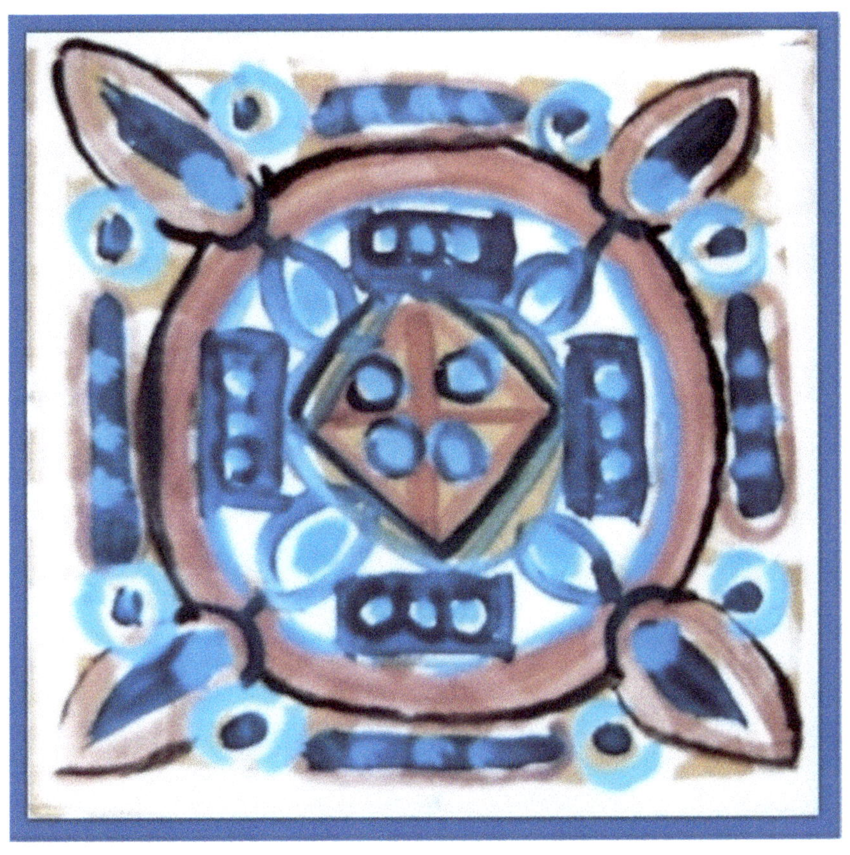

Oriental

Acrylic on paper, 27 x 27 cm, 2005

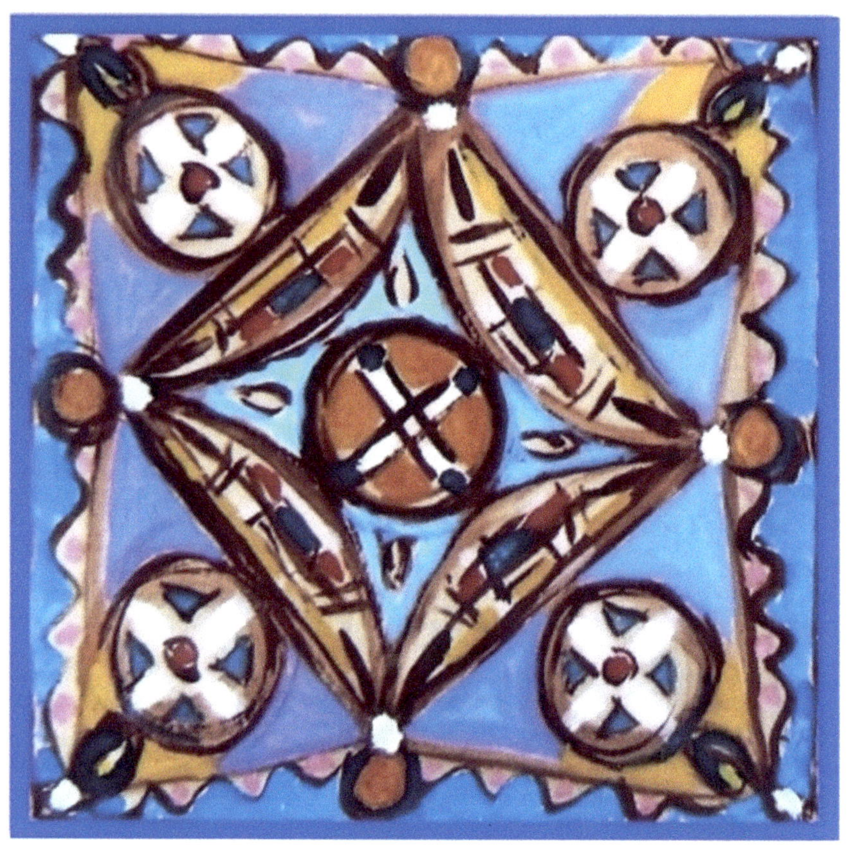

Curtain

Acrylic on paper, 28 x 28 cm, 2007

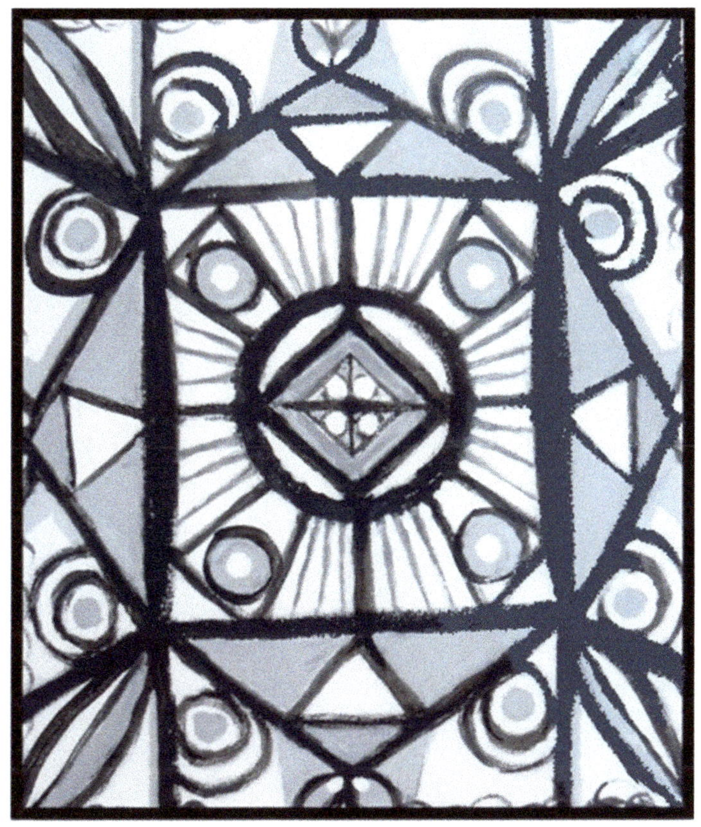

Decoratively Speaking

Acrylic on canvas, 60 x 50 cm, 2005

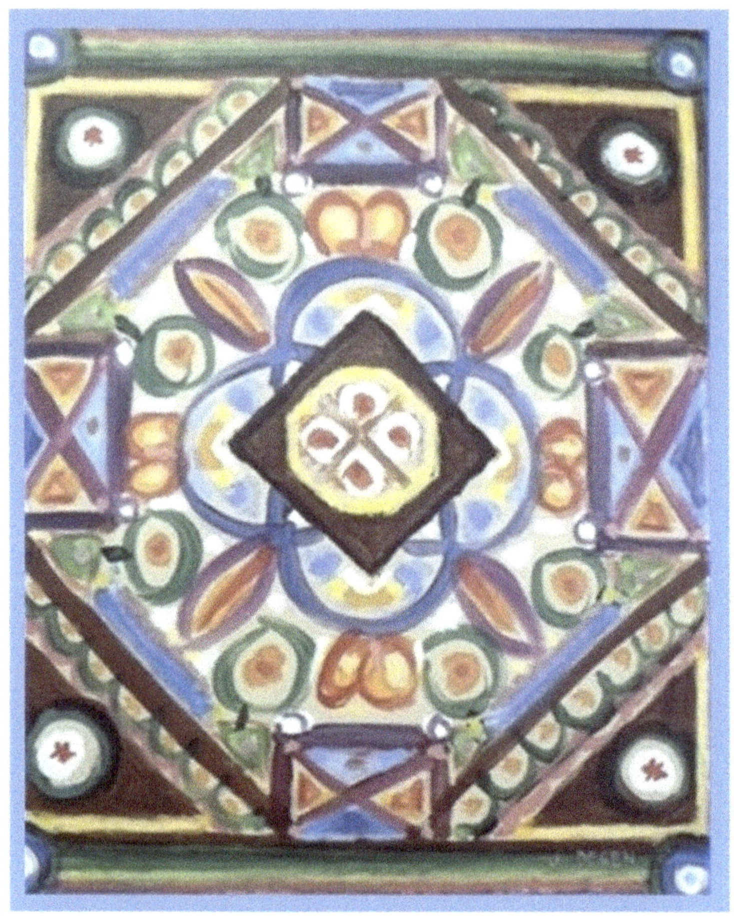

Alla Rustica

Acrylic and pastel on paper, 38 x 27 cm, 2004

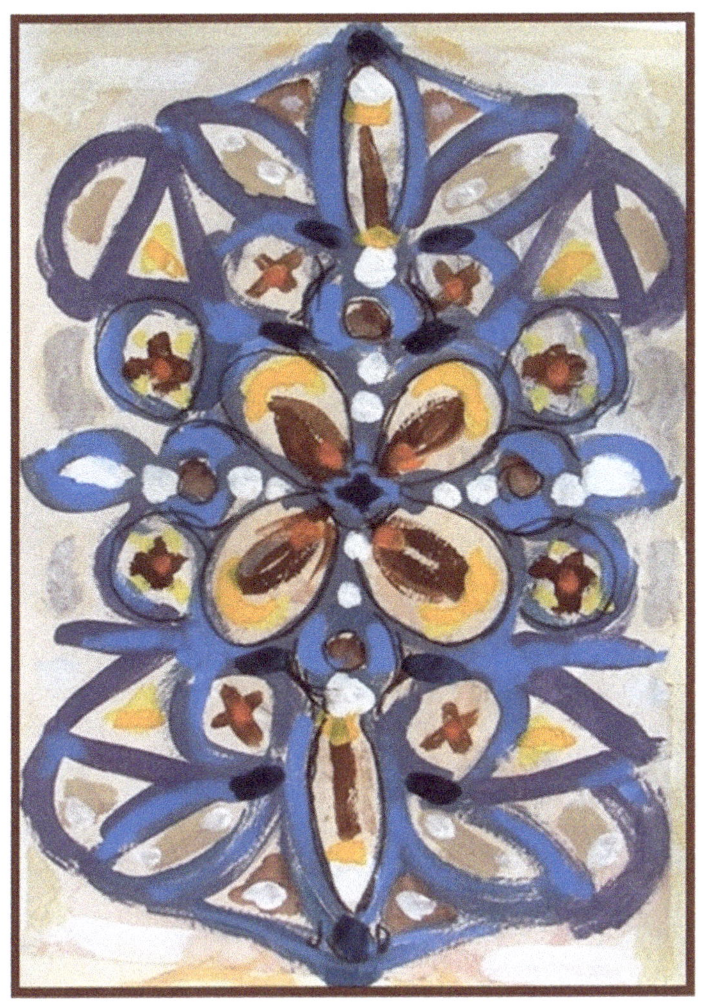

Lantern

Acrylic on paper, 30 x 24 cm, 2008

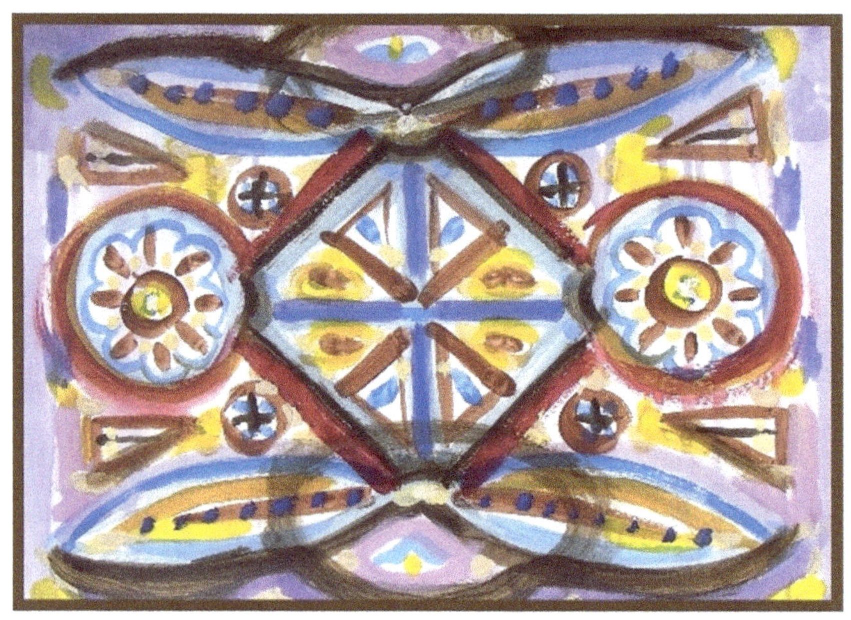

Observation

Mixed media on paper, 27 x 38 cm, 2009

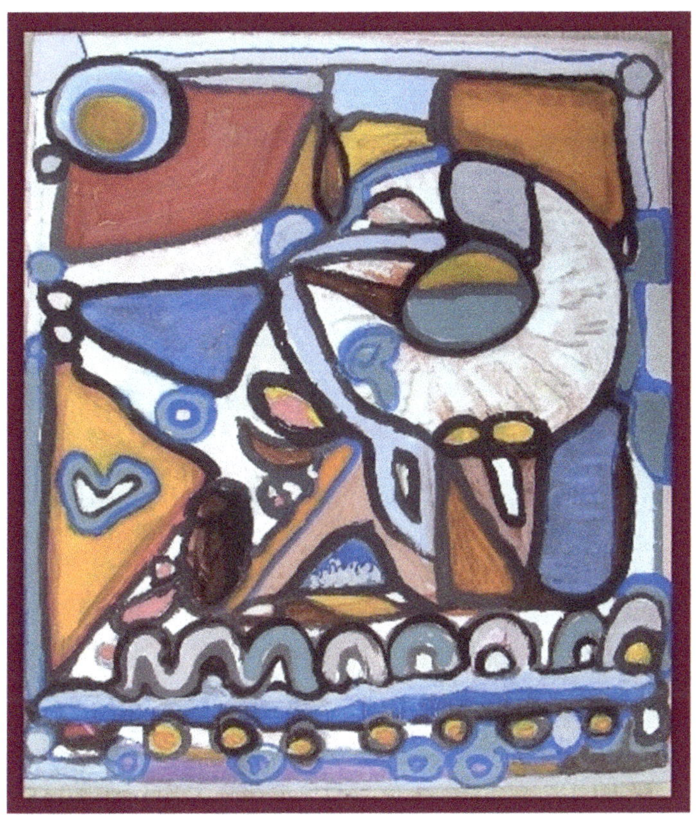

Light Baroque

Gouache on carton, 37 x 32 cm, 2009

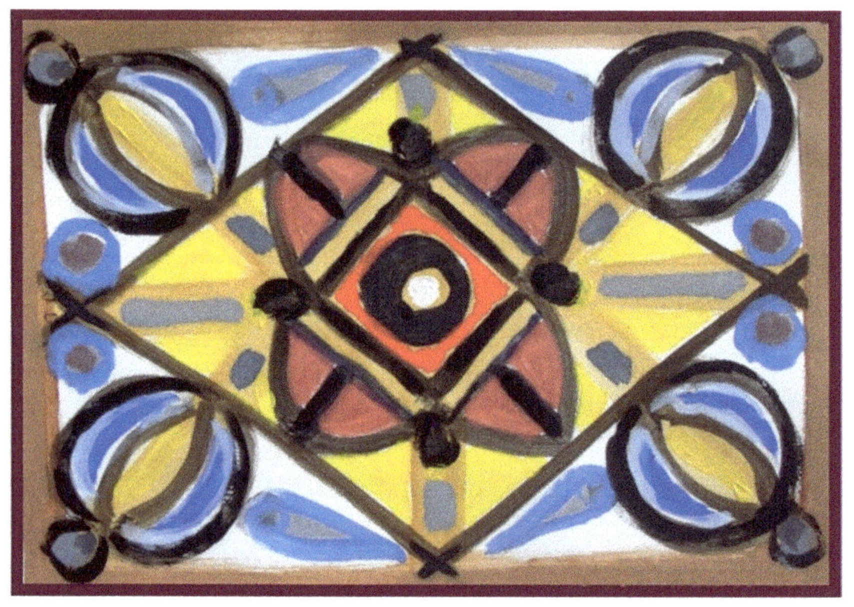

Stained Glass

Acrylic on paper, 26 x 38 cm, 2009

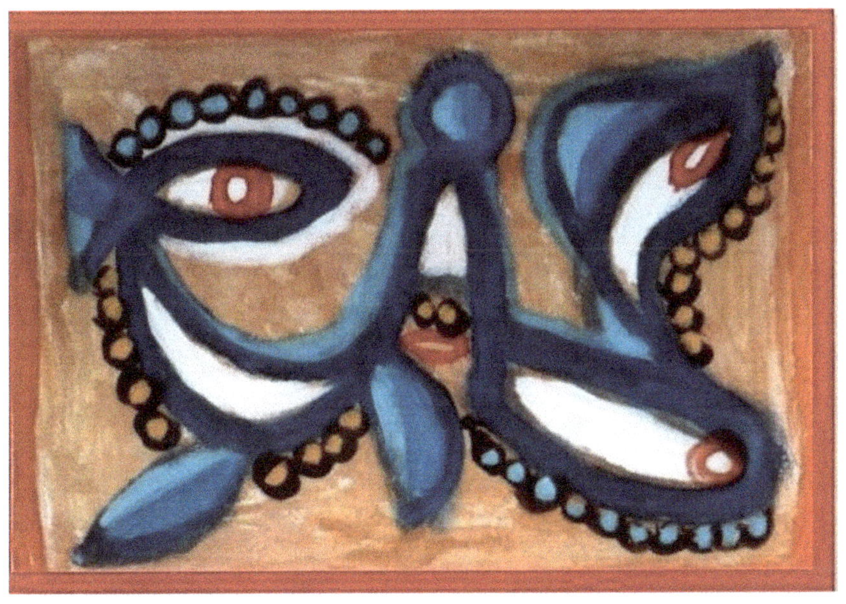

Ornaments

Acrylic on paper, 27 x 37 cm, 2005

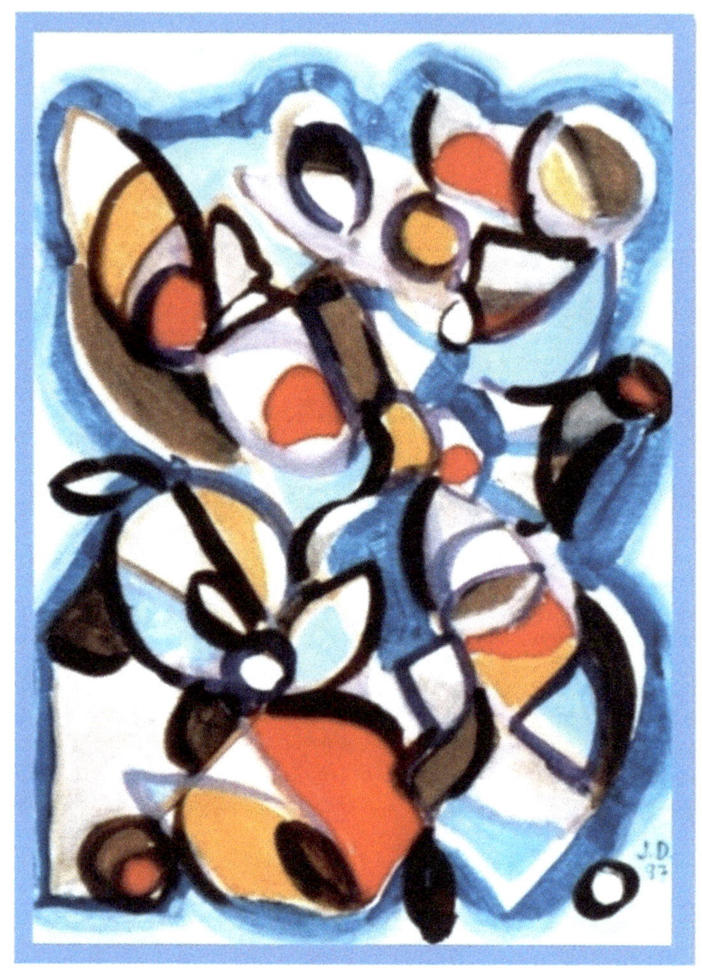

Untitled 1

Acrylic on paper, 36 x 28 cm, 1997

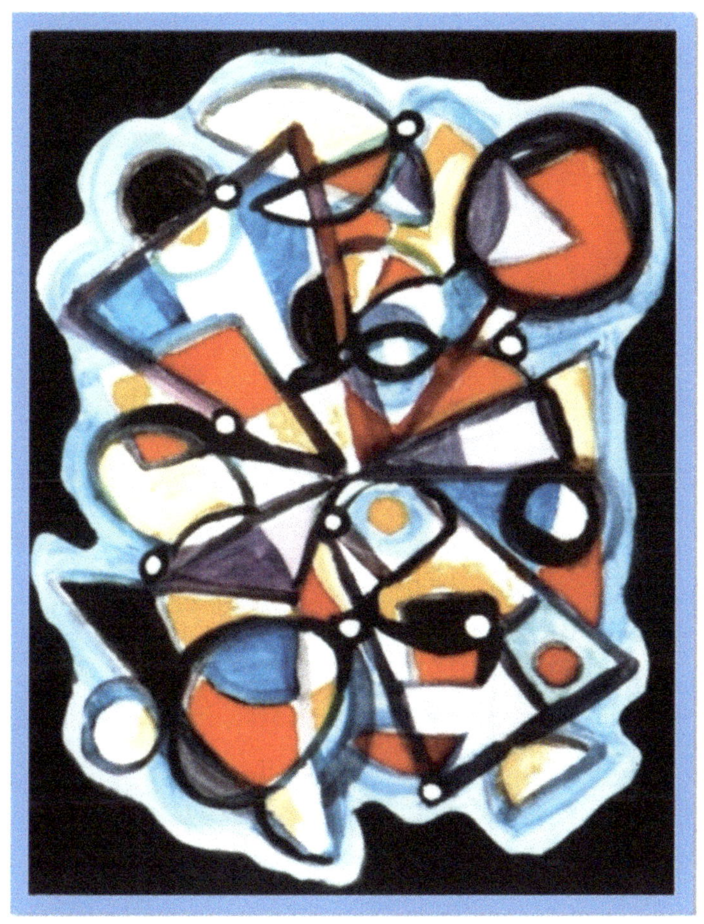

Untitled 2

Acrylic on paper, 40 x 30 cm, 1997

Just as a candle cannot burn without fire,
men cannot live without a spiritual life.
(The Buddha)

Every painting is a voyage into a sacred harbour.
(Giotto di Bondone)

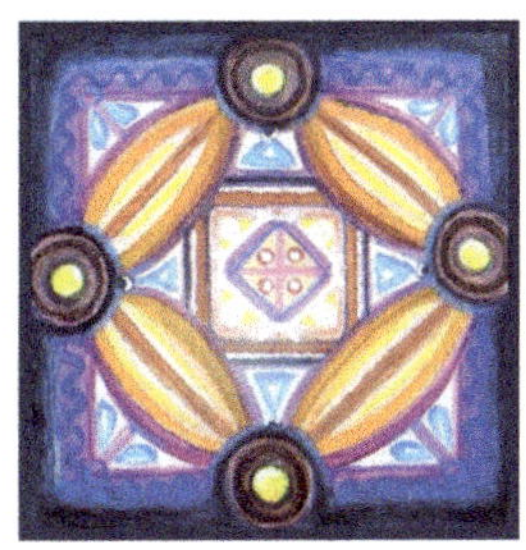

Spirituality

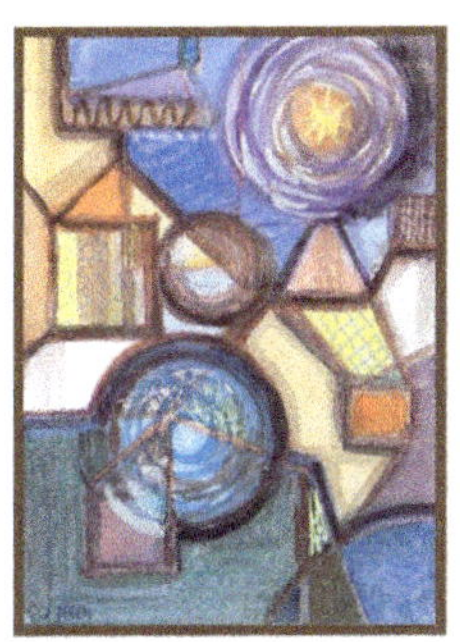

Christian Memories

Oil on board, 60 x 50 cm, 2009

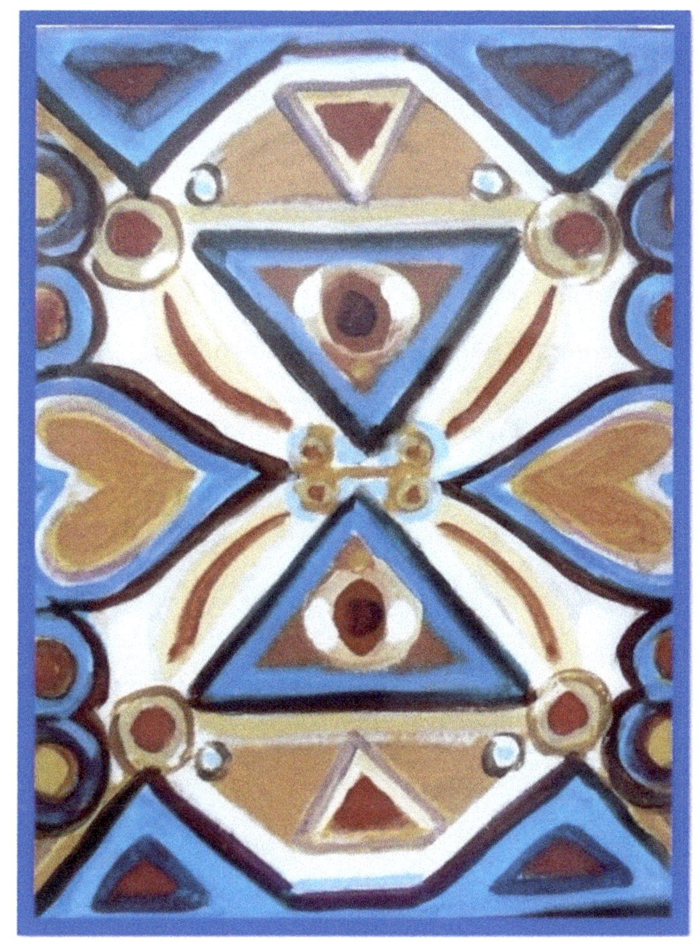

Awakening

Acrylic on board, 54 x 41 cm, 2008

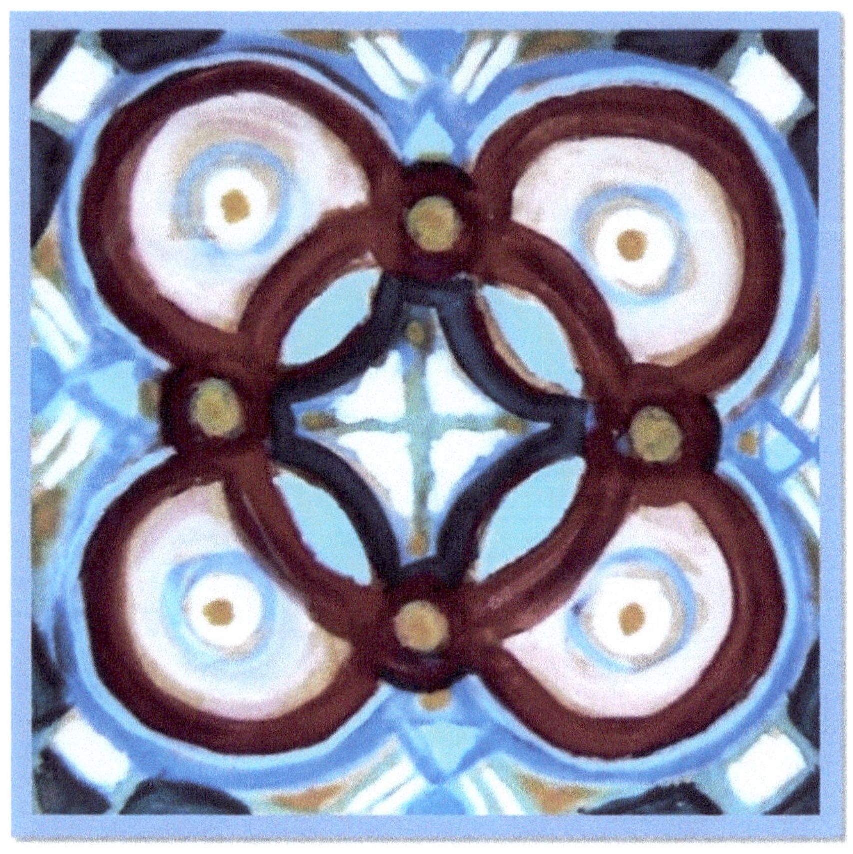

Basilica

Acrylic on paper, 28 x 28 cm, 2007

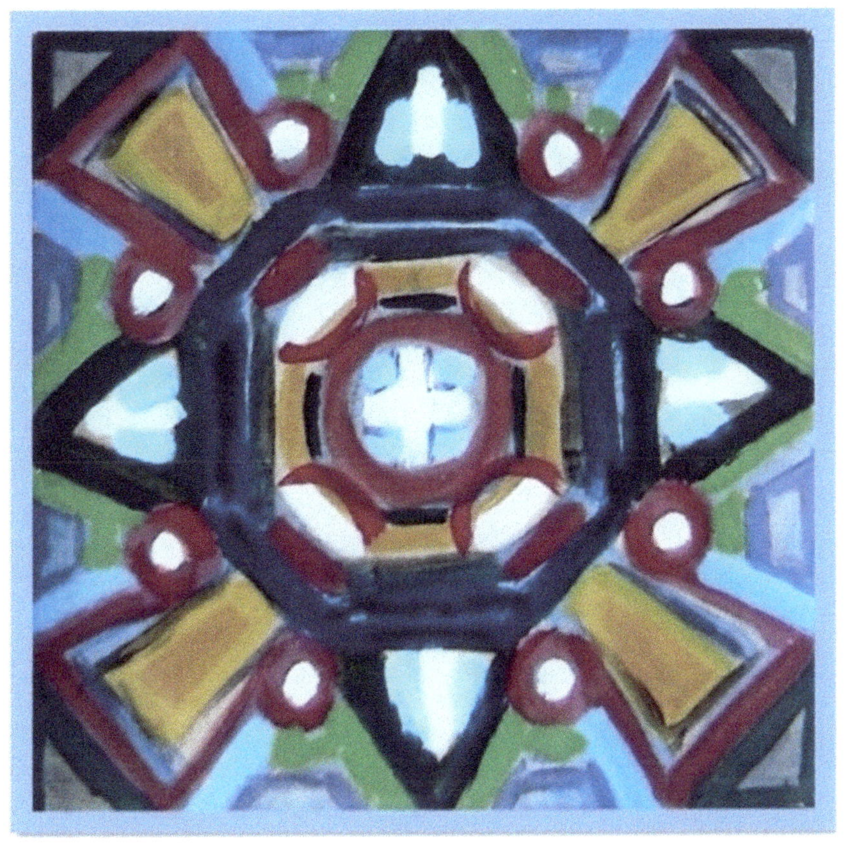

Basilica Dome

Acrylic on paper, 28 x 28 cm, 2005

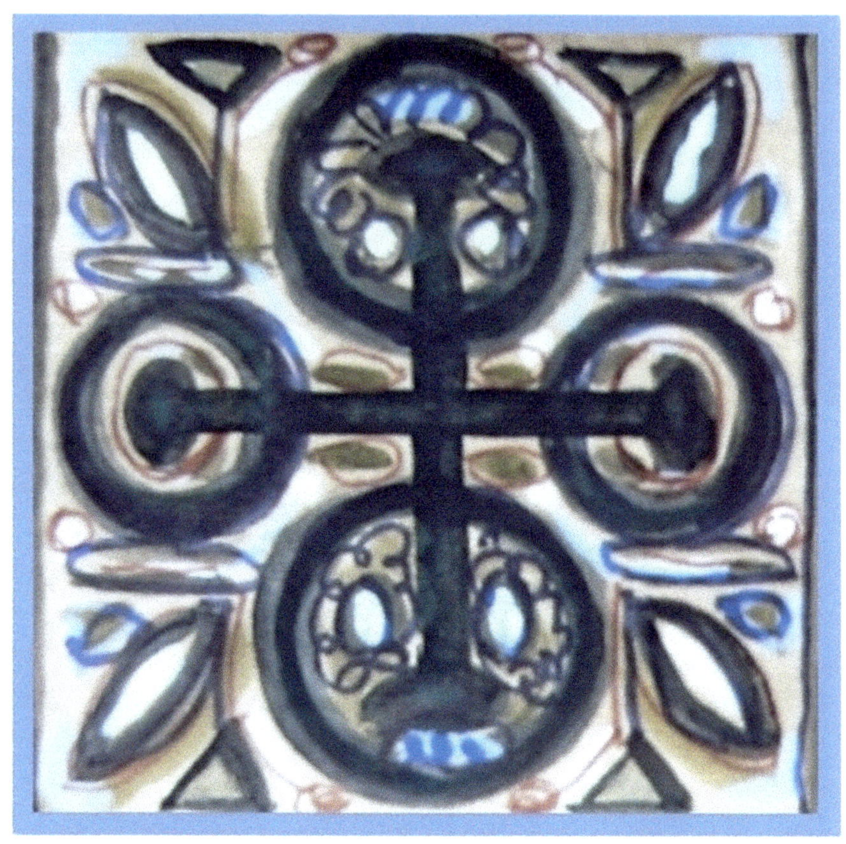

Byzantium

Acrylic on paper, 27 x 27 cm, 2006

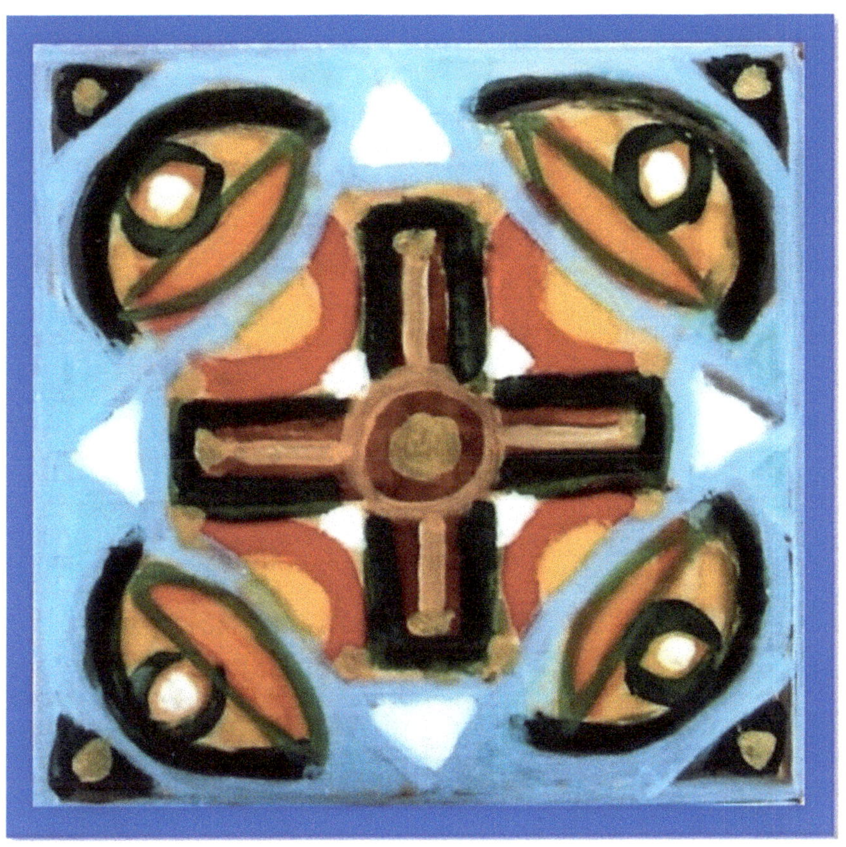

Peace

Acrylic on paper, 28 x 28 cm, 2007

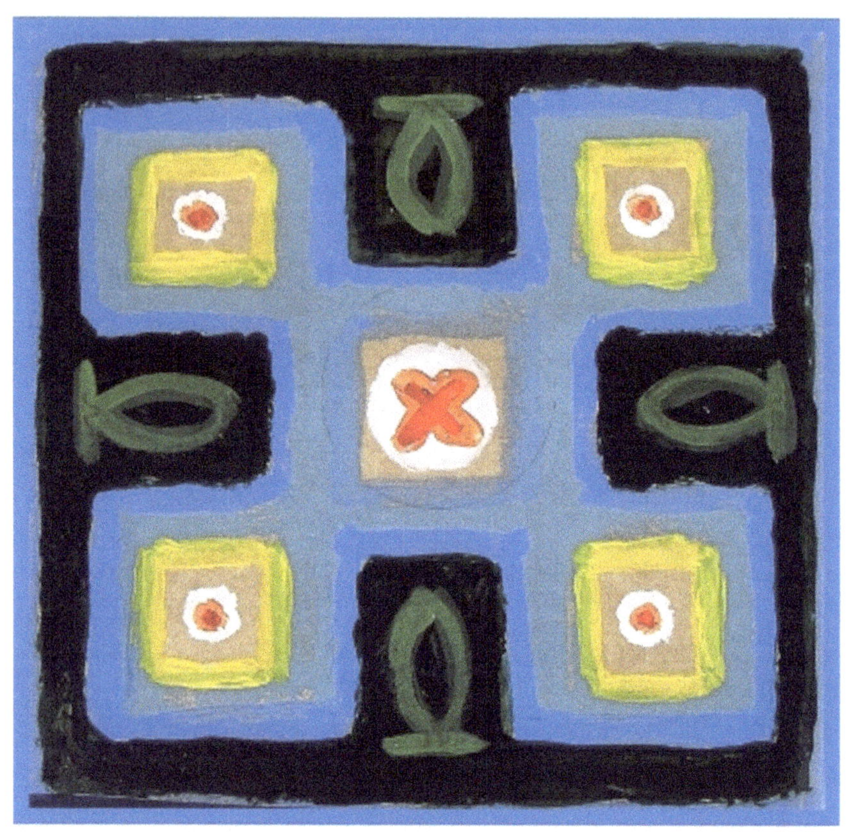

Blue Cross

Acrylic on paper, 28 x 28 cm, 2010

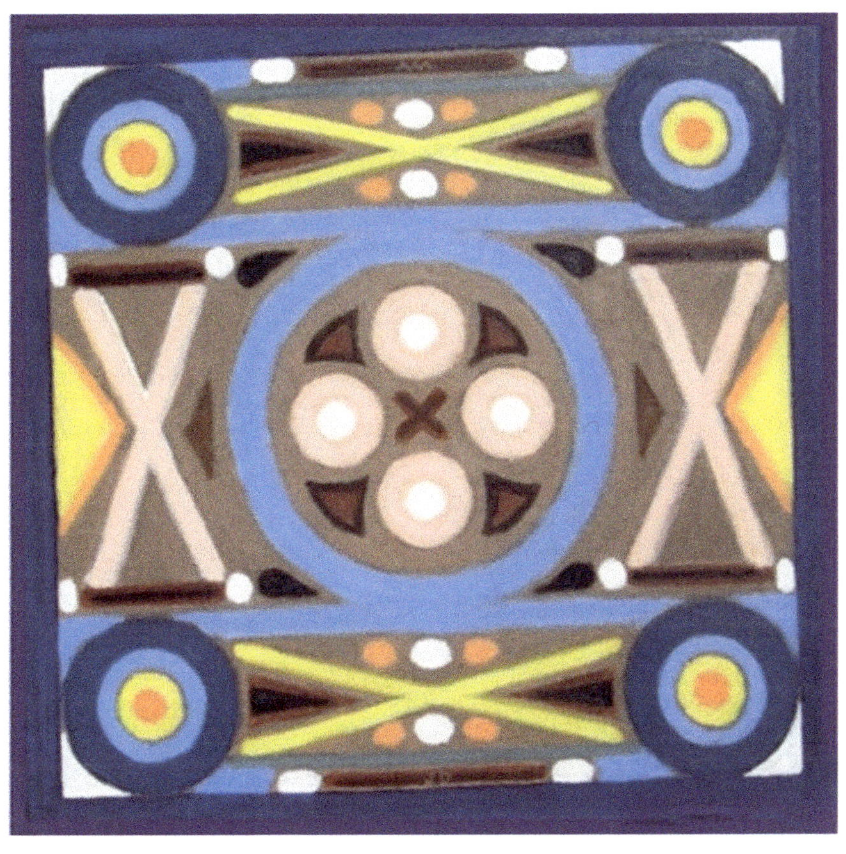

Meditation

Acrylic on paper, 60 x 60 cm, 2007

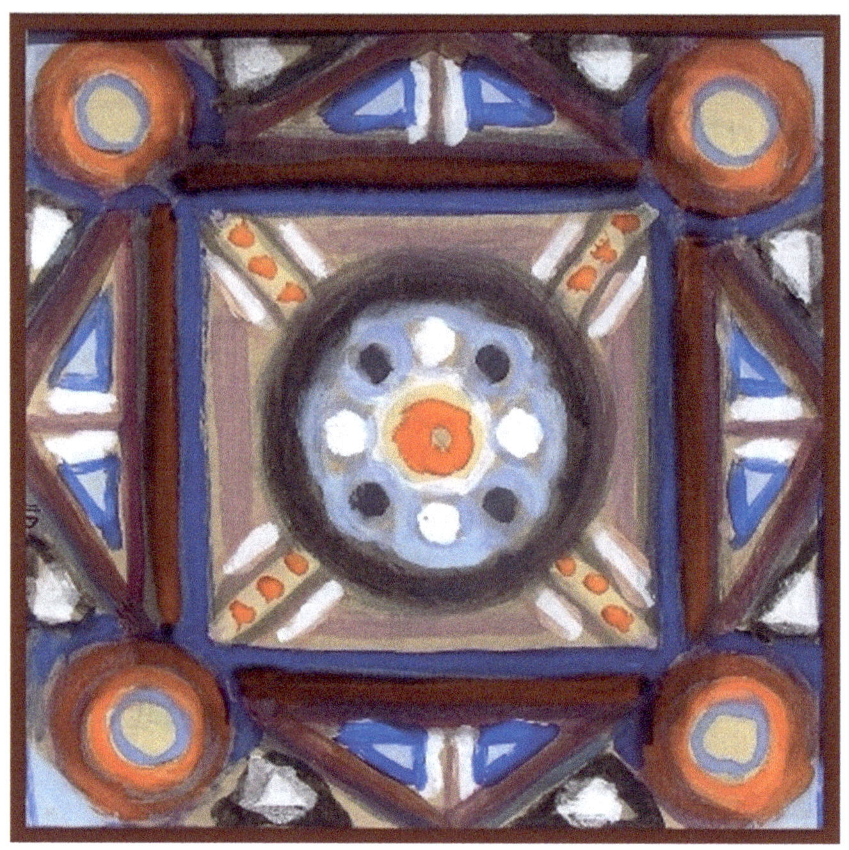

Silence

Acrylic on paper 28 x 28 cm, 2010

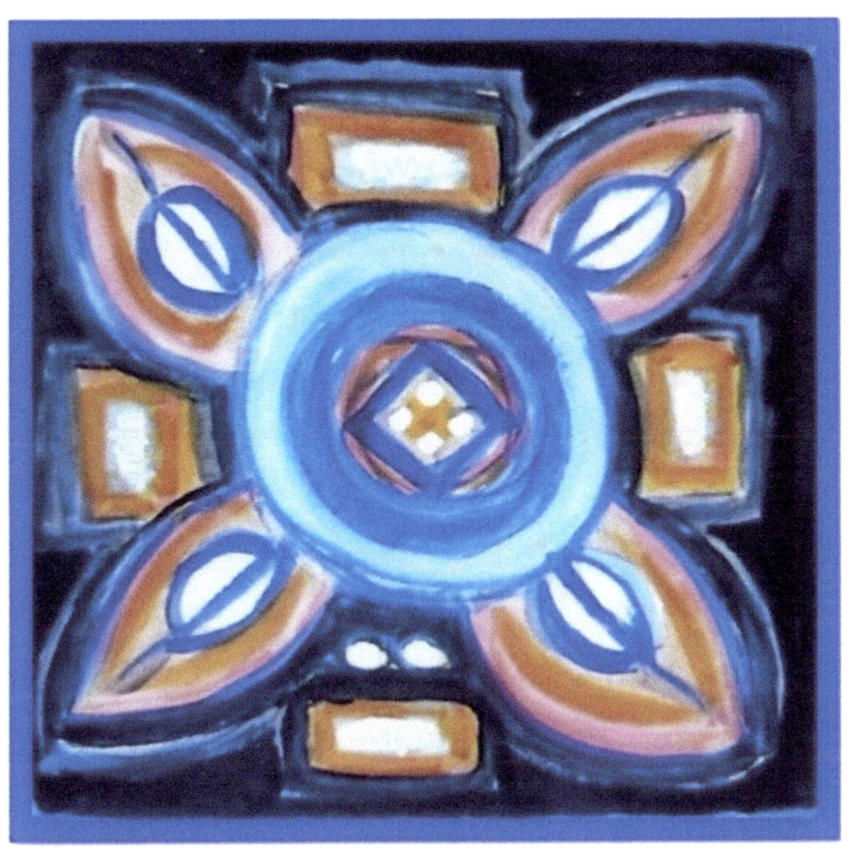

Clear Sight

Acrylic on paper, 27 x 27 cm, 2004

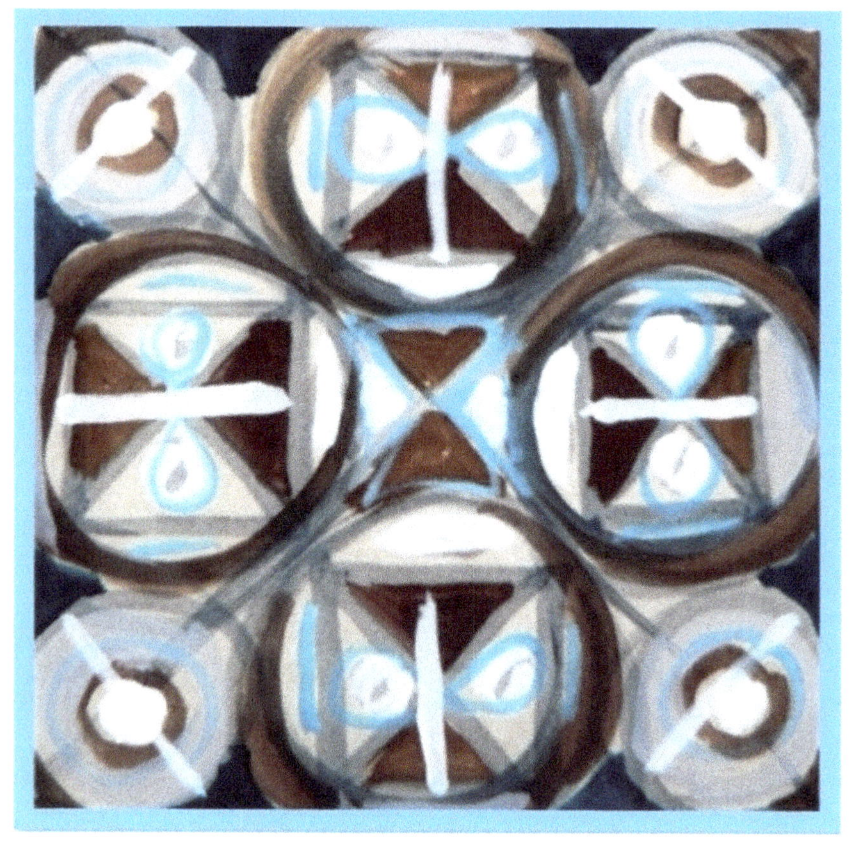

Memory

Acrylic on paper, 28 x 28 cm, 2007

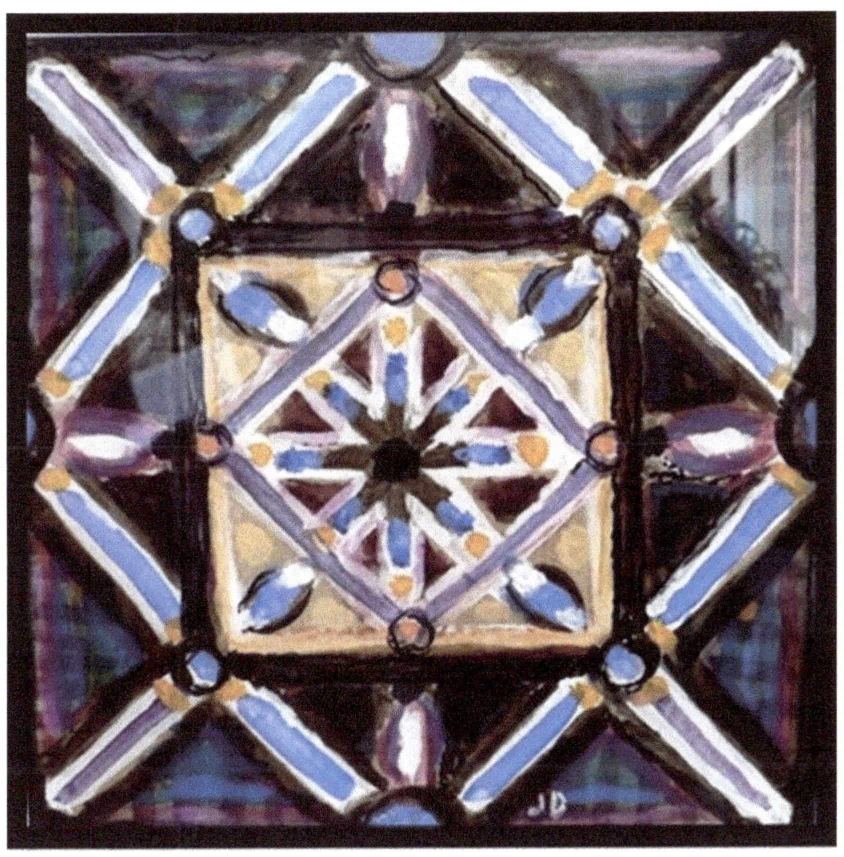

Contemplation

Acrylic on paper 28 x 28 cm, 2010

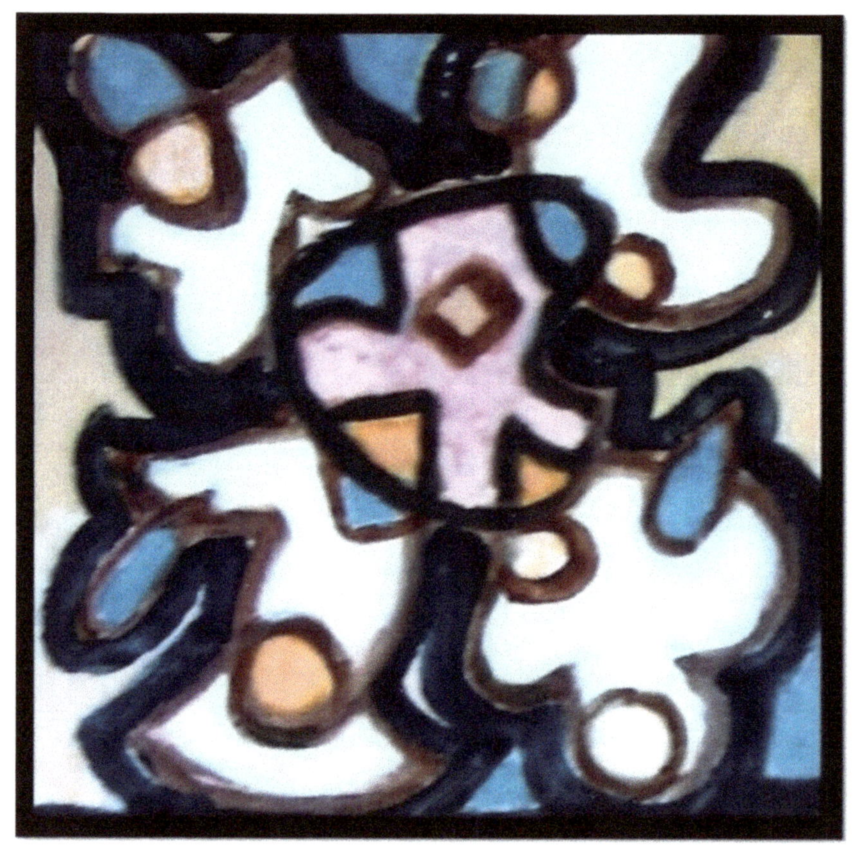

Company

Acrylic on paper, 27 x 27 cm, 2007

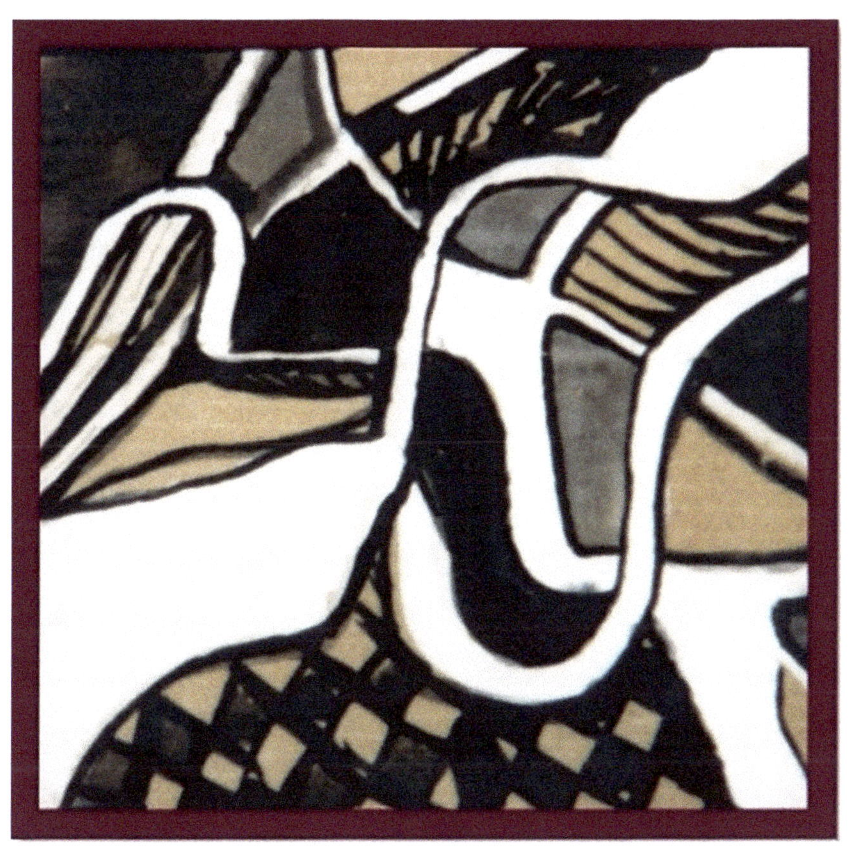

Different Ways

Acrylic on paper, 27 x 27 cm, 2002

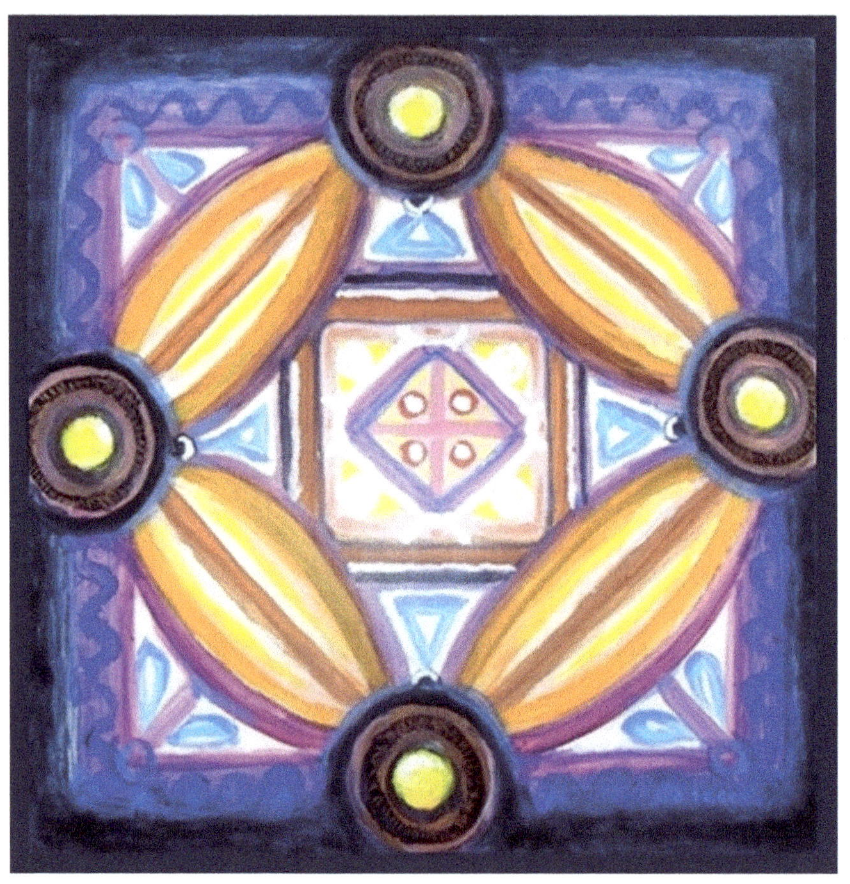

Message

Acrylic on board, 60 x 59 cm, 2010

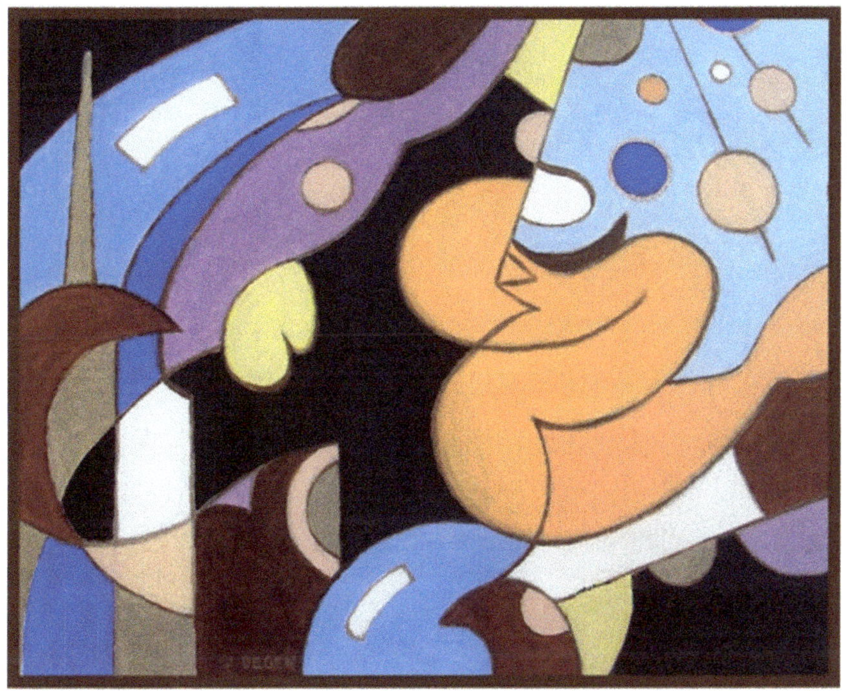

View in the Dark

Acrylic on canvas, 61 x 76 cm, 2009

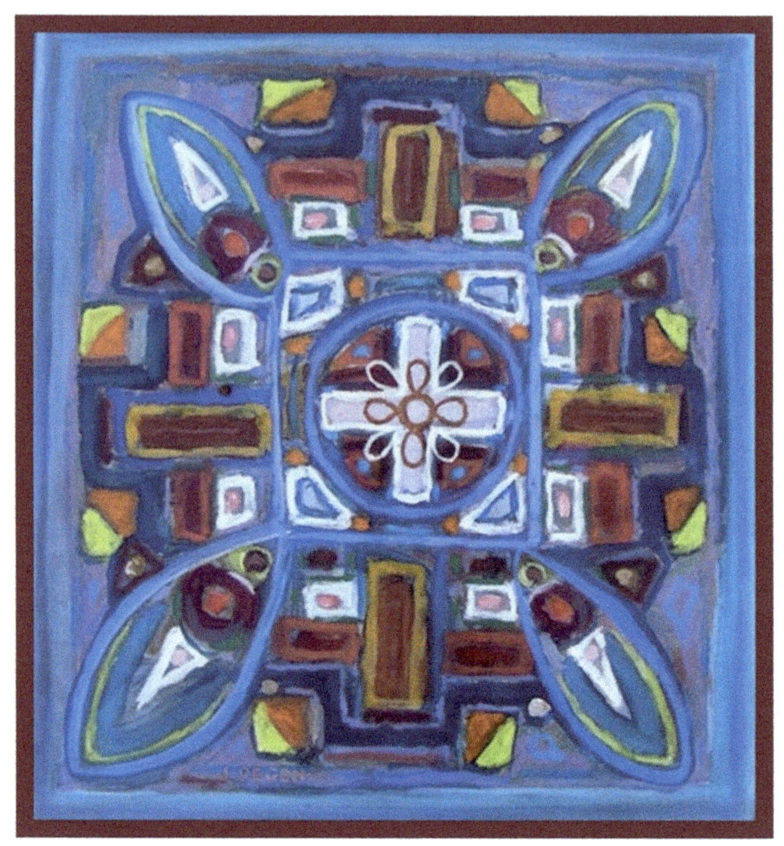

Mandala in Blue

Oil on board, 50 x 45 cm, 1997

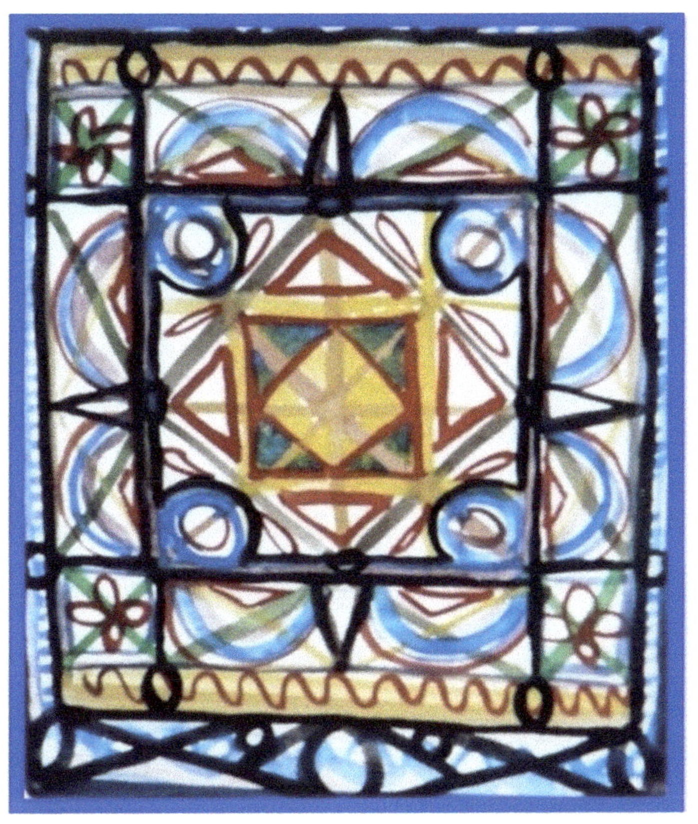

The Hope

Acrylic on paper, 32 x 28 cm, 2007

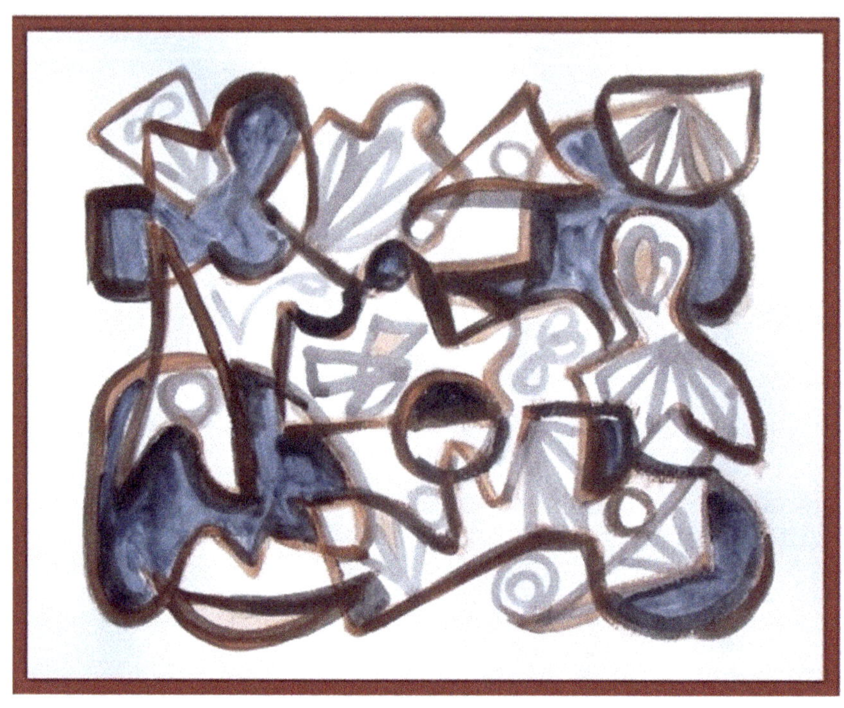

Silent Celebration

Acrylic on paper, 28 x 36 cm, 2009

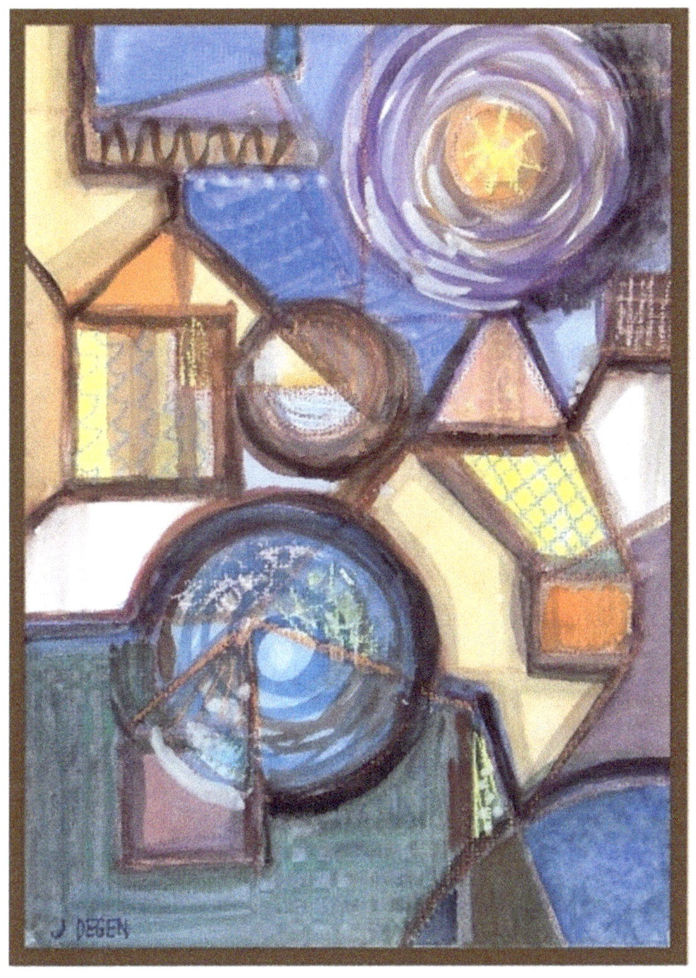

The Feast

Acrylic on board, 43.5 x 36 cm, 2009

MORE ABOUT JINDRICH'S OTHER BOOKS

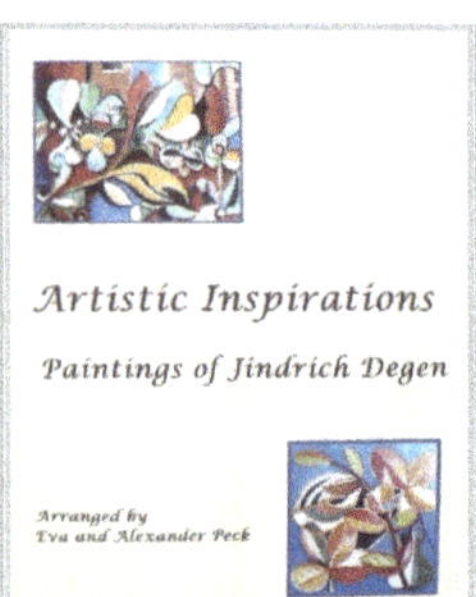

Artistic Inspirations – Paintings of Jindrich Degen The book features 200 of Henry Degen's paintings. The range of subjects is diverse, presented in both realism and abstract art. The art works, produced in various media, are organized under twelve themes.

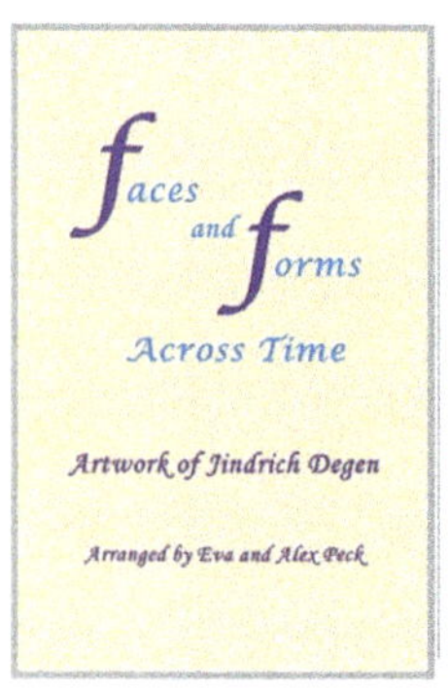

Faces and Forms Across Time – Artwork of Jindrich Degen This collection features real-life portraits, as well as images and portraits based on the works of other artists. In addition, two sections portray animals (domestic and wild) and one section presents icons and symbols.

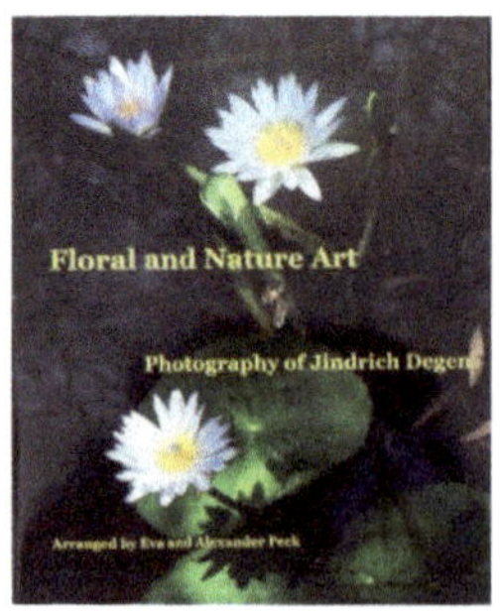

Floral and Nature Art – Photography of Jindrich Degen This book presents digital photography of Henry Degen. The images of flowers and bushland settings, captured through the eyes of an artist, are arranged under the themes of floral art and nature art. Inspirational quotations on each page complement the photographic beauty.

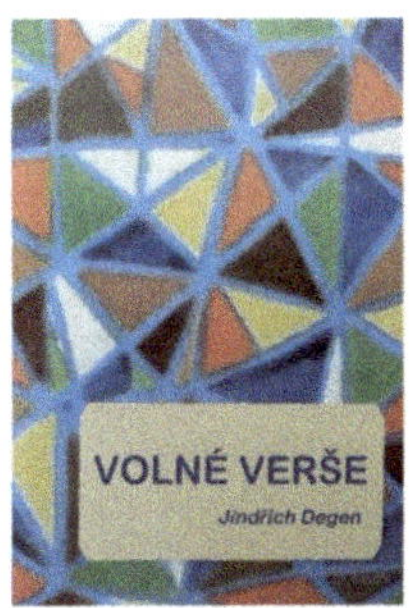

Volné verše (Free Verse) A diverse collection of Czech verse and prose, often in a light-hearted form, created over a decade and inspired by life's circumstances, this book addresses current issues of science and technology, as well as capturing experiences, dreams and fantasies of the author. The verses speak to us today as much as in the time they were written.

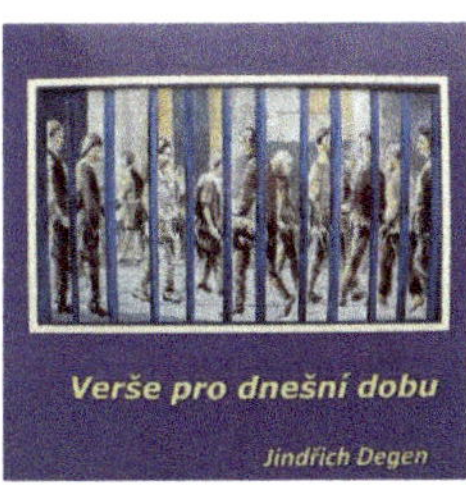

Verše pro dnešní dobu (Contemporary Verse) This small book is a selection of eleven works from *Volné verše*, presented as a graphically illustrated colour version.

ABOUT PATHWAY PUBLISHING

Pathway Publishing (www.pathway-publishing.org) is dedicated to sharing truth and beauty through books that present what is true to life and reality, as well as what is lovely and inspirational. The goal is to not only provide sound information, but also to lift the human spirit.

Pathway Publishing has a vision of helping readers on their path of enlightenment and spiritual transformation. The wisdom and experience of spiritual teachers, thinkers and visionary writers from various backgrounds and faith traditions are recognized and valued. Books produced by Pathway Publishing include:

- *Artistic Inspirations - Paintings of Jindrich Degen*, arranged by Eva and Alexander Peck

- *Colour and Contrast – Artwork of Jindrich Degen*, arranged by Eva and Alexander Peck

- *Faces and Forms Across Time – Artwork of Jindrich Degen*, arranged by Eva and Alex Peck

- *Floral and Nature Art – Photography of Jindrich Degen*, arranged by Eva and Alexander Peck

- *Volné verše*, Jindrich Degen (poetry in Czech)

- *Verše pro dnešní dobu*, Jindrich Degen (poetry in Czech)

- *Memories of Times with Dad – Poems and Letters*, Alexander and Eva Peck
- *Divine Reflections in Times and Seasons*, Eva Peck
- *Divine Reflections in Natural Phenomena*, Eva Peck
- *Divine Reflections in Living Things*, Eva Peck
- *Divine Insights from Human Life*, Eva Peck
- *Pathway to Life - Through the Holy Scriptures*, Eva and Alexander Peck
- *Journey to the Divine Within – Through Silence, Stillness and Simplicity*, Alexander and Eva Peck

Some of the publications are also available as e-books.

Pathway Publishing

Seeking truth and beauty

www.ingramcontent.com/pod-product-compliance
Ingram Content Group UK Ltd.
Pitfield, Milton Keynes, MK11 3LW, UK
UKHW062302290726
14090UKWH00017B/851